Family Wellness

Raising Resilient, Christ-Purposed Children

John D. Eckrich, MD

CONCORDIA PUBLISHING HOUSE · SAINT LOUIS

Published by Concordia Publishing House
3558 S. Jefferson Ave., St. Louis, MO 63118-3968
1-800-325-3040 • cph.org

Manufactured in the United States of America

1 2 3 4 5 6 7 8 9 10   29 28 27 26 25 24 23 22 21 20

Endorsements

Brimming with practical suggestions and encouragement while emphasizing positive health and wellness in parenting, this work by John Eckrich is bathed in spiritual reflection and care. Lots and lots of great resources for parents here!

Bruce M. Hartung, Ph.D.
Professor Emeritus, Practical Theology, Concordia Seminary, Saint Louis

Dr. John Eckrich, as physician, father, and grandfather, tackles all aspects of wellness in this book, which is specifically geared toward parents and families. Very practical tips are included, along with critical foundational thoughts on wellness related to raising children to be more resilient and more focused to become children (and ultimately adults) of high integrity who have servant hearts and are strong followers of Christ. I highly recommend this book to all parents in their joyful challenge to raise healthy children in all areas of their lives.

Debra Arfsten, Ph.D.
Professor of Christian Education, Director of Christian Education (DCE) Program, Director of Synodical Placement, Concordia University Chicago

This is a delightful, stimulating book to read and digest. It gives the blueprint for raising children with integrity who are resilient, courageous, and compassionate. Dr. Eckrich blends together his deep understanding of wellness from his work as a physician with an amazing perspective of the developmental process. Throughout the book, the wisdom of the Christian faith shines through in an uplifting fashion! I love this book!

David Ludwig, Ph.D.
Professor Emeritus, Lenoir-Rhyne University,
Author of *Christian Concepts for Care*

Table of Contents

Section 1: Getting Started, Led by the Spirit

Section 2: Character Values of Spirit-Led Health and Wellness

Section 3: Models of Health and Wellness

Section 4: Spirit-Led Stewardship of Health and Wellness

Section 5: Helpful Additions to Your Conversations as Parents

Message to Readers

The medical, behavioral, educational, and scriptural descriptors and opinions in this book are intended to provide helpful and informative material to you as a parent or grandparent, or for a parents' discussion group. The author and publisher are not engaged in rendering medical, health, theological, or cognitive personal professional services in the book. The book is not meant to be a substitute for discussing all physical, mental health, educational, and spiritual concerns with and consulting with appropriate professionals before adopting any of its suggestions or drawing inferences from it.

The author and publisher specifically disclaim all responsibility for any liability, loss, or risk, personal or otherwise, which is incurred as a direct or indirect consequence of the use and application of any of the contents in this book.

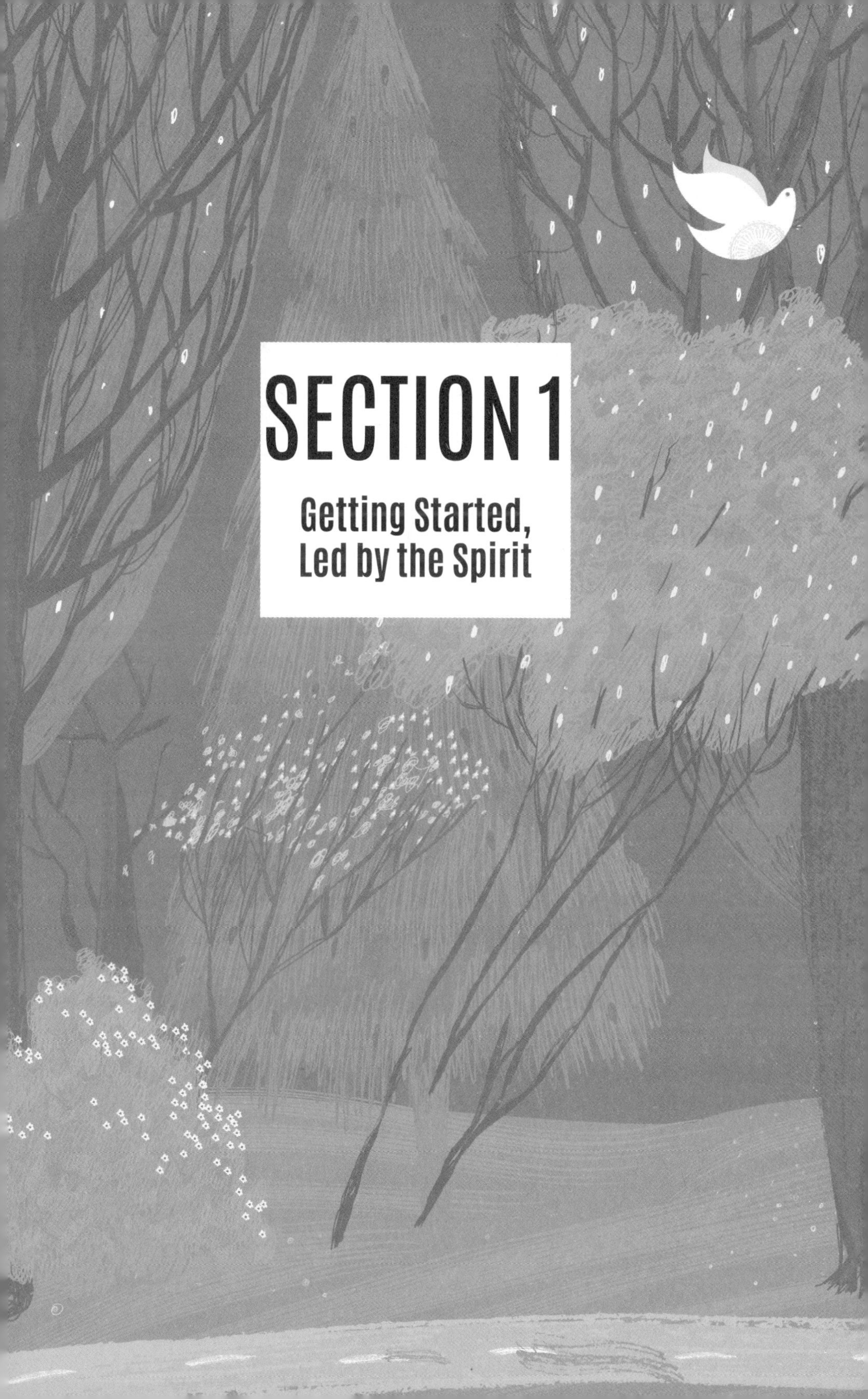

SECTION 1

Getting Started, Led by the Spirit

Introduction

When God places a child in your life, He calls you to loving leadership. Your divinely issued vocation is to diligently guide your child toward maturity, showing him or her the same respect and honor God affords all of His children in equal measure. The Holy Spirit gives you the desire and ability to live joyfully with your child in the arms of your Savior, here and into eternity.

To live respectfully and joyfully necessitates being raised in a faithful family to fear, love, and trust God, as Martin Luther reminds us in his Small Catechism explanation of the First Commandment. Children today are simultaneously developing within a democratic society in a culture that often appears devoid of the recognition of a present and active Creator, let alone a Redeemer and Sanctifier.

Even so, as a Christian parent, you strive to give your child values centered on God's will that are necessary to help him or her become an effective and fruitful citizen in your home and in your faith and public communities. You hope to raise a loving, faith-filled, resilient, honest and upright, securely purposed, and compassionate member of the human race. Along with those values, it is complementary for your child to learn stewardship of body, mind, and spirit—the very attribute God gives us for life and service.

Faced with extraordinary healthy and unhealthy options for his or her health and well-being, your child needs to learn to make choices with an understanding of the consequences of those choices—both the blessings and the curses. Therefore, we should not be surprised that God has laid out the ramifications of our choices with clarity in His Holy Word. Additionally, we have significant medical and behavioral science to validate the importance of wellness behavior.

Whether you have been parenting for a while or you are new to the role, you are discovering how joyful it can be. You also know that it can be frustrating. This dichotomy is exemplified by a culture aspiring to live peacefully, democratically, and in pursuit of happiness even as it is populated with fractured families, distraught communities, and inequalities of means of subsistence.

Not since we left the Garden have we had such access to the bounty of God's creation, yet the headlines shout news of anxiety, hunger, violence, poverty, political conflict, injustice, and despair. Truly, there is darkness in the light of such abundance. Among the significant contributions to this shadowy discord are the challenges of neighbors who do not share common bonds of resources, who do not accept the same standard for truth, and who do not find the same strength in the family unit as the anchor for dealing with the ills of the world.

If you are leading a family today, you are well aware of these detriments to relational harmony in your "village." Even with an enormous reserve of energy, persistence, and patience, a parent needs more than self-reliance. Christian parents long for the power of the Holy Spirit and the companionship of fellow followers of Christ to help them lead their children well. I believe good parenting is deeply enhanced by a Christ-centered perspective and is amplified by a strong faith family. God's Word provides a lamp to illumine our way through a landscape darkened by parenting strategies that focus on the enhancement of ME: child-raising scenarios to advance *my* child's ability to strive and thrive ahead of others. Instead, God's Word shows us a parenting path best walked as WE: child raising directed first toward our relationship to God, then with our child and all of God's creation.

Parenting with the goal of forming relationships—WE—requires more than conversation; it requires action that anchors our verbiage. Children absorb what they observe far more effectively than what they hear. Therefore, the wellness choices shared in this book are as valuable to your own health and wellness as they are for your child's. *Family Wellness* promotes a whole and well child in the setting of a whole and well family. Grandparents, siblings, extended family, teachers, pastors, and caring neighbors, as God has provided them, are your village. They are your support team by their deeds and as expressed and reinforced by their words. Parents and their cohorts lead by acting from the foundation of their own healthy behavior, rather than merely lecturing at or reacting to the child's behavior.

Accordingly, the foundation for our conversation will first examine parenting styles and the challenges and chances for producing faithful, morally sound, and healthy kids in the twenty-first century. Second, we will review the knowledge of God-designed, natural human development, illuminated by leading educators, physicians, behaviorists, and theologians. Third, we will consider the integration of physical, cognitive, and spiritual elements for preparing our children to live in a diverse society and, better still, to live with the joy afforded them by Christ.

To begin our wellness-parenting conversation, then, I invite you to explore with me several important objectives. Entrusting our steps to the triune God, our parental hope is to rear our children and realize eternity with them by emphasizing these core character values:

- *Love:* An abiding faith in the incarnate Jesus, who restores us in a loving relationship with our heavenly Father. By faith, we live that love within our life together with others.
- *Resilience:* The ability and confidence to face any challenge, to try again and again, and to live in Christ free from the debilitating anxiety of discouragement.
- *Integrity:* The ability to make responsible decisions and accept the consequences; honesty; strong moral principles, especially respect for others, centered in God's will.
- *Security:* The clear understanding of self and purpose as one clinging securely to Christ of the cross and His resurrection.
- *Compassion:* The commitment to live with a servant heart and thus contribute to the wellness of family and society by fostering healthy relationships.

Acquiring a high capacity for these character values (among others you may hold dear) is very significant in order for children to be empowered family members and effective constituents of our faith communities and in society at large.

Intentional behavior is a fundamental component for wellness within our families and culture. Therefore, we will look at five lifestyle choices that can be encouraged beginning early in a child's life and that can contribute to personal as well as community well-being. They include the following:

- Natural movement
- Plant-dominated nutrition
- Regular rest
- Focus on faith and loved ones
- Purposeful contribution to good outside of self

I will clarify and expand these strategies to address age-appropriate abilities in separate chapters.

The Appendix (page 233) provides discussion questions that are anchored in God's Word. Use these to prompt Spirit-inspired conversations that can encourage you and your parenting partner or small group to think creatively and learn from each other's expertise and experience.

The last chapter is devoted to grandparenting. I, like many of you, have found the joys and challenges of grandparenting to be a greatly rejuvenating booster shot to purposeful living. In turn, I am confident that I am blessing my grandchildren's and children's lives as well.

Be assured that as the father of three and the grandfather of two, I am on the parenting journey with you. I readily recognize mistakes I have made along the way, and I give myself permission to learn from my mistakes and then let loose of them. Faith assures me that God forgives me in Christ. Furthermore, I cannot express more fervently the importance of the grace and forgiveness I've received often from my spouse and children. God's grace and that of my family continuously helps me grow into a more enlightened parenting role.

I urge you to seek forgiveness and readily forgive, even if you are parenting for the first time. We should not be deceived; we all will make mistakes. By God's grace, He continues to shower us with His forgiveness through His Son and gives renewed opportunities to grow well and whole in His Word. By that same grace, may we inform and reform our parenting each and every day. Thanks be to God.

John D. Eckrich, MD

CHAPTER 1

Parenting Roles and Relationships with Children

Train up a child in the way he should go;
even when he is old he will not depart from it.

Proverbs 22:6

We are called to lovingly lead our children in the way of Christ throughout their earthly life and to prepare them for their eternal life in God's presence. As most of us realize, the vocation of parent stretches from womb to tomb (Proverbs 2:6). Parenting input modulates over time to meet our children's maturity and circumstances, but we are never done parenting. Significant persistence and consistency is required of parental leadership.

As we parent in and with faith in Christ, we know we need to prepare our children to live with God's creation and with His people, who are broken by sin. Children enter a culture and society in which its members express diverse moral values, vast choices, self-focus, and often a misunderstanding of identity and purpose. We live in a democratic republic that has a primary objective of equality within a disparate society: equal value of human life, equal freedom to live however we choose within the law, and equal opportunity to fulfill hopes and ambitions. Can we identify core relationship values consistent with the Christian faith that parents can instill in their children who are entering such a world? It is a worthwhile question and conversation. I'll refresh a discussion of those values in a moment, but first let's look at the ways we can parent to produce good citizens for our country and for our faith community.

TODAY'S PARENTING STYLES

Our democracy professes equal rights, respect, and opportunity for all of society. That proposition has been present since the founding of our nation; and democratic principles have existed in some form in other civilizations and eras. Indeed, our equality dates to Christ's work on the cross:

> For in Christ Jesus you are all sons of God, through faith. For as many of you as were baptized into Christ have put on Christ. There is neither Jew nor Greek, there is neither slave nor free, there is no male and female, for you are all one in Christ Jesus.
>
> (Galatians 3:26–28)

In our country, however, we are increasingly seeking to realize this ideal through political, legal, and social discourse addressing inequalities in civil rights, socioeconomics, gender, age, ability, and race. As Christians, we realize that equality and mutual respect do not always exist in society because of our egocentric human nature and the nature of sin—after all, sin arose when Adam and Eve tried to equate themselves with the Creator. Equality and respect are, nonetheless, worthy best practices for living in relationship with others because they are based on our equal standing as children of God. Furthermore, I believe that the statement of allegiance to our country—"one nation under God, indivisible, with liberty and justice for all"—has contemporary worth, meaning, and empowerment.

St. Paul addresses these ideals in his letter to the Christians in the republic of Rome:

> Let love be genuine. . . . Love one another with brotherly affection. Outdo one another in showing honor. . . . Contribute to the needs of the saints and seek to show hospitality. . . . Live in harmony with one another. Do not be haughty, but associate with the lowly. . . . If possible, so far as it depends on you, live peaceably with all.
>
> (Romans 12:9–18)

Paul expands on this topic in his letters to the Christians at Colossae (also a Roman republic):

> Put on then, as God's chosen ones, holy and beloved, compassionate hearts, kindness, humility, meekness, and patience, bearing with one another and, if one has a complaint against another, forgiving each other. . . . And above all these put on love, which binds everything together in perfect harmony. And let the peace of Christ rule in your hearts, to which indeed you were called in one body.
>
> (Colossians 3:12–15)

Christian parents and their children share an identical relationship with God. They share the same worthiness to be members of God's family through the water and Word of Holy Baptism. They are equally loved and receive the same respect and honor in God's eyes, afforded them only by Christ's life, death, and resurrection. In response, each parent and child is called to live in the manner worthy of being a child of God. Each is to fear, love, and trust God above all things.

Although equal to one another in the family of God, their relationship to the Creator is *not* democratic. Humans are created in God's image—but not as equals to Him. In addition, parents and children are called to different roles and responsibilities within the family in order to bring about unity and harmony in their life together and to be stewards of all of God's creation. For children, following the will of their parents comes with an important promise:

> Children, obey your parents in the Lord, for this is right. "Honor your father and mother" (this is the first commandment with a promise), "that it may go well with you and that you may live long in the land."
>
> (Ephesians 6:1–3)

Martin Luther describes these responsive, clearly delineated roles of children this way:

> *Honor your father and your mother.* . . . We should fear and

> love God so that we do not despise or anger our parents and other authorities, but honor them, serve and obey them, love and cherish them.
>
> (SC, Fourth Commandment and its explanation)

What about parents' responsibilities? Parents, Paul reminds us, are not to raise children in a cruel manner or without compassion but rather have an ordered, responsible, instructive, and caring approach to parenting:

> Fathers, do not provoke your children to anger, but bring them up in the discipline and instruction of the Lord.
>
> (Ephesians 6:4)

Parenting should be done with compassion and with an understanding of our child's human limits and frailty, which is the same compassion God shows each of us:

> As a father shows compassion to his children, so the LORD shows compassion to those who fear Him. For He knows our frame; He remembers that we are dust.
>
> (Psalm 103:13–14)

Therefore, compassionate discipline is the delicate, deliberate dance parents perform to raise their children so that they treasure compassion in their relationships with others.

Parenting also requires us to make tough choices with awareness and acceptance of associated consequences. It calls for fair discipline and justice. For parenting merely to be permissive is not healthy. We are to train our children and others assigned to our care as God guides us:

> It is for discipline that you have to endure. God is treating you as sons. For what son is there whom his father does not discipline? If you are left without discipline, in which all have participated, then you are illegitimate children and not sons. Besides this, we have had earthly fathers who disciplined us and we respected them. Shall we not much more be subject to the Father of spirits and live? For they disciplined us for a short time as it seemed

> best to them, but He disciplines us for our good, that we may share His holiness. For the moment all discipline seems painful rather than pleasant, but later it yields the peaceful fruit of righteousness to those who have been trained by it.
>
> (Hebrews 12:7–11)

Additionally and unceasingly, parents should raise their children in God's Word:

> From childhood you have been acquainted with the sacred writings, which are able to make you wise for salvation through faith in Christ Jesus.
>
> (2 Timothy 3:15)

At first glance, these guidelines may seem to demand a rather authoritative or strictly controlling parenting practice. The authoritative parent requires absolute control, total obedience, and even breaking the child's will to conform to the parent's will. There were times and places in society where that was the typical parenting approach. Your parents may have been raised with the "father [or mother] knows best, and I turned out fine" mentality, and if stringent control worked with their generation, some would reason, it is appropriate for every generation. Generally speaking, the parent was the ultimate authority and provided rewards or punishment to achieve his or her goals. The child was left without equal standing and no opportunity to legitimately question, challenge, or disagree. Certainly, there was a time in our culture when inequality in gender, race, physical and mental capacity, and age was commonplace. Often, the response was rebellion. Increasingly, that is not the social and political environment our children inherit.

After World War II, parenting practices shifted so that a permissive or nonrestrictive approach became more acceptable.[1] Some parents allowed their children to "do their own thing" without many strings. Permissive homes had few rules, guidelines, or restrictions on the child's freedom. Nonrestrictive parenting may have come about in part as a backlash against the authoritarianism of previous generations. The result, however, is that without boundaries, a substantial number of permissively raised children now live insecurely.[2] They do not experience or appreciate boundaries or a sense of belonging to a closely knit family or family-based society. They may struggle with any type of authority. Furthermore, they are challenged by a lack of effective skills for child rearing themselves since they have no model of the support with accountability that comes from a family life with healthy boundaries. This can be true for single- or dual-parent homes. I believe this is a major contributor to the breakdown of the family unit we see so abundantly in our society today.

You may have been raised with few boundaries and cannot imagine restricting your child's ability to express him- or herself or to make choices. Consider, however, that there could be a parenting style that combines the better qualities of authoritative and permissive parenting that is more effective for the challenges and threats children in the twenty-first century face.

In the last hundred years, behavioral physicians and psychotherapists like Dr. Alfred Adler and Dr. Rudolf Dreikurs have laid the foundation for contemporary parenting pioneers like Dr. Michael Popkin. Dr. Popkin, through writings and workshops, has helped millions of parents to develop responsible, cooperative, and courageous children.[3] His parenting practice, called *democratic parenting*, points to equality and freedom as an ideal but adds much more to give structure and support to child rearing. Parents are leaders (as Luther advocates in his Small Catechism), not dictators. They establish order by facilitating cooperative contributions to the family good by members (parents, children, grandparents) who are mutually respected and respectful. All family members learn from one another continuously; the family becomes the workshop for mutual care and living. Every member of the family has a distinct purpose that adds to the harmony and good of the family (see Colossians 3:12–15). Parents and children have social equality defined by mutual respect and honor and delineated by individual rights and responsibilities.

Parents' and children's roles, rights, and responsibilities are clarified in democratic parenting to bring harmony, unity, and mutual care to both the earthly family and to society at large. I believe that if our society were filled with families with similar tenets for life together, we would more likely be able to approach our ideals of a truly democratic society.

Obviously, flawed and sinful humans that we are, we still fall short of that; nonetheless, we realize that our children are entering a culture that has as its goal equality of human worth. In the following chapters, we dissect the five relationship values mentioned earlier to train our children to be members of God's family and to help them better live in and serve as citizens in our culture. What would these character values look like in our children?

- *Love, filled with faith:* Loving, faith-filled children have hearts that are anchored in their Christian faith. They know the Bible stories and logic of their faith, which the Spirit uses to help them know and love God. They think and discern with the mind of the incarnate, crucified, risen, and persistently loving Christ, who restores them in their relationship with God. They can express their faith through unconditional love, not just in words but also in the way they live, including insisting on esteem, justice, and liberty for all.
- *Resilience:* Resilient children live with the ability to be persistent in their efforts to accomplish goals creatively, cooperatively, and adaptably. And because they trust Christ Jesus even when they fall short, they know they have forgiveness and mercy to live boldly for Him. This allows them to live resiliently, courageously, and, therefore, with less anxiety.
- *Integrity:* Children with integrity take responsibility for their choices. They are honest and upright. That means they also develop the maturity to accept the outcomes of their choices and do not blame others for the ramifications if those decisions go awry. They are morally sound and respectful of others. They learn to make decisions based on God's will revealed in the Bible.
- *Secure:* Secure children are anchored by their faith in their baptismal identity, as those saved and restored by Christ's death on the cross. They know they are purchased for a purpose, so they live securely, despite the threats of sin, in their vocation as children and the call to be purposed for Christ.
- *Compassion:* Compassionate children possess a servant heart. They value and understand themselves in a servant posture. Their energy

flows outward for mission and service rather than inward to self because they have put on sympathy and concern for other. This servant posture is exemplified by the work of their Savior in His earthly ministry and His sacrificial death for our sins.

In the next several chapters, we examine these character values as infrastructure for health and wellness in our biological, faith, and societal communities.

NOTES

1. Michael H. Popkin, *Active Parenting 4th Edition Parent's Guide* (Marietta, GA: Active Parenting Publishers, 2015), 7.
2. Ibid., 6–8.
3. Ibid., 16.

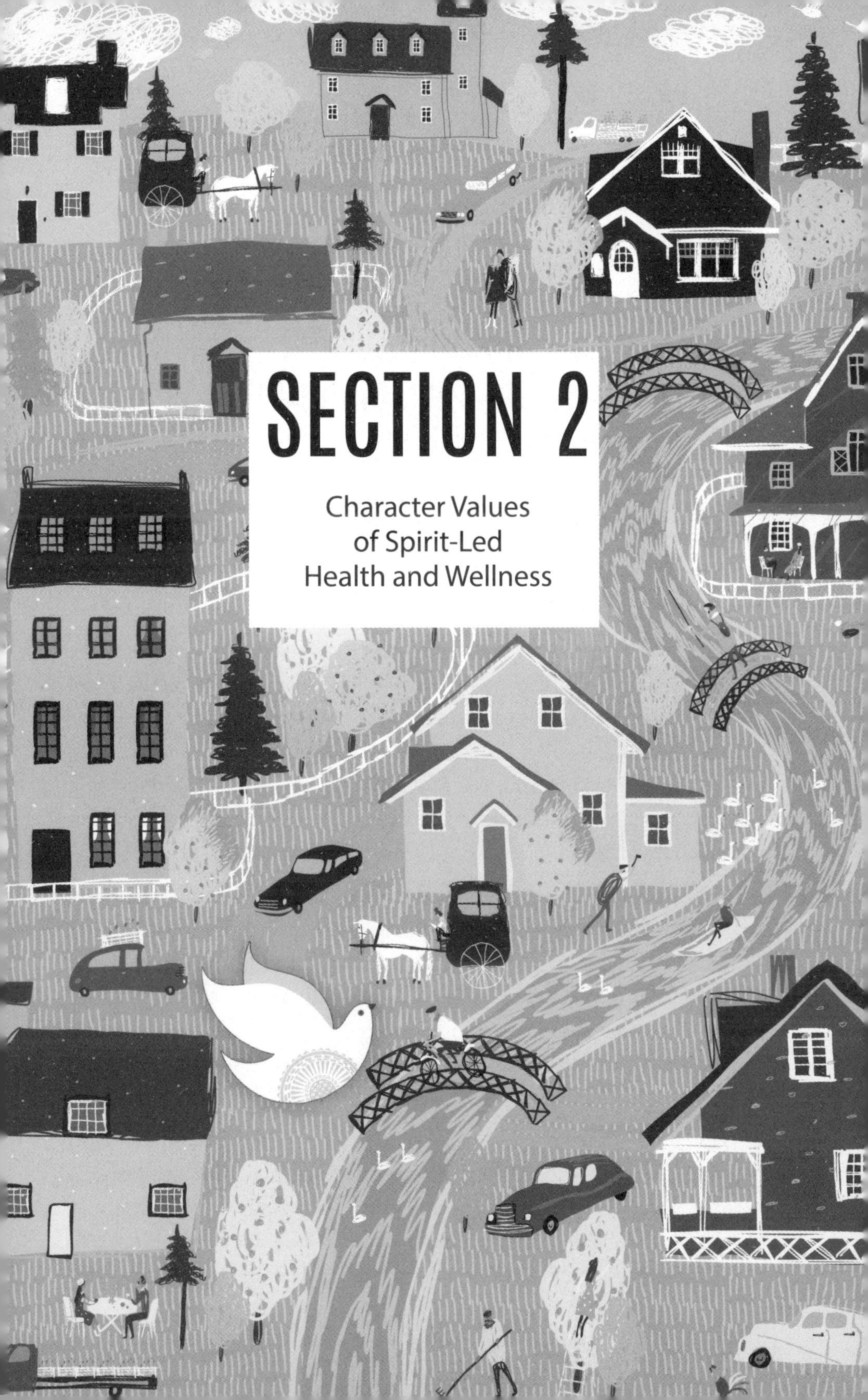

SECTION 2

Character Values of Spirit-Led Health and Wellness

CHAPTER 2

Parenting Loving, Faith-Filled Children

> But as for you, continue in what you have learned and have firmly believed, knowing from whom you learned it and how from childhood you have been acquainted with the sacred writings, which are able to make you wise for salvation through faith in Christ Jesus.
>
> 2 Timothy 3:14–15

Faith-filled children, versed and living in God's Holy Word and in the Confessions, are Christ-centered people who fear and honor the Lord. They love the Lord with heart, soul, mind, and strength. They recognize both the abundance of grace readily available to them from moment to moment and the daily presence of sin, as they and their parents cannot of their own strength or reason live up to the pile of dirty laundry that makes up their lives.

Faith-filled children place their trust in Jesus, their Lord and Savior. Their parents help them learn that God created them and all things and loves them unconditionally and intimately. God is daily present and active in their lives. God loves them so much that He sent His only Son to earth, incarnate as a man, to live and then suffer and die for them on a cross. Jesus' death and resurrection restores these children to be with God and to be members of His family.

God put His very name on your child when you brought him or her to the baptismal font, where your child received the gifts of the Spirit through Word and water, namely, forgiveness of sins, the promise of salvation, and the faith to believe that these gifts are real and true. By the Sacrament of Holy Baptism, your child now joins you as a member of God's family.

God provides His children with an earthly family, by birth or adoption. Parents' primary role is to love and care for their children, provide for their physical needs, and teach them about God's love and continuous care for them. Faith-filled children learn how to fear, love, and trust both God and the earthly parents given by God. Even Jesus, as a human child, displayed these character values:

> Now His parents went to Jerusalem every year at the Feast of the Passover. And when He was twelve years old, they went up according to custom. And when the feast was ended, as they were returning, the boy Jesus stayed behind in Jerusalem. His parents did not know it, but supposing Him to be in the group, they went a day's journey, but then they began to search for Him among their relatives and acquaintances. . . . After three days they found Him in the temple, sitting among the teachers, listening to them and asking them questions. And all who heard Him were amazed at His understanding and His answers. And when His parents saw Him, they were astonished. . . . And He said to them, "Why were you looking for Me? Did you not know that I must be in My Father's house?"
>
> (Luke 2:41–49)

We know that Jesus was without sin (1 Peter 2:22; Hebrews 4:15; 2 Corinthians 5:21; 1 John 3:5, and others), and so we know that He was obedient to His parents, completely trustworthy, and a perfect decision maker. For these first-time parents, God worked faith in their hearts as well as discernment and adaptability. They did not punish Jesus for causing their delay and distress. Rather, we read that they didn't understand what He said, but that Mary "treasured up all these things in her heart" (Luke 2:51). This Bible story includes parents, extended family members, and a child who are all faith filled; Jesus is a whole child in a whole family!

God the Father tells us about Himself in the Bible. The Word is God's voice and communication to each of us. When God speaks His Word, He speaks only truth. He can do no other. So what our loving God tells you is good and healthy for you. God tells you His design and what He wants you to know—which includes what not to do and what is not good for you. But many children grow up in a culture and educational system without the knowledge of God or a sense of absolute truth.

God the Holy Spirit gives His children an understanding of His will, which provides guidance for how His creation lives best in relationship with Himself and with others. This guidance is God's Law, the Ten Commandments, which is the standard for relational life together. The Commandments are a curb to order our behavior, a mirror to reveal our wrongdoing, and a guide for our lives together. As we learn the Commandments, we learn that God is just and that He expects His children to be just as they relate to others. Through His Son, who suffered under the world's sin and went to hell to pay for that sin, God provides His children release from the bondage of the self-destruction of sin.

God's Son gives us the Lord's Prayer, which is the model for how we are to communicate with His Father. God initiates communication with us in His Word, and we respond with prayer in Jesus' name. The Lord's Prayer is the perfect example because it is from Jesus Himself and its seven petitions cover all aspects of our life in and with Him. It teaches us that we are to go to God for everything we need. Faith-filled children learn this prayer from their parents and repeat it often, imprinting it firmly in the mind.

God the Son gives us Sacraments, or visible signs, under His Word. These visible signs are the tangible elements of water, bread, and wine. The Sacraments are the means by which God forgives our sins and sustains us in the faith. Faith-filled children understand that the identity given them in their Baptism is that of God's adopted sons and daughters, and they understand that when older family members are given bread and wine at the altar, they are receiving God's true body and blood for the forgiveness of their sins.

God provides faith-filled children with parents, grandparents, godparents, caregivers, pastors, and teachers to lead them in the mind of Christ, to show them His love, and to teach them the ways they can love Him and all He has created for them. Faith leaders, along with parents, have the responsibility to teach children to fear God (both to be afraid of

God's anger if they disobey His rules and also to have awe and respect for His might), who unconditionally loves them and who created them in His image. Parents, pastors, and teachers strive to teach faith-filled children how to trust God and how to place all fears, concerns, and anxieties into God's hands.

Parents lead and teach children by the words they speak. Far more effectively, however, parents guide children by what they do, how they act, and how they treat their children and others. Children are extraordinarily efficient sponges, and they pattern their actions after those of their parents. Children learn justice, for example, by the way parents treat others within and outside the family.

One additional, practical observation applies to an effective setting for leading and teaching faith to children: make the breaking of bread, mealtime, a classroom for faith formation. A friend of mine observed that a major reason he and his seven siblings were God-fearing, faithful people was that they shared twenty-one meals together each week with their parents. Impossible in the twenty-first century? Challenging, yes, but not impossible. Eating, praying, and singing together around God's bountiful goodness (especially without the distraction of cell phones, handheld games, earbuds, or tablets) allows the transfer of living skills, knowledge, wisdom, patience, gratefulness, kindness, and love. Allow your family meal to be a temple for worshiping God. Be there in body, mind, and spirit; be there in love.

> Let the word of Christ dwell in you richly, teaching and admonishing one another in all wisdom, singing psalms and hymns and spiritual songs, with thankfulness in your hearts to God.
>
> (Colossians 3:16)

Specifically, in addition to gathering the entire family for meals, how can you encourage loving, faith-filled children?

- Develop the practice of regular prayer at mealtime and bedtime. Consider also gathering at the start of the day, before family members leave home for school, work, and day care. Praying together is a particularly effective way to anchor hearts and minds in faith and to strengthen family bonds.

- Hold regular family devotions. A wonderful connection point is bedtime, when families can also read stories from the Bible. This is an opportunity to discuss questions and to encourage emerging and early readers by having them read the devotions or stories from a children's Bible.
- Be an active Christian by regularly attending worship services, Bible study, and Sunday School. Engage in volunteer opportunities in your congregation, such as serving on committees or boards, ushering, serving on the altar guild, or teaching VBS. Most congregations have ample opportunities for members of all ages to participate.
- Have Bible- and faith-based books in your home. Keep a Bible, hymnal, catechism, prayer book, devotional, and other printed resources in sight and at hand. Your faith community can assist you in teaching Bible stories and help you introduce Luther's Small Catechism, portions of the Confessions from the Book of Concord, and other explanatory writings that our faith family holds true. Use these resources as memory work to develop a spiritual grammar.
- Explore nature, from the backyard to public spaces, and describe how God is present in all settings and the loving way He actively cares for all. Remind children that God is present when they are sick or go to the doctor, and that He is to be thanked when they get well.
- Live out your faith and your identity as a child of God in a manner visible to children: make faithful choices; steward God's gifts of body and mind; verbally honor God; treat others justly; and strive to show respect for all God's creation.
- Have fun! Remind children that God is joyful when they are close to Him. Sing Christian songs at devotions; listen to radio with Christian music and messages; take them to Vacation Bible School, youth retreats, and other gatherings. Laughing together strengthens bonds.

Learn love; teach love; live love. Being assured that we are loved and having the capacity to be loving form the bedrock for our next character traits of courage and resilience.

CHAPTER 3

Parenting Resilient, Courageous, Less Anxious Children

I can do all things through Him who strengthens me.

Philippians 4:13

Daily, we observe the number of discouraged and demoralized people in our society. I believe many are not sure if anyone loves them. Concurrently, reports of anxiety-driven illnesses continue to dramatically mount among all generations. Resilient people, on the other hand, develop motivation and energy, and they can learn to persist despite setbacks and deterrents to living abundantly.

Christian parenting aims to raise awareness of God's unremitting mercy and forgiveness in Christ, which allows children to live with less anxiety and apprehension because they understand that failing at a task is not the same as failing as a person. No matter what they do, they cannot lose God's love for them in His Son. Because of Jesus, they daily have unconditional love, mercy, forgiveness, and another chance to live according to God's will. They have new opportunities to live out their faith. Their worth is assured by Christ rather than the world:

> Blessed be the God and Father of our Lord Jesus Christ! According to His great mercy, He has caused us to be born again to a living hope through the resurrection of Jesus Christ from the dead. . . . You have been born again, not of perishable seed but of imperishable, through the living and abiding word of God.
>
> (1 Peter 1:3, 23)

Furthermore, as they are brought up in a Christian home, our baptized children learn to understand the moment-to-moment presence of God in all aspects of life. Since God is always with them, they are empowered to live boldly. God tells us this in both the Old and New Testaments:

> Be strong and courageous. Do not fear or be in dread of them, for it is the LORD your God who goes with you. He will not leave you or forsake you.
>
> (Deuteronomy 31:6)

> For God gave us a spirit not of fear but of power and love and self-control.
>
> (2 Timothy 1:7)

Children are growing up in a society that espouses equality in gender, race, ability, age, and values. Secular child-rearing educators like Drs. Alfred Adler and Michael Popkin emphasize the need for children to be resilient and courageous as the basis for cooperative behavior and effective learning. These traits allow children to try, fail, learn, and try again. Those who lack courage to try again can't learn and can't grow. Eventually, if discouraged often enough, they stop trying. They may resolve to be a failure, cautions Popkin.[1] That is a huge injury to children's spirit and future ability to learn. The Scriptures remind us that resilient children need love, guidance, and wise pruning to become courageous and to grow:

> I am the vine, and My Father is the vinedresser. Every branch in Me that does not bear fruit He takes away, and every branch that does bear fruit He prunes, that it may bear more fruit. . . . As the branch cannot bear fruit by itself, unless it abides in the vine, neither can you, unless you abide in Me. . . . As the Father has loved Me, so have I loved you. Abide in My love. If you keep My commandments, you will abide in My love, just as I have kept My Father's commandments and abide in His love. These things I have spoken to you, that My joy may be in you, and that your joy may be full.
>
> (John 15:1–11)

Courage also is an anchor for the development of a stable personality. Look at the characteristics God develops in His beloved King David:

> And Saul and the men of Israel were gathered, and encamped in the Valley of Elah, and drew up in line of battle against the Philistines. . . . And there came out from the camp of the Philistines a champion named Goliath . . . whose height was six cubits and a span. . . . "I defy the ranks of Israel this day." . . . When Saul and all Israel heard these words of the Philistine, they were dismayed and greatly afraid. Now David was the son of an Ephrathite of Bethlehem. . . . David was the youngest [son]. . . . David heard [Goliath]. . . . And David said to Saul, "Let no man's heart fail because of him. Your servant will go and fight with this Philistine." . . . David said to Saul, "Your servant used to keep sheep for his father. And when there came a lion, or a bear, and took a lamb from the flock, I went after him and struck him and delivered it out of his mouth. And if he arose against me, I caught him by his beard and struck him and killed him. . . . The LORD who delivered me from the paw of the lion and from the paw of the bear will deliver me from the hand of this Philistine."
>
> (1 Samuel 17:1–37)

From youth on, David was given a chance to try, fail, learn, and try again. His courage increased. He became resilient. Drawing on that courage, David reached his full potential as king of Israel, not for his own glory but to demonstrate the amazing purposes of God. David's father, Jesse of Bethlehem, gave him encouragement and responsibility for the care of family resources such as precious livestock, and assigned David critical tasks, such as providing his brothers in the army with supplies for battle. Then King Saul demonstrated trust and encouragement in young David when he put the fate of all Israel in this resourceful shepherd's hands.

When people of power and authority encourage a child, that child grows in courage and confidence. However, some parents may assume the child can do nothing on his or her own and complete tasks for the child. The child who isn't challenged or held responsible doesn't mature. Conversely, some parents may stress perfection over incremental improvement. They set expectations too high, assuming their child will achieve even unrealistic goals. When the child can't achieve a successful result, rather than reassessing the goal or making failure a teachable moment, parents may reprimand or even berate the child for his or her mistakes.

An adult's negative reaction when a child falls short of high standards injures the child's courage by deriding his or her personhood or worth rather than addressing the unmet results. Consequently, the child begins to feel guilt over the failure to meet expectations. If repeatedly chided, the child internalizes guilt and develops shame when he or she perceives that not only what he or she attempted to do fell short of a standard but also he or she is subpar and inadequate.

The uncomfortable reality is that shame may lead to extreme anxiety, withdrawal, and loss of self-worth. Some children express shame-driven anxiety by either shutting down emotionally or acting out with malice, an intent to harm others. Others respond to shame by self-injury: alcohol or drug abuse; smoking or marijuana use; cutting or self-mutilation; anorexia, bulimia, or overeating; sex; or even attempting suicide.

Let's look further at the anxiety of childhood and then address parenting that offers hope, calm, and courage.

THE ANXIETY SPECTRUM

To be sure, some level of anxiety or worry is a part of typical childhood development, whether your child is in an encouraging or discouraging household. The Christian home cannot completely buffer a child from stress.

Stress produces physical and emotional responses in everyone. It causes the body and brain centers, called the *hypothalamic-pituitary-adrenal* (HPA) axis, to release hormones and nerve transmissions that produce recognizable stress responses: flushed face, jitteriness, elevated pulse and blood pressure, headache, and sleep disturbances. These are responses to anxiety—fight, flight, or freeze.

All children suffer anxiety, but it is usually temporary and relatively harmless, especially if addressed promptly by parents and teachers. It is critical to talk to your children, because their perception of what is stressful or what provokes anxiety might be substantially different from yours.

Generally, anxiety will not significantly disrupt daily function. Once the stress is addressed through various forms of behavior modification or talk therapies, or the cause of the stress is diminished, the secretion of stress hormones lessens and the body and mind return to a peaceful state.

Sometimes, though, the stresses recur and the body is continuously bathed in stress hormones; anxiety becomes prolonged and intensified; unhealthy patterns of behavior may become established. There may also be genetic or environmental factors that modulate the person's ability to react or recover from stresses. No matter the cause, normal daily function becomes altered. At this point, it is time to consult your pediatrician.

Recurrent or deeply inculcated anxieties that truly alter daily function are called *anxiety disorders*. Some of the common ones are generalized anxiety disorder (GAD), obsessive-compulsive disorder (OCD), attention deficit hyperactivity disorder (ADHD), post-traumatic stress disorder (PTSD), and phobias. More-disruptive mental health disorders include major or clinical depression, manic-depressive illness (bipolar disorder), dissociative identity disorders, and schizophrenia. These illnesses may require significantly more intensive or even lifelong medications, treatments, and cognitive therapies to bring people to better function. These disorders may have structural or chemical changes within the nervous system, contributing to the intellectual or emotional dysfunction.[2]

Integration disorders are sensory-processing disorders in which the brain struggles to receive and respond to information coming in through the senses: how we see, hear, smell, taste, or touch. These disorders present themselves in a variety of ways and degrees and may be temporary. Some children are simply oversensitive to one sensory stimulus or another, and others exhibit integration disorders as part of another disorder (anxiety, for example).

In any case, it is a disturbing reality that mental health experts reveal that 80 percent of kids with a diagnosable anxiety disorder and 60 percent of children with diagnosable depression are not receiving adequate treatment.[3]

It is important for parents to know that mental health caregivers do not link every discouraged child with the group of mental illnesses we call anxiety disorders or integration disorders. However, a parent's discouraging responses to a child can be a contributing and complicating factor of these dysfunctions.

Parents need to be aware of and seek resources that will help them differentiate between basic anxiety and life-interfering anxiety. While that is not always as easy as it sounds, you can use your powers of observation and what you know to be usual, baseline behavior and activity in your child to assist you and your counseling resource person. Also, you can seek the opinions of other family members, teachers, or care providers who interact with your child. If your child is demonstrating persistent, irrational, and overwhelming worry, fear, or apprehension that is interfering with daily activities, consider that he or she may need intervention from an adult to change a situation. In most cases, the situation is improved or resolved when a caring adult with the authority to intervene gets involved, respectfully listens to the child, and takes action. In some cases, though, the child may need more.

If you suspect that your child is suffering from an anxiety disorder, significant depression, or dissociative illness, seek help as soon as possible, starting with his pediatrician. The pediatrician may prescribe medications or refer the child to a counselor, psychologist, or psychiatrist.

If your child is so discouraged that she is experiencing problems at home, in school, or in social settings; is showing signs of physical deterioration; or has attempted self-injury, you need to seek immediate assistance from medical and mental health professionals, and you need to speak with your pastor. These are red warning lights on your parental dashboard! These may also be warning lights on your own mental health monitor; your child's mental and emotional wellness often is highly connected to your own well-being as a parent and what is going on in the home. So be sure to care for yourself as well, seeking conversation with trusted others and receiving grace from your Lord Jesus.

Parents in these situations often feel a heavy burden of guilt. Remind yourself that Jesus has compassion for you and for your child. He fully and completely restores you. And He invites you to rest in Him:

> Come to Me, all who labor and are heavy laden, and I will give you rest. Take My yoke upon you, and learn from Me, for I am gentle and lowly in heart, and you will find rest for your souls. (Matthew 11:28–29)

SUGGESTIONS TO ENCOURAGE RESILIENCE IN ALL CHILDREN

Every child benefits from encouragement. A number of family resources for building courage and mental health resilience are available; check with your pastor, pediatrician, library, or other parents for their recommendations. Trust your instincts, though, and look for naturally occurring opportunities to be an encourager. For example, build opportunities for encouraging your spouse and your children into the morning routine and at mealtime. Use this as an entry point to explore situations that have been encouraging or discouraging to you and to them. Ask your children to share a story of someone who made them feel low or someone who made them feel valued that particular day.

We live in a rapidly changing world. Encourage your child to be creative and work in collaboration with friends. Instead of trying the same action or approach to solving a problem, help him or her to think creatively toward new solutions. Show your child how to work with others to accomplish a goal. Teach him to be adaptable to changing circumstances and environments.

Popkin[4] suggests additional strategies to help build courage and resilience that are worth repeating here, again considering mealtime as an effective entry point for introduction:

- Begin by giving the child responsibility consistent with her ability. Start by valuing your child by asking her opinion or asking how she might tackle a challenge that is appropriate to her age. Let her discover the consequences of her approaches to problem solving (within safe boundaries), and avoid bailing her out. Let her even be uncomfortable in taking on a responsibility.

- Praise your child for what he accomplishes on his own, remembering to seek improvement rather than perfection. Provide positive feedback even when he doesn't accomplish tasks as you expect. It is important to affirm his self-worth and his worth to the family even when he fails to fully accomplish goals and tasks to your expectation. Clearly differentiate between worth and accomplishments.
- If your child misbehaves, clarify your negative feelings toward the behavior and emphasize that you still love her. This greatly blunts the emotion of shame from establishing itself in her personality and the hiding and secretiveness that accompany shame.
- Make sure your child understands and believes in his unique gifts to the family and to the world.
- Popkin advocates writing personal "improvement" letters. He suggests that children love to receive a handwritten note saying how they are progressing; it is an intentional and visible sign of your confidence in them.[5]
- Be observant of changes in the mood or behavior of your child, especially when those changes last beyond a day or two. If the changes persist, it is time to explore further, perhaps with professional help.
- Make life together fun. Play board games that teach courageous choices. Consider simple games like stacking blocks; organized sports (de-emphasizing winning at all costs); and skills like sewing, cooking, coloring or painting, or playing a musical instrument. Recall that play often is a child's work and daily classroom.
- Make sure, as a parent, that you are addressing your own stresses and anxieties. If you need guidance and encouragement, it is critical that you address the challenges that frequently are reflected in the anxieties of your children.

Resilient children develop the courage and integrity to make responsible decisions in their daily lives and within their families and communities. Next, we examine how we can help children understand how to make thoughtful and moral decisions and then live with their choices rather than blame others for unhealthy outcomes.

NOTES

1. Michael H. Popkin, *Active Parenting 4th Edition Parent's Guide* (Marietta, GA: Active Parenting Publishers, 2015), 13, 111–118.
2. John D. Eckrich, *Fear, Anxiety and Wellness: Journey to a Heart at Peace* (n.p.: Tenth Power Publishing, 2017), 151–200.
3. Child Mind Institute Children's Mental Health Report: Anxiety and Depression Association of America, 2016, www.adaa.org.
4. Popkin, 13, 111, 118.
5. Popkin, 13, 111–118

CHAPTER 4

Parenting Children with Integrity

Do not be conformed to this world, but be transformed by the renewal of your mind, that by testing you may discern what is the will of God, what is good and acceptable and perfect.

Romans 12:2

Children readily acquire the tendency to play the blame game. For proof, we need only to look at the precedent set in Genesis 3 by Adam, Eve, and the serpent. We have an anxious world, and at the center of it is a mistaken understanding that an appropriate technique for reducing anxiety is blaming someone else for the negative consequences of a decision. Owning and acknowledging the results of the choices we make, especially the bad results, is known in our faith as *confession*, to which we are called daily. Despite the forces in this world that entice us and our children to make other than God-fearing, loving, and trusting choices, we know the Holy Spirit works in the Christian to guide us to God's will and way.

Life is full of choices. All Christian parents should understand the urgency of teaching their children to make choices that align with God's will as expressed in His Word and that are consistent with helpful outcomes. Children also need to understand, accept, and learn from choices that might result in harmful or negative consequences. Children need to know it is important to "fess up when you mess up."

Parents continuously observe that their children's choices may be guided by an enormous array of influences, particularly in areas related to health and wellness. Parents may feel, and with some cause, that their influence does not dominate in their child's mind, especially as he or she enters teenage years. That is where active, consistent parenting and parental modeling can have the greatest impact.

As mentioned, children learn good choices from watching the choices of their parents. This is particularly true in the area of wellness:

- Smoking
- Nutrition
- Maintaining a healthy recommended weight
- Physical activity and regular exercise
- Keeping alcohol use to a minimum
- Proper use of prescription drugs
- Fiscal responsibility and generosity with charities, including the local congregation
- Rest
- Personal growth (education)
- Cell phone and internet use
- Media consumption
- Relationships, including marriage

If you as a parent can say that you make good choices with regard to all of the above, then you are to be highly commended. Many of us struggle in one or more of these areas and may be discovering and suffering the consequences of our choices. Yet we can learn from poor choices, of course, and can become wiser when we experience the results. Then we have the opportunity to adopt new behaviors and share our knowledge of consequences with our children. The Lord continuously grants His people the chance to repent and start anew; parents should afford that same renewal to themselves and to their children.

Parents also must demonstrate the principles of honesty, honor, decency, respect, and fairness. Children see this in their parents' marriage and home life; in how they deal with neighbors, relatives, and business associates; and at sporting events, for instance. Children observe parents' respect for each other and for others outside the family, whether they're in a position of authority, a peer, or a subordinate.

If children do not learn from those who have their best interests at heart and who love them most dearly, they will surely turn to peers, the internet, social trends, or more nefarious sources for wellness knowledge.

As mentioned above, the corollary to raising children with the wisdom to make well-reasoned choices is to raise them with the willingness to live with the consequences of their decisions. Our desire as parents is to give our children a Christ-centered, morally sound, healthy foundation on which to base decisions that lead to God-fearing, God-loving, and God-trusting results. There is an additional caveat: if our children make poor choices, they benefit from understanding that they need to accept the responsibility and appropriate punishment for adverse results. They are not maturing well or learning from their mistakes and failures if they are not held accountable or if they continuously blame others. Blaming others is disrespectful; it is a sign of immaturity.

It is important that we also allow our children to make independent, age-appropriate, and, we hope, Spirit-inspired choices. If we make the choices for them, they cannot learn and they cannot grow. It is also necessary to help our children understand that there are limits to all choices. We cannot make choices with resources that we do not control (that is, things that do not belong to us), nor can we base our choices on imagination and nonrealities. Parents should be willing to teach these limits, as children likely have already experienced restrictions in some aspects of their lives.

It is a narrow road for parents to walk between complete dominance of their children and permissiveness. As children are entering a world with democratic ideals, parents can allow increments of freedom with appropriate limits based on the child's age and maturity. Little children can be given the choice among healthy food and drink options. Early elementary schoolkids can choose when to play and when to do homework. Middle schoolers can regulate bedtime, social time, which sports to participate in, how to spend an allowance. As they demonstrate the ability to make wise choices, limits can be expanded.

There are practical guidelines for families to help children make responsible decisions. For younger children, family meals are a wonderful setting for allowing age-appropriate choices: milk or water; peas or beans; rice or sweet potatoes, and so forth. Popkin suggests beginning by posing either-or choices: "You may choose a kiwi slice or an orange slice"; "You may do your homework before supper or after."[1] Make sure you as the parent are honestly comfortable with either choice.

Next, Popkin suggests adding when-then choices: "When you do homework before supper and you're tired as bedtime approaches, then you may play relaxing games or read your favorite book."[2] Give a choice only once, then act and stick to it: "I would like you to clean your room tonight, or you may not watch movies or play video games with your friends." And give children a do-over after they have experienced a negative outcome: "You didn't completely finish your cleaning as asked and missed going with your friends to the movies. Why don't you clean your room as asked this week, and then earn the privilege to go with your friends?"

Sudden shifts in your mood or parenting approach are very confusing to children. Try to eliminate the element of surprise in your parenting; be consistent in the way you make decisions so your children can learn a stable model of thinking through challenges.

Being respectful of others is a key component of building relationships. If you observe your child being disrespectful to you or to another person, stop and immediately make that a teaching moment to discuss, amend, and correct—but do so respectfully. Berating or lecturing a child in front of others is humiliating for the child and embarrassing for the adult.

Don't be afraid to share with older children a situation when you were faced with the moral dilemma to be dishonest and what influenced your decision to tell the truth or act honorably. If you have the courage, share a situation where your integrity failed and what you learned from it.

Encourage decision-making to be fun rather than fearful. Couple verbal praise or reinforcement for good choices with expanding freedom, and add a tangible, nonmonetary reward when consistently good choices are made: cook a favorite meal, read a favorite book, or attend a favorite sporting event or concert. Select rewards that involve you as parent, another relative, or close friends. Good choices have good outcomes for the family. Reinforce choices with consequences that are good for the WE, rather than for ME alone.

Clearly, these choice settings require consistent parenting and an agreement to parent jointly if parenting as a couple, whether you are married or divorced.[3] The worst situation is when one parent is the disciplinarian and one is the friend. This only teaches the child to manipulate one authority figure against the other, and it leads him or her to self-serving decision-making.

Finally, and particularly in preteen, teen, and young-adult years, your child may make choices that have traumatic results: traffic accidents with injury or death; drug, tobacco, and alcohol use and abuse; pregnancy; sexually transmitted infection; financial distress; probation or incarceration; suicide attempt or success. These are the nightmares of parenting that we try to keep in the most distant places in our minds. Should such a crisis arise, though, we need to find the balance between rationalization, rejection, forgiveness, love, and reconciliation. Children must suffer the repercussions, including punishment, for their decisions. These repercussions may be public and come with social fallout.

They should be encouraged to confess and repent, submitting to God's will and parental authority. Then, by Jesus' grace and forgiveness, they are reconciled with the God of mercy. We, as parents, guided by the Holy Spirit, must repent and confess ourselves, seek counsel for ourselves and for our children, and resume the loving leadership mantle of guiding our children in the will and ways of the Lord. For that we surely will need the power of the Holy Spirit, and most likely the fellowship and companionship of fellow members in the Body of Christ. God, grant these gifts to us all.

As our children realize the well-being that comes from being loved and loving, they are living resiliently and courageously and are developing moral integrity through making and living with godly decisions. And they now are ready to comprehend the callings and purposes Christ already has in place for them within His kingdom.

NOTES

1. Michael H. Popkin, *Active Parenting 4th Edition Parent's Guide* (Marietta, GA: Active Parenting Publishers, 2015), pp. 13, 111–118.
2. Ibid.
3. Catherine K. Buckley, "Co-parenting after Divorce: Opportunities and Challenges" (Evanston, IL: The Family Institute at Northwestern University, 2013).

CHAPTER 5

Parenting Secure, Christ-Purposed Children

God is our refuge and strength, a very present help in trouble. Therefore we will not fear though the earth gives way, though the mountains be moved into the heart of the sea, though its waters roar and foam, though the mountains tremble at its swelling. . . . The God of Jacob is our fortress.

Psalm 46:1–3, 7

No temptation has overtaken you that is not common to man. God is faithful, and He will not let you be tempted beyond your ability, but with the temptation He will also provide the way of escape, that you may be able to endure it.

1 Corinthians 10:13

"A Mighty Fortress Is Our God," one of Martin Luther's best-known hymns, paraphrases the powerful statement of security in Psalm 46. Despite the target painted on the hearts of all of God's children, Satan and the powers of evil have no ability to separate you or your child from the grasp of God's protection. It is important to teach your child Luther's Morning and Evening Prayers to reinforce this truth. We remember and rehearse daily that Jesus has "kept me this night from all harm and danger; and I pray that You would keep me this day also from sin and every evil, that all my doings and life may please You. For into Your hands I commend myself, my body and soul, and all things" (SC, Luther's Morning Prayer).

Baptized into Christ, your child lives, studies, and plays safely because Jesus sends His holy angels to guard over all aspects of life. In addition, the God who protects us sets purpose and mission within the life of each of His children:

> For You formed my inward parts; You knitted me together in my mother's womb. I praise You, for I am fearfully and wonderfully made. Wonderful are Your works; my soul knows it very well. My frame was not hidden from You, when I was being made in secret, intricately woven in the depths of the earth. Your eyes saw my unformed substance; in Your book were written, every one of them, the days that were formed for me, when as yet there was none of them.
>
> (Psalm 139:13–16)

Jesus has a plan for each of us. He identifies purpose and direction, as we are told in Psalm 139. That meaning and purpose is sacred because it was bought with such a price, Jesus' own death:

> You were bought with a price; do not become bondservants of men. So, brothers, in whatever condition each was called, there let him remain with God.
>
> (1 Corinthians 7:23–24)

Jesus spent His life and death in our stead restoring us in relationship with the triune God. For me, it is said best in Martin Luther's explanation of the Second Article of the Apostles' Creed: "[He] has redeemed me, a lost and condemned person, purchased and won me from all sins, from death, and from the power of the devil; not with gold or silver, but with His holy, precious blood and with His innocent suffering and death, that I may be His own and live under Him in His kingdom and serve Him in everlasting righteousness, innocence, and blessedness" (SC).

As parents, we begin instilling the value of purpose by teaching our children about their place in their family: first, as a member of God's family, baptized and redeemed by the triune God Himself; and second, as a member of an earthly, faith-filled family that understands its purpose to glorify God and serve His people.

God equips each child with spiritual gifts, and each God-given gift has value in God's sight—and should in the earthly family's eyes as well. Those spiritual gifts, along with the unique talents, strengths, abilities, and feelings God has given each of us, are very important to the family's function and harmony. And when we make individual choices with consequences, those choices have repercussions for the whole family.

We can observe our children's personality traits and physical and mental capabilities at the youngest of ages. One child may have coordination, physical strength, and size to nurture athletic talents; another, the strength and coordination to dance. One child may appreciate color and design. Another may be a gifted communicator, a gentle spirit, a reconciler, or a strong scholar. It is never too early to encourage and expand on God-given gifts through simple words and actions of support or expanded opportunity.

We may also observe behaviors not centered in Christ that we know will lead to ill purposes. When we do, we have opportunities to try to direct those behaviors to better use by changing channels for expressing energy and emotional drives.

Again, your children will observe the ways you express the purpose and direction of your own journey as a follower of Christ. Take every opportunity to show, by word and deed, how you live out your faith and the Christian love instilled in your heart as you care for God's people and all of God's creation:

> Truly, I say to you, as you did it to one of the least of these My brothers, you did it to Me.
>
> (Matthew 25:40)

It is also important to teach children that fulfilling their missional walk means they may experience hard times. Living out a Christ-centered purpose is quite countercultural. As Christ-purposed, by walking a faithful path, they could experience rejection by some people, especially their peers; they risk being ridiculed and rejected. As a parent and faith teacher, you will need to help your children discover the joy, fulfillment, and security of being different because of Jesus. This message is especially challenging to communicate to teenagers and young adults. But it is far easier to encourage the more difficult path in the way of Christ because you are walking in the same direction, expressing the confidence you experience as one unconditionally loved by Christ.

> For to this you have been called, because Christ also suffered for you, leaving you an example, so that you might follow in His steps.
>
> (1 Peter 2:21)

Furthermore, being Christ-purposed means growing in the knowledge of God, gaining increased insight into God's presence among us, and growing in God's grace.

> And it is my prayer that your love may abound more and more, with knowledge and all discernment, so that you may approve what is excellent, and so be pure and blameless for the day of Christ, filled with the fruit of righteousness that comes through Jesus Christ, to the glory and praise of God.
>
> (Philippians 1:9–11)

Finally, being Christ-purposed and Spirit-nurtured uplifts us to hearten our children in character virtues—fruit of the Spirit—that are wellness gifts of that very work of the Spirit:

> By this My Father is glorified, that you bear much fruit and so prove to be My disciples.
>
> (John 15:8)

We are given specifics by St. Paul in Galatians 5:22–23: love, joy, peace, patience, kindness, goodness, faithfulness, gentleness, self-control. These are virtues and characteristics instilled by the Holy Spirit that all Christian parents hope to model and instill in their children as citizens in both God's heavenly and earthly kingdoms.

Here are a few suggestions for encouraging highly secure, Christ-purposed children to highlight family purposes and goals:

- Periodically ask your family these questions: How are we doing in accomplishing the purpose for the resources God has given us?

What have we done today for the good of God's kingdom?

- Discuss the security of knowing that God loves them unconditionally, will never leave or forsake them, and is always near them, "our refuge and strength, a very present help in trouble" (Psalm 46:1). Similarly, their family must always be their safe harbor through any of life's storms where they find unconditional love and acceptance for who and whose they are.
- As a family, participate in service projects at church, school, or community so children can model faith in action. This might be serving meals at shelters; setting up Christmas decorations at church; contributing pocket change to bell ringers, firefighters, or other volunteers. Explain why being generous is important. Make service fun. Your attitude is highly transparent; show positive energy and excitement when you volunteer. After the task is completed, discuss how it made everyone feel and the joy you experienced.
- Let children contribute when the offering plate comes around, and extol the purpose of family giving—why and how you choose your offering amounts and directives. Encourage them to give a portion of their allowance, joyfully. Again, your attitude is highly transparent.
- Frequently discuss the importance of being honest, especially about who they are. For teens, the influence of "internet identity" rather than their true identity as a child of God can become overwhelming and destructive. As a parent, be honest and encourage and expect the same in your child.

With the bulwark of their identity anchored securely in Christ's love, resilient with integrity, and armed with the conviction of being Christ-purposed, we encourage our children to have a servant heart and compassion for all of God's creatures and cosmos. That love and compassion led our Lord to the cross. His death forgives our sins. His death restores our hope for wellness.

CHAPTER 6

Parenting Compassionate Children with Servant Hearts

> And let us consider how to stir up one another to love
> and good works, not neglecting to meet together, as
> is the habit of some, but encouraging one another,
> and all the more as you see the Day drawing near.
>
> (Hebrews 10:24–25)

God's gifts of His Son, an eternal home, and earthly families are utmost expressions of our heavenly Father's desire for His children to be in close relationship with Him and with others. His intention is for us to characterize the same relational harmony that is shown in the three persons of the Trinity: Father, Son, and Holy Spirit. Love flows continuously outward from each person of the Trinity into one another and from the triune God into His creation. God also shows us that the strength of relationships is not just encouragement and care but also accountability:

> Two are better than one, because they have a good reward for their toil. For if they fall, one will lift up his fellow. But woe to him who is alone when he falls and has not another to lift him up! Again, if two lie together, they keep warm, but how can one keep warm alone? And though a man might prevail against one who is alone, two will withstand him—a threefold cord is not quickly broken.
>
> (Ecclesiastes 4:9–12)

We want to raise children who understand that joy resides in and flows from serving one another in healthy relationships. Ultimate joy flows from our relationship with Jesus. When relationships are modeled after the example of Christ's love for His Church, they fully display the posture of being mutual servants.

What does it mean to teach relational servanthood? It means to inspire children with a guiding principle of living outside of self, of serving and living as WE rather than ME, as David Ludwig, pastor and psychologist, eloquently identifies it in his writings.[1] We want children who are not focused on themselves but who gladly turn their energy and spirit for living into cooperative associations with and for the care of others. We want our children to understand that this is the very nature of Christ's relationship within the triune God—Father, Son, and Holy Spirit—and this is the model Jesus has given to us to care for one another.

God tells us of the harmonious dance of the Trinity from Genesis to Revelation as He refers to Himself as "Us" and "Our." The word *trinity* means "three in unity." "Yet for us there is one God, the Father, from whom are all things and for whom we exist, and one Lord, Jesus Christ, through whom are all things and through whom we exist" (1 Corinthians 8:6). And Jesus Himself tells us, "I and the Father are one" (John 10:30). Finally, we are sent into mission in the name of this relational God: "Go therefore and make disciples of all nations, baptizing them in the name of the Father and of the Son and of the Holy Spirit" (Matthew 28:19).

Divine unity flows into us as love, trust, and respect. In John 14:16–17, we hear Jesus' voice: "And I will ask the Father, and He will give you another Helper, to be with you forever, even the Spirit of truth, whom the world cannot receive, because it neither sees Him nor knows Him. You know Him, for He dwells with you and will be in you."

Jesus speaks to us from the depth of the triune relationship: "But God shows His love for us in that while we were still sinners, Christ died for us" (Romans 5:8). Our Christian faith family is to be Christ-centered in love: "Beloved, let us love one another, for love is from God, and whoever loves has been born of God and knows God. Anyone who does not love does not know God, because God is love" (1 John 4:7–8).

Paul further explains this love in his letter to the faithful in Corinth:

> Love is patient and kind; love does not envy or boast; it is not arrogant or rude. It does not insist on its own way; it is not irritable or resentful; it does not rejoice at wrongdoing, but rejoices with the truth. Love bears all things, believes all things, hopes all things, endures all things. Love never ends. As for prophecies, they will pass away; as for tongues, they will cease; as for knowledge, it will pass away.
>
> (1 Corinthians 13:4–8)

All of these "love passages" emphasize the strength of loving by serving one another as the basis of Christlike relationships, relationships lived as WE. Living as WE is the very definition of Christ's compassion:

- We show one another sympathy, empathy, understanding, and care.
- We are lenient and tolerant; we are kind and gentle; we are humble.
- We are forgiving.

One further example of the forcefulness and effectiveness of compassionate WE living comes in Paul's description of human nature in the value-laden Greek words he uses to describe the natural man and the Spirit-led man. Our natural self is turned inward toward self (ME)—*incurvatus in se* in St. Augustine's[2] and Luther's terms.[3] The man, filled and informed (breathed into) by the Holy Spirit, lives the way God intends for His children to live (WE). This person is enlivened, empowered, transformed, nonanxious, and focused outward into loving and effective relationships: love-filled WEs, harmonious in the triune God, harmonious with others and all of creation.

Jesus calls us into a posture as a servant, which He demonstrated in His relationship with the Father:

> Have this mind among yourselves, which is yours in Christ Jesus, who, though He was in the form of God, did not count equality with God a thing to be grasped, but emptied Himself, by taking the form of a servant, being born in the likeness of men. And being found in human form, He humbled Himself by

> becoming obedient to the point of death, even death on a cross.
> (Philippians 2:5–8)

Our core beliefs, stated in the Apostles', Nicene, and Athanasian creeds, define the divine relationship.

Therefore, Christians are relational people, service people. The Christian home is the incubator for instilling and encouraging humble, compassionate servanthood. And our congregations are relational workshops. Our mission and purpose are established in the hearts, minds, and spirits of congregation members, who effectively lead through relating to and caring for one another. We live out compassion by our actions.

To take this one step further, how do we go about making sure our children understand how relationships function best? We help them understand that relationships work best when each person in the relationship is focused on making the relationship itself the best it can be. That does not mean abandoning one's wholeness, wellness, or rights. But it can mean that rather than looking at our own feelings and behaviors as a sacrifice of self for others, we see the great joy in choosing (not being forced) to contribute individual entitlements if they can produce good for the whole relationship. Cooperation rather than competition can produce more satisfaction and positive results. This stands in contrast to a "survival of the fittest" mentality that exists in much of our world. Christians are called to countercultural behavior when the situation demands following in the way of the cross.

How can we encourage relational, servant-hearted children in our families? At the risk of being repetitive, I cannot help but emphasize family meals as the prime location for relationship strengthening and for contributing:

- Encourage children to plan, shop, serve, and clean up after meals.
- Allow children to lead prayers and offer prayer requests.
- Ask children to supply topics for mealtime discussion.

Use mealtime to initiate regular, structured family meetings. Give each child a position, title, and job. Use this forum to share events, situations, and feelings openly. Make decisions that might impact the family members. Discuss activities, schedules, vacations, or large purchases. Encourage everyone to share their viewpoints. And use a democratic voting process. (Note that this does not imply that all decisions are made by a family vote. As parents, you retain the authority to decide family health and welfare decisions, but you can allow children to express their opinions and concerns so they feel respected and honored.)

Point out examples where your children have demonstrated compassion, but also point out opportunities within family life to be compassionate, where they can show leniency or mercy to a brother or sister or friend. Reinforce the importance of this value by your commendation.

Just an FYI: conclude family meetings with a fun activity, even if it's just sharing a food treat or playing a game. The message is "We are a family, even when we face tough decisions and have differing opinions; in the end, we can have fun with one another."

Hold regular family devotions, and as children are able, allow them to choose or read the devotions. Allow children periodically to lead family prayers. End each devotion with the same question: "What can I do today and tomorrow to serve you in Jesus' name?"

It is critical to actively listen to your children. Look them in the eye, stop watching TV or looking at your phone, sit and face them directly, and direct all your attention to their concerns. You will instill great value and purpose in honoring their feelings and thoughts.

Encourage children to contribute to major family purchases and activities. Giving something from their hearts, whatever the amount, teaches them that their contribution is valued and necessary for the good of the family. Make giving fun! In a broader sense, help them understand and see how their contributions make it possible for the whole family to have joy-filled experiences together. Within means, have family vacations or staycations with the children's contributions buying food or tickets for fun activities. Encourage church offerings from their own resources and explain to them the ministries those gifts will support.

Anchored in love; resilient with courage; honest, respectful, and armed with the ability to make good decisions; securely Christ-purposed; and compassionate—how do we now connect these fundamental character traits to parenting individual, family, and societal health and wellness behaviors that honor God and bless all? That is the challenge of the remainder of this book. Are you ready to apply practical wellness applications to this parenting journey with your children? Read on!

NOTES

1. David Ludwig, *Renewing the Family Spirit: Overcoming Conflict to Enjoy Stronger Family Ties* (St. Louis: Concordia Publishing House, 1989).
2. *Augustine, City of God* (Kindle edition), book XII, chapter vi.
3. Matt Jenson, *The Gravity of Sin: Augustine, Luther and Barth on "homo incurvatus in se"* (London: Bloomsbury T & T Clark, 2007), 2, 15, 45, 128, 130, 183.

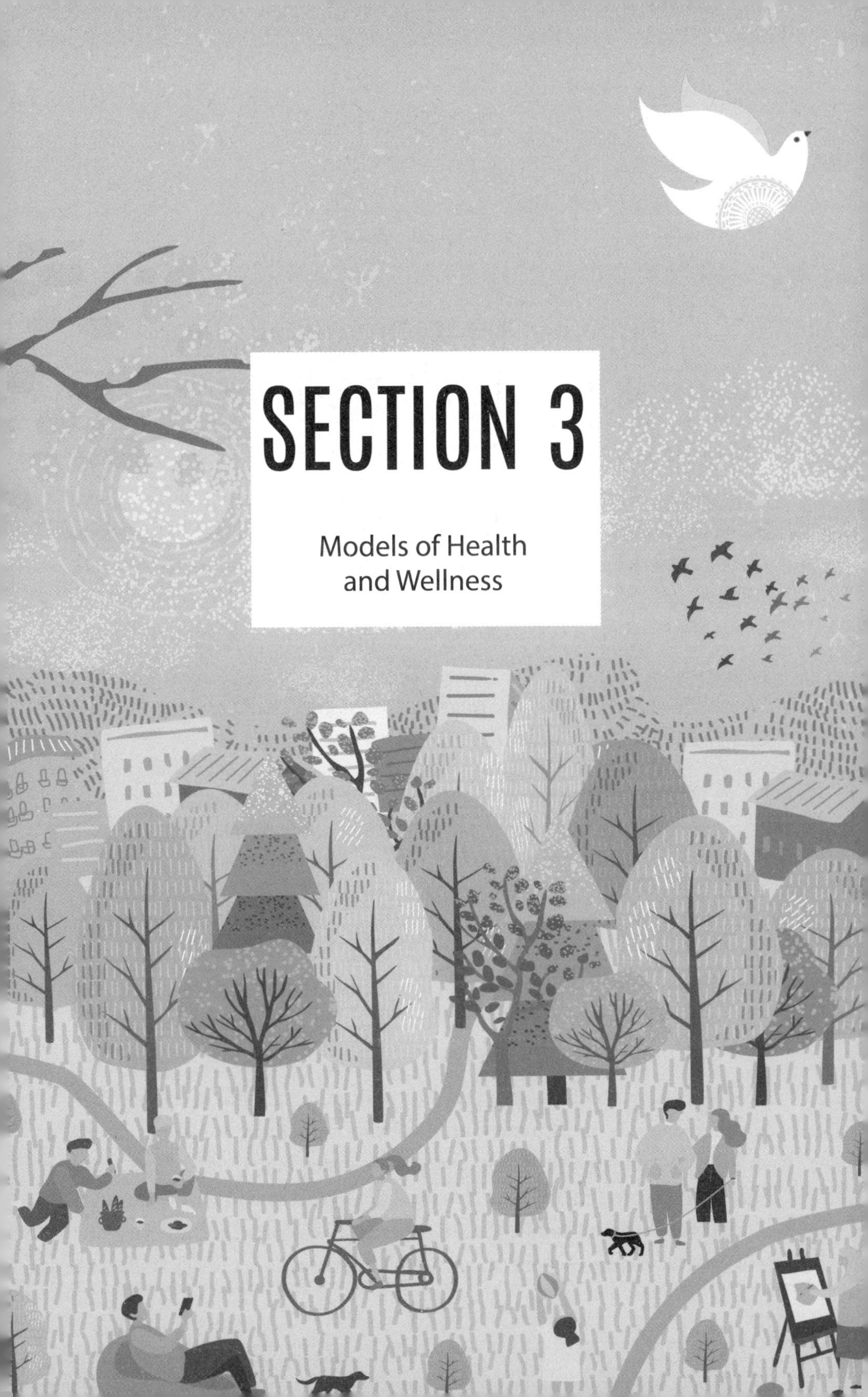

SECTION 3

Models of Health and Wellness

CHAPTER 7

Pathways for Wellness Behavior in Both Parents and Children

The first part of our discussion has focused on the role of parental leadership in instilling core values in our children to better live and serve in the home and outside it in a democratic society—to strive to be loving, Christ-centered, resilient, upright, secure, and compassionate children, siblings, and citizens.

The rest of this book points to Spirit-inspired wellness behaviors and patterns that support those values. Therefore, it makes sense to explore how wellness behavior encourages the development of God-fearing, virtuous children. The Gospel of Luke shares this insight:

> And when [Jesus' earthly parents] had performed everything according to the Law of the Lord, they returned into Galilee, to their own town of Nazareth. And the child grew and became strong, filled with wisdom. And the favor of God was upon Him. (Luke 2:39–40)

Parental leadership, guided by the Spirit, stewards physical, cognitive, and spiritual wellness in children by anchoring that stewardship in the Word made flesh, Jesus, and in the Sacraments He instituted.

The connection between children's core values and their wellness behavior occurs in an understanding of who and whose we are as God's children. When we are baptized with the water and Word of the Holy Spirit, we are brought into the covenant of God's love and family through Christ. However, although we are now God's children, we are not, nor will we ever be, the owners (masters) of God's creation. Our own life and the life of the universe is placed into our active management by the owner, God. This management includes our vocations, emotions, relationships, physique, intellect, finances, environment, and fellow creatures. That makes us caretakers of the gifts that help us accomplish this work—our body, mind, and spirit.

We are reminded in God's Word that He expects us to be working both to steward well and steward wellness:

> The LORD God took the man and put him in the garden of Eden to work it and keep it.
>
> (Genesis 2:15)

> "For it will be like a man going on a journey, who called his servants and entrusted to them his property." [The master expected all to be working, but his displeasure with the servant who did not steward his gifts was clear:] "And cast the worthless servant into the outer darkness. In that place there will be weeping and gnashing of teeth."
>
> (Matthew 25:14, 30)

> This is how one should regard us, as servants of Christ and stewards of the mysteries of God. Moreover, it is required of stewards that they be found faithful.
>
> (1 Corinthians 4:1–2)

In my faith community, we have developed a helpful model to depict and encourage the stewardship of wellness among Lutheran professional church workers and laity. It is called the Lutheran Wellness Wheel.*

Grace Place Wellness Ministries (GPWM) is a Recognized Service Organization in the LCMS that nurtures vitality and joy in ministry by inspiring and equipping church workers to lead healthy lives. GPWM utilizes two scriptural anchors, Galatians 5:22–23 and Ephesians 4, for discussing wellness and exploring God's gracious provision for wellness for His creatures through the Holy Spirit.

* I invite you to visit the websites of The Lutheran Church—Missouri Synod (LCMS) or Grace Place Wellness Ministries (GPWM) to explore this concept further.

THE LUTHERAN WELLNESS WHEEL

This teaching model identifies a centering value, or center "bore," of our new creation in Christ through Baptism. We have an identity as a child of God, who loves us through Christ's death and resurrection (Galatians 5:22–23; Ephesians 4:21–24). Surrounding the entire wheel is our spiritual well-being, our daily transforming by the Holy Spirit as we die to sin and arise to newness of life through God's Word and Sacraments. With thankfulness and praise, we live out our faith joyfully in all aspects as the Spirit works mercy, witness, and life together among us. The six spokes of this wheel help us understand how God's presence actively fills all components of daily living: Relational, Intellectual, Emotional, Physical, Financial, and Vocational. (We will explore the application of Galatians 5 and Ephesians 4 to the Wellness Wheel in depth in Chapter 12.)

Luther sets an appropriate tone for a discussion of stewardship of wellness in his "Defense and Explanation of All the Articles," penned in 1521. His perspective is most useful as we advocate stewardship principles for parents and children:

> This life, therefore, is not godliness but the process of becoming godly, not health but getting well, not being but becoming, not rest but exercise. We are not now what we shall be, but we are on the way.[1]

Baptized into faith, each of us is a work in progress, being molded, sculpted, and healed from day to day by the Holy Spirit. We are "on the way," as Luther describes the work of the Spirit upon our faith journey.

Furthermore, St. Paul reminds us of the disposition, or "fragrance," of a well person in process:

> For we are the aroma of Christ to God among those who are being saved and among those who are perishing, to one a fragrance from death to death, to the other a fragrance from life to life. Who is sufficient for these things? For we are not, like so many, peddlers of God's word, but as men of sincerity, as commissioned by God, in the sight of God we speak in Christ.
> (2 Corinthians 2:15–17)

Again, the Christ-modeled characteristics are the wellness gifts from the Spirit to those who live, breathe, and move in Christ. You might ask yourself, "What is my fragrance?" or "What is our aroma as parents?" or "What do my children breathe in when they're in my presence?"

Therefore, with fruit of the Spirit in mind, we examine how parents can encourage growth, joyful living, and servanthood in our dear children, remembering Luther's perspective regarding the Holy Spirit's daily ripening of our faith.

I am going to introduce you, as loving parent-leader, to five wellness behaviors that complement the relationship and character traits discussed in the early chapters of this book:

- Movement
- Plant-based nutrition
- Regular rest
- Focus on faith and family
- Purposeful and missional living

The chapters ahead look at the scriptural basis for these five wellness disciplines, but be assured that there is strong evidence in science and medicine as well that validates these behaviors. The five wellness behaviors are verified by some of the most instructive studies on human well-being that have been done in half a millennium. Chapter 8 is concerned specifically with how they are presented by author and lecturer Dan Buettner, a Fellow of the National Geographic Society. His insight is readily accessible and easily understandable. And the later chapters of this book focus on age-specific parameters that allow you to better address your child's specific stage in growth and development.

NOTES

1. *Career of the Reformer II, Luther's Works*: American Edition, vol. 32, George W. Forell, ed., (St. Louis: Concordia Publishing House, 1958), 24.

CHAPTER 8

Contemporary Examples of Wellness: The Blue Zones

To prepare our children to live in a twenty-first-century democracy, in addition to the five character values (page 10), I suggested that there are at least five complementary wellness behaviors—or health-and-wellness stewardship principles—that appear to enhance the longevity, quality, and joyfulness of life's journey. These behaviors are modeled in the earthly walk of our Savior. Examples include the following:

- Regular physical activity. As a carpenter's son (Matthew 13:55), Jesus would have done physical work regularly as He learned His earthly father's trade. And there are many examples in Scripture of Jesus walking everywhere, including to Jerusalem (John 2:13), a round trip of 240 miles from Nazareth.
- Plant-based nutrition (John 6:9).
- Periodic rest (Mark 4:35–40).
- Focus on faith and loved ones (John 19:25–27).
- Relational living with outward mission and purpose (Luke 9:11; Matthew 11:28–29).

In addition to biblical examples, how do we know these behaviors are valuable? How do we incorporate them practically into daily family life?

THE BLUE ZONES[1]

In 1550, eighty-three-year-old Luigi Cornaro wrote a best seller titled *The Sure and Certain Method of Attaining a Long and Healthful Life.*[2] Cornaro proposed that his readers could extend the length of life by practicing moderation. He lived well into his nineties during an era when the average age of death was around seventy. Many of the great ancient philosophers and spiritualists dating to before the time of Christ had advised their listeners on issues of aging, but Cornaro's writings provided a zenith for this topic. That is, until the publication of Dan Buettner's findings on the Blue Zones in the November 2005 edition of *National Geographic Magazine*.[3]

Since 2002, Mr. Buettner, a National Geographic Fellow and *New York Times* best-selling author, explorer, educator, speaker, and storyteller, has been illuminating the world on living longer, more happily, and, I think, more effectively through his meticulous and informative work. That first cover article for *National Geographic* was titled "Secrets of Long Life." Subsequently, he has published multiple books, articles, blog posts, and podcasts and has spoken publicly on not merely living longer but on thriving as well. Furthermore, Buettner encourages us to make wellness choices and behavior changes to enhance not just our personal and family well-being but also that of our community and society.[4, 5]

Buettner collaborated with demographer Dr. Luis Roseto-Bixby to identify five locations around the globe that are centers of long life: Ikaria, Greece; Okinawa, Japan; Sardinia, Italy; Loma Linda, California; and the Nicoya Peninsula, Costa Rica. Buettner discovered life-extending wellness behaviors common to these locations:[6]

- Natural movement
- Understanding purpose
- Downshifting (rest)
- 80 percent rule (moderate food consumption)
- Plant slant to nutrition
- A glass or two of wine (for nonalcoholics) combined with nutritious diet
- Putting family first
- Belonging to community
- Being with supportive friends and relatives

An extraordinarily complex interplay between nature and nurture is expressed in physical and cognitive disorders (obesity and attention deficit disorder, for example). Researchers in a recent, enormous, Harvard-led twin study suggest that about 40 percent of conditions appear primarily inheritable and that at least 25 percent of ills could have causal social or environmental factors.[7] It is instructive to look at Buettner's findings and other science to give us perspective on wellness behaviors that complement the character values listed in the earlier chapters.

- *Natural movement:* Make lifestyle choices that encourage physical activity. Choose walking rather than riding, and use physical effort to perform household chores and to grow, harvest, and prepare meals. Make natural movement regular and touching all aspects of daily living.
- *Plant-based nutrition:* Follow a predominantly vegetarian nutrition plan. Most residents in Blue Zone locations eat little meat, preferring fruits and vegetables as 90 percent or more of their intake. Protein often comes from beans. Inhabitants don't eat to excess. Some follow an 80 percent rule to help them determine when they have had enough to eat: when they sense that their stomachs are 80 percent full, they stop eating. It is estimated that if we Americans were to follow this rule, we might lose as much as 17 pounds in the first year of modified intake.
- *Systemic and periodic rest (downshifting):* Reduce the negative effects of stress by regularly slowing down life's pace, or downshifting; diminishing stresses; and resting throughout the day. During these quiet times, our stress-response system (hypothalamus-pituitary-adrenal axis) slows, stress hormone secretions diminish, blood pressure lowers, and pulse rate decreases. We can nap, pray, or meditate. We can share a "happy hour" (a time of face-to-face conversation with our family). Certainly, we can share meals more often than the average American family tends to do.
- *Prioritizing faith and loved ones:* Place spiritual life, faith, and family above other competing choices and commitments. This adds longevity and vitality to life. Investing in the physical, cognitive, and spiritual well-being of your children and grandchildren empowers the whole family. Having a spouse or even a significant friend adds not only support but also accountability, and it also contributes significantly to longevity. A complementary component to the definition of *family* includes friendship circles and members of your spiritual community. Regularly attend worship services with friends and family. Participating in a spiritual community adds four to fourteen years

to life expectancy and untold value to quality of life. Again, interpersonal accountability in addition to mere friendship is value added.

As a Christian reference point, Luther noted that every Christian—in fact, every human being—has been called by God into a family, a relationship. Luther states, "God has given this walk of life, fatherhood and motherhood, a special position of honor, higher than that of any other walk of life under it."[8]

- *Purposeful and missional living:* Wake up each morning with an intentional acknowledgment of your vocation as parent and family leader, a purpose that is beyond your career or job. Having missional incentive may add up to seven extra years to life.[9] By comparison, in our Western culture, the greatest risk factor for dying in your mid-sixties is retirement.[10]

Perhaps the most insightful finding from the Blue Zones is that you have opportunities to make choices and behavioral changes in your personal environment, little changes that produce wellness for the long term. These changes can gently motivate you to be more social, more mobile, less consuming, and more conscious about what you are doing, eating, and drinking on a daily basis. And no matter when you make these lifestyle changes, you will benefit. The key to these wellness behaviors is that you just need to start now. Since there are benefits to beginning at any point, even adulthood and old age, think of the advantages of instilling these attitudes, behaviors, and choices into children from birth!

Here are suggestions from Blue Zone inhabitants, especially those living in the United States, that you can integrate into your home environment to promote wellness:[11]

- *Create a Blue Zone kitchen.* Place healthy ingredients in easy reach and in plain sight. Equip your kitchen with utensils and cookware that encourages physical effort. Reduce reliance on mechanized equipment. Lay out your kitchen in a triangle with the stove, sink, and refrigerator at the tips of the triangle so you have to take steps between them. Have good lighting. Use a smaller, energy-efficient refrigerator that is not overstuffed, and keep a smaller pantry to discourage waste. Stand while preparing food. Wash dishes by hand.
- *Redesign your bedroom to encourage good sleep.* Buy a comfortable mattress and pillows. Keep your thermostat between 62 and 65 de-

grees Fahrenheit at night. Keep your room dark during sleep, and dim the room an hour before bedtime. Keep your TV, computer, and cell phone out of the bedroom.

- *Make your entire home a Blue Zone.* Keep a scale in a prominent place and get on it regularly. Have just one TV in your home and keep it turned off most of the time to discourage mindless viewing. Switch from power tools to hand tools. Plant a vegetable garden and eat from it. Walk a dog; ride a bike; choose an active sport as a hobby. Consider buying a few pillows or beanbag chairs to give your thighs an extra daily workout. Consider replacing chairs with stools to encourage better posture and core strength.
- *Get into a social group, book club, or mutual care group, or actively participate in your faith community.* Remember that people who belong to a faith-based community and attend community functions at least four times per month live four to fourteen years longer than people who don't. Sing in the choir; serve as an usher; work on a committee.
- *Stop drinking soft drinks, including diet sodas and diet teas.* Do not drink energy drinks. Water, coffee, and natural teas clearly have been shown to have substantial health benefits over soft drinks, including producing better blood flow, lower rates of Parkinson's and dementia, strong cancer prevention, and anti-inflammatory properties. Some studies indicate that one glass of red wine daily has heart-healthy benefits. (Put this in perspective with overall health.)
- *Make smart dietary choices.* Snack on nuts. Eat sourdough and whole-grain bread. Eat beans daily. Cut sugar. Retreat from meat. Reduce cow dairy by switching to soy, almond, sheep, or goat's milk (you may need to add vitamin B12). Eat fish frequently, but in moderation (3–4 ounces per serving).

Can we create a Blue Zone community of our own? As good stewards, we can also encourage our community to be healthy. In California, Iowa, Oregon, Florida, Hawaii, Minnesota, Oklahoma, Texas, and Wisconsin, entire communities have created public environments for walking paths connecting neighborhood gardens, grocers, and restaurants offering healthy food and snacks, and intentional opportunities for quiet space and rest.[12]

As we explore further in this book, we will see the importance of integrating wellness behavior into your parenting as soon as possible, hopefully even before the birth of your children. However, hear this loud and clear: any time you can introduce healthy choices and behavior to your children has benefits. The starting is often the most difficult task. How does one find motivation to begin? Where do you find the impetus to change from physical, emotional, and spiritual funk to joy and abundant living and parenting?

Here are a few suggestions.

- *Physically,* you can find motivation by taking an honest look at your current level of health. Are you moving with ease and without distracting stiffness or pain? Is any dysfunction making it hard to parent vibrantly and caringly? Are you comfortable with your level of health, with how you project our interest in others, especially your children? As you age, do you treat your body like a being who wants to be around to see your children become adults and parents themselves?
- *Intellectually and emotionally,* are you as bright and clear as you would like to be as you deal with your children? Are you focused on your children rather than your social media accounts, being truly present when you are conversing or listening to your children? Do you prioritize your responsibilities to place faith and family above other pulls and desires within our culture? Are you doing thinking activities or exercises and avoiding substances that dull mental clarity and emotional responsiveness? Are your thoughts of peace or of turmoil? What is your self-talk like? Is it harsh, accusatory, and judgmental? Or is it forgiving, calming, and content? Are you continuing to learn? Do you experience new things with excitement? Do you have a clearer understanding and commitment to your vocation as parent?
- *Spiritually,* are you taking your concerns to God, leaning on His wisdom revealed in the Bible? Do you regularly acknowledge your humanity, repent of your sin, and receive Holy Communion? Are you confident in Jesus' work on your behalf—suffering, dying, and rising for you—and in the gifts of your Baptism?

Your responses to these questions are telling. We all age. We can age resiliently and purposefully, or, if we don't steward these good gifts of God, we can stagnate and experience increasing deterioration.

We can make a difference in the lives of our children and grandchildren, beginning with changing our health choices and behaviors. Begin with small and encouraging baby steps, gradually incorporated until they become daily disciplines. Then we can share them by example and word to our children. God's calling to parents is most enjoyable when it is accompanied by vitality and persistence that can come from a healthy body, mind, and spirit.

NOTES

1. Dan Buettner, *Blue Zones: The Science of Living Longer; 9 Lessons for Living Longer from the People Who've Lived the Longest*, second ed. (Washington, DC: National Geographic Society, 2008, 2012).
2. Luigi Cornaro, *The Art of Living Longer*, Pantianos Classics, Large Print Edition, translation first published in 1917.
3. Dan Buettner, "The Secrets of Living Longer," *National Geographic*, (November 2005).
4. Buettner, "The Finnish Town That Went on a Diet," *The Atlantic*, Atlantic Media Company, April 7, 2012.
5. Anne Underwood, "How Public Policy Can Prevent Heart Disease," *NewsWeek* (April 2, 2010), accessed June 24, 2015 Newsweek.com/how-public-policy-can-prevent-heart-disease-75073.
6. Buettner, *The Blue Zones Solution: Eating and Living Like the World's Healthiest People* (Washington, DC: National Geographic Society, 2015), 20–21.
7. Rich Haridy, "Massive Harvard-Led Genetic Twin Study Homes in on the Nature versus Nurture Debate," New Atlas (January 14, 2019), www.newatlas.com/harvard-gene-twin-study-catch/58038/.
8. "LCMS Life Library—Vocation," lcms.org/life-ministry/library/vocation.
9. Cari Shane, "The Secrets of a Long Life from the U.S.'s Top Longevity Hot Spot," Leapsmag (Jan. 10, 2020), leapsmag.com/the-secrets-of-a-long-life-from-the-u-s-s-toop-longevity-spot.
10. G. Mannes, "Would It Kill You to Retire? Maybe," *AARP* (December 22, 2017), http://www.aarp.org.
11. Buettner, *The Blue Zones Solution*, 205–227.
12. Buettner, *Blue Zones: The Science of Living Longer.*

CHAPTER 9

Parameters of Wellness Behavior in Parents and Children

As a physician, parent, and grandparent, I see children who are born with or develop a vast spectrum of physical and mental abilities. All people have imprinted in them the image of God. All baptized people have unfathomable value and worth because they have been purchased through Christ's death on the cross for us. Young and old, all of God's children are precious in His eyes, forgiven and redeemed because of Jesus. Our wellness is not an indicator of our value or worth.

When I speak of individual wellness, then, I am referring to the finest quality of health that Spirit-inspired care and stewardship of God's gifts can offer. We hold dual "wellness passports." Just as we acknowledge our dual human citizenship as saint and sinner (St. Augustine's and Luther's Latin phrase *Simul Justus et Peccator* comes to mind[1]), we are also physically perishable (biodegradable or easily spoiled), yet destined for imperishability through Christ (1 Corinthians 15:52).

Being perishable means we will experience various disorders due to the limitations of our genes and gene mutations, birth defects, mental and emotional distress, wellness choices, environment, illness, injury, and disease. The markers for physical, cognitive, and spiritual childhood development I will share (see Section 4) derive from scientific, medical, psychological, and theological observations on the diversity of humanity. All people fall somewhere along a developmental bell-shaped curve in each of these three areas.

A BELL-SHAPED CURVE

This does *not* mean that anyone anywhere along the curve has less or more worth in the eyes of God, nor should it mean that they have less or more value in the eyes of society. That is the ideal of a democracy to which we subscribe with vigor. Living accordingly, in the face of sin, remains a great challenge to us all.

This *does* mean, for example, that a larger number of children may begin to crawl at 6–8 months old while some may crawl at 5 months and some at 10. But children who achieve physical milestones early are no more valuable to God or to the family than those who develop at a more typical rate. Children with developmental disabilities can live joyful, productive lives and should be welcomed in the collective arms of our society just as they are welcomed in the arms of our Savior.

As a parent, your expectations for your child must be adjusted according to many variables, and it is here that health professionals provide specific guidance. Parents need up-to-date scientific and medical information to support the wellness choices they make for their children. For our purposes in this book, then, some sections may seem overly scientific or academic. You can skim those or use them as more in-depth references as you desire; and you may read this book sequentially or skip to parts that pertain to your child's age. Whatever your child's age, it is important to have strategies based on sound evidence as you lead your family toward wellness.

Here are the age categories:

- Prenatal
- Birth to 12 months
- Early Childhood: toddler stage (ages 1–3 years) and preschool (ages 3–5)
- Early Elementary: kindergarten–grade 3
- Late Elementary: grades 4–8
- High School: grades 9–12

These categories may not align with the academic structure of your community's educational system, so you may need to make appropriate adjustments.

At the outset of our exploration of health behaviors for specific age groups, we will look at prenatal wellness. Your baby needs care even before it is born.

NOTES

1. See the Apology of the Augsburg Confession Article II, paragraphs 38–41.

SECTION 4

Spirit-Led Stewardship of Health and Wellness

CHAPTER 10

Prenatal Wellness

In those days Mary arose and went with haste into the hill country, to a town in Judah, and she entered the house of Zechariah and greeted Elizabeth. And when Elizabeth heard the greeting of Mary, the baby leaped in her womb. And Elizabeth was filled with the Holy Spirit, and she exclaimed with a loud cry, "Blessed are you among women, and blessed is the fruit of your womb! And why is this granted to me that the mother of my Lord should come to me? For behold, when the sound of your greeting came to my ears, the baby in my womb leaped for joy. And blessed is she who believed that there would be a fulfillment of what was spoken to her from the Lord."

Luke 1:39–45

Following this, we hear Mary's hymn of praise for her Lord and our song of thanksgiving for our deliverance from sin, death, and the power of the devil:

> My soul magnifies the Lord, and my spirit rejoices in God my Savior, for He has looked on the humble estate of His servant.
> (Luke 1:46–48)

Together with the story of Abraham and Sarah (Genesis 18:1–15), these are beautiful examples of prenatal parenting. These parents experience joy and preparation. The Spirit is maturing their faith. They are physically active, sharing meals, and resting, even with Mary traveling difficult paths to visit her cousin Elizabeth. They understand the strong bonds of family support. These prenatal parents understand God's mission and purpose for them and their offspring.

There is enormous and highly justified emphasis these days on maternal well-being even before conception and especially during the prenatal period of fetal development. Pregnancy comes with substantial bodily changes, anticipation, and apprehension. It is an important nine months for asking questions and understanding the realities of parenting.

Conceiving a healthy child also pertains to the father's health, not merely the mother's wellness.[1] Both parents' health in the three to six months before conception is critical, especially as it relates to their control of obesity, hypertension, and diabetes. Science informs us that healthy couples have a better chance to birth healthy babies. Couples who moderate weight, alcohol and drug consumption, diet, and smoking and who exercise regularly have a better chance of having healthy kids. Good prenatal care decreases the child's propensity to develop obesity, diabetes, hypertension, and heart disease in later life. It can also affect the expression or repression of potential genetic tendencies to certain diseases.

While I will address much of this chapter to the expectant mother, it is important for expectant fathers to be well aware and supportive of these wellness choices. You are a team.

MOVEMENT FOR EXPECTANT MOTHERS

Even if you are not a regular exerciser, your physician will recommend a compatible regimen of walking, moderate strength training, low-impact aerobics (such as swimming), yoga, or Pilates, all designed specifically for pregnancy. While this applies to both parents, this is especially important for mothers. Commonly, we see many pregnant women continue their established workout regimen with minor modification as pregnancy advances. If your pregnancy is healthy, exercise does not produce an increased risk of miscarriage, premature birth, or low-birth-weight babies. As always, it is prudent to start out by exercising slowly and to include adequate stretching. Be sure to stay well hydrated with water and minimize jarring and jumping movements where you might risk a fall or suffer blunt trauma to your belly.

Exercise during pregnancy also helps reduce stress; diminishes some of the discomfort of constipation, leg swelling, and back pain; and helps reduce the risks of gestational diabetes and preeclampsia.

Exercise helps prepare the woman's body for labor and delivery, improving flexibility, and strengthening and stretching heart, lungs, muscles, ligaments, and joints, which will be challenged during the actual course of childbirth.

PLANT-BASED NUTRITION FOR THE EXPECTANT MOTHER

A plant-based, whole-food diet is essential before, during, and after pregnancy for good health. Discuss with your physician your caloric needs at the various trimesters of your pregnancy. Pregnant women must consume balanced meals that provide adequate nutrition and calories for themselves and their developing fetus. Unless your ob-gyn specifies, your pregnancy is not the time for low-calorie diets. The rule of thumb is to eat normal caloric amounts in the first trimester and follow your physician's recommendations in the second and third trimesters. Many physicians will recommend consuming at least 200–300 more calories per day during the second and third trimesters than before pregnancy. That may not seem like a lot, but it is a critical increase for your baby to grow well in the womb. Please discuss this with your physician.

Your ob-gyn, physician assistant, or nurse practitioner will advise you regarding the need for prenatal supplemental vitamins, but the advice is to take only the recommended amount of vitamins and minerals. The most important supplement is folic acid, a B vitamin found in fruits and vegetables. You should make sure you are taking at least 400 micrograms per day. Adequate folic acid consumption can reduce the risks of certain birth defects like spina bifida. Your prenatal vitamins should contain iron, calcium, additional minerals, and good fatty acids, which are especially important for your baby's eyes and brain. Human breast milk contains these good fatty acids, called *arachidonic acid* (ARA) and *docosahexaenoic acid* (DHA), so that fatty acid consumption can continue from the mother who breastfeeds. Please be sure your doctors are well aware of any supplements you are taking during pregnancy, including herbal products, and discuss risks and benefits with them.

A few additional diet-related issues during the prenatal period are worth mentioning here.

Lead

It is well documented that excessive maternal lead levels during pregnancy can lead to low birth weight, miscarriage, stillbirth, and early childhood learning and behavior problems.

With the banning of lead content in most house paints, you might believe that there is little risk of exposure; yet homes built before 1978 likely contain some lead-based paints. Therefore, it is important if you are renovating an older home that you or your contractor follow safe and approved procedures for lead mitigation. Perhaps more threatening is the possibility of excessive lead concentrations in the public water supply of some municipalities. Pay attention to the standards in your community. If your home gets water from a well, have it tested regularly. Toys and jewelry can also contain lead, so be alert to where and how items are made that come in contact with you and your child.

You may increase your risk of lead contamination if you are not eating regularly, as lead is more easily absorbed on an empty stomach. Also, if your diet is lacking in vitamins C, D, or E, or short on zinc, iron, or calcium, you may be at risk for absorbing more lead.

Alcohol

Avoid alcohol during pregnancy—period. If a mother does not drink alcohol during pregnancy, she is absolutely guaranteed not to give birth to a child with *fetal alcohol spectrum disorder* (FASD).

FASD affects approximately 40,000 babies born each year. They have a far higher risk of birth defects, learning disabilities, and behavioral disorders, and they struggle to learn necessary life skills. These disabilities last a lifetime.

There is no safe amount or type of alcohol that the mother can consume, nor is there a safe time during pregnancy that Mommy can get away with a drink. Remember that if you are breastfeeding, your baby also will consume alcohol you have ingested.

Tobacco

None of us should consume nicotine. This includes smoking, vaping, snuffing, chewing, and other avenues. Particularly during pregnancy, there is enormous evidence that smoking and exposure to secondhand smoke may lead to premature labor or smaller-than-normal birth weight. Additional negative effects for babies include increased risk of *sudden infant death syndrome* (SIDS), breathing complications, and learning disorders, and for adults, lung, respiratory, and heart disease.

Children who are exposed to secondhand smoke after birth have far more respiratory infections, pneumonia, diminished lung function, and asthma.

The bottom line is if you smoke, quit now! And if you struggle to quit, at least make your home and car smoke-free zones. (An increasing number of states prohibit smoking in vehicles when people under age 18 are present.) If your spouse or others in the house smoke, do everything you can to urge them to quit for the sake of all in the home, especially the children.

Cannabis

Studies from the Centers for Disease Control and Prevention suggest that one in twenty women consumes cannabis during pregnancy by smoking, vaping, dabbing, eating, drinking, or applying creams or lotions to her skin. Health officials agree that the tetrahydrocannabinol (THC) in marijuana does pass through your blood system to your baby (including breastfeeding postpartum). Although much more scientific study is in the pipeline (so to speak), the recommendation of the CDC is that mothers should *not* consume marijuana in any form during pregnancy.

If you have been smoking nicotine or cannabis during pregnancy, it is imperative that you let your pediatrician know because your baby may experience withdrawal from these drugs during the first few days after birth.

Opiates

The consumption of opiates by pregnant mothers is staggering.[2] The health risks to the child are enormous and include birth defects, low birth weight, and neonatal abstinence syndrome (NAS). Therefore, pregnant women *must* be honest with their obstetrician and pediatrician so the safest care can be given to the child. Quitting suddenly can cause severe problems for both mother and fetus. Even if a physician has prescribed opiate medications, the ob-gyn must know so he or she can safely bring the mother through her pregnancy.

REST

Mother's rest is important in that it protects both her and her baby from the psychological stresses and strains of pregnancy. Fatigue is common during pregnancy, however, and the only solution is more rest.

The hormone progesterone, which increases in pregnancy in order to prepare the uterus to support the fetus, is a major culprit in the experience of fatigue. Weight gain and fluid retention cause discomfort, which affects good rest. Excitement or fearful anticipation (especially in first-time mothers) can disrupt sleep and therefore contribute to tiredness. Leg cramps and heartburn often cause mothers to wake from sleep. And the pressure from a burgeoning abdomen can arrest good sleep, especially in the third trimester, by pressing on the bladder and creating the need for more frequent urination.

Despite all of these challenges, most OBs recommend that women spend at least eight hours in bed each day and get at least seven hours of restful sleep. As a woman's body changes and the pressures on the body advance, it may be more difficult to achieve this goal.

What happens if Mommy doesn't get enough sleep? There appears to be an increased risk of requiring a C-section, prolonged labor, elevated discomfort during labor, and postpartum depression.

Mothers can try to resist lying on their back, because the heavy uterus can press on the nerves, spine, and blood vessels in the back. Sleeping on the left side can help reduce back discomfort and can lessen heartburn by relieving pressure on the stomach. (It also improves blood and nutrient flow to the fetus.) Lying on the left side with a pillow between the knees can relieve back and hip discomfort. And intentional breathing, massage, and prayer can lessen negative emotions so the mother can relax. Finally, nothing beats a nice afternoon nap, best held to 20–30 minutes so as to not further disturb nighttime rest.

FOCUS ON FAITH AND FAMILY

Prenatal days are perfect "pause points" for parents to spend in prayer, devotions, and reading the Scriptures. We find Mary and Elizabeth doing just that: reflecting, praying, praising, and relishing the gifts of God. In their pregnancies, the Spirit is preparing the world for those Hebrew cousins, John and Jesus, one to prepare the way and one who *is* the Way.

Parents might spend time reflecting on how an addition to their family will affect existing relationships. This new being brings enormous opportunities for fulfillment and joy but also physical, mental, relational, spiritual, and financial challenges. Actively preparing through parenting classes, fellowship groups, or devotional materials is helpful. But just as important is setting aside time to talk face-to-face with your spouse and express all fears and anticipation openly and honestly and without distraction. This conversation will afford huge dividends when this new life is upon you. Do not be afraid to seek outside counseling. Many congregations, social service ministries, OB-GYN practices, maternity hospitals, and even baby clothing and supply stores offer classes to help expectant parents.

Couples typically draw closer together to plan and prepare for their expanding family. Some document the prenatal period with photos, milestone calendars, and journals. An effective faith- and family-building activity is to create a prayer journal to record daily prayers for the baby and for one another.

The parents should consider making arrangements with their pastor to plan for the baby's Baptism and to thoughtfully choose godparents.

If both parents work outside the home, day-care provisions for the baby should be in place. Ideally, the day-care provider is of the same faith tradition as the parents or at least supports the family's faith values.

Additionally, the prenatal period is a time for young parents to connect more deeply with their family support system. It does take a community to raise children. Grandparents-to-be, siblings of the parents, and friends can be invaluable resources. It also may be a good time to begin discussing boundaries for parenting responsibility. As much as your family might be interested in your pregnancy and assure you of their child-rearing expertise, it is important for the baby's parents to understand and establish their authority and responsibility as primary. These discussions may not be completed in a single session or two. Ongoing, loving, and understanding conversation is essential and needs to be continued throughout the child's life.

Shared worship, reading, devotional resources, Bible study, and counseling where available can set important foundations for the village. Here are a few wonderful resources for parents in their prenatal journey:

- *Blessings and Prayers for Expectant Moms: A Devotional Companion*, Rachel C. Hoyer (2011, Concordia Publishing House)
- *Dear Mother—Devotions for New Mothers*, Mary J. Moerbe (2017, Concordia Publishing House/LWML)
- *The Power of a Godly Grandparent: Building a Spiritual Inheritance for Your Grandchildren*, Edition 1, Stephen Bly, Janet Bly (2003, Beacon Hill Press of Kansas City)
- *Godly Moms: Strength from the Inside Out*, Lenore Buth (2013, Concordia Publishing House)
- *Teaching the Faith at Home: What Does This Mean? How Is This Done?* David Rueter (2015, Concordia Publishing House)

Introducing the New Baby to Siblings

An additional challenge arises for your family as you introduce a newborn to his or her siblings. Children in the 1- to 2-year-old range may not fully comprehend what it means to have a new baby sharing the love, time, and space of the existing family; however, they can feel the excitement you express. You can help siblings prepare for a new brother or sister as someone who belongs to "our" family by reading picture books together, discussing the baby in Mommy's expanding belly, and preparing space and baby items together.

Parents can engage in special activities with the toddler to let the child know he or she is still loved dearly. This might involve reasonable gifts such as dolls, books, or stuffed animals, but it is more important to create opportunities to spend dedicated one-on-one time with Mommy, Daddy, and grandparents as well. A bedtime routine or other regular daily activity will reassure the toddler.

Two- to four-year-olds become very sensitive about sharing parents with someone new. Sometimes preschoolers feel jealous or threatened. Children this age are concrete thinkers and may not readily comprehend a baby that isn't visible just yet. Therefore, you might want to wait to break the news until the pregnancy is visible or you're bringing new furniture or baby clothing into the home so the older sibling can see the reality of what is coming. Certainly, show respect to him or her by making every effort to be the one to announce the pending arrival rather than letting your child learn by overhearing conversation or from someone else.

Be honest with children this age; the new baby may be fun and cuddly, but it may also be noisy, smelly, and time-consuming for parents. Involve your preschooler in the planning: let him or her help decorate the room or pick out some of the baby clothing. You can also buy a baby doll so the big brother or sister can take care of his or her own baby.

Don't be surprised if there is some regression in toilet training or a desire to return to bottle feeding or a pacifier. Children just want to know they are still loved, so be gentle and reassuring. Encourage Dad or another father figure to spend time with these siblings. This is a most important chance for both parent and child to have a wonderful opportunity to bond.

Children older than age 5 are not as threatened as younger children because they are more aware of their place in the family and their individual worth. It is still important, however, to use age-appropriate language and to communicate frequently. Give older children simple responsibilities in child care, and have them come to the hospital as soon as possible after the birth to see their new sibling and their mother so they can begin to understand the new family unit. They need to recognize their significance to the health, wellness, and happiness of your family.

Reassure them of your love; this is always the bottom line and can't be done often enough.

PURPOSEFUL AND MISSIONAL LIVING

Preparing for a new child offers a wonderful time to review your mission and purpose in life. A helpful first step, before looking at your family's mission, is a profound examination of your own life as it relates to the confessions of your faith. Understanding biblically based, God-inspired directives for life together provides the foundation for thinking through purpose and mission. First-time parents are assuming an entirely new role, so how do you prepare for new purposes as parents with a child? The Holy Scriptures provide topics to study individually and to discuss with each other during the prenatal period:

- The family is the fundamental building block of both faith formation and societal order and peace; children are God's gift. (Psalm 127:3–5)
- The family is the place to reflect on and explore the spiritual truth found in God's Word. (John 17:17)
- The family is the model for understanding our relationship with God in Christ. (Romans 8:15–17; Ephesians 1:11; 3:6; Hebrews 12:5–11; 1 John 3:1)
- The Christian home creates the atmosphere to show love, forgiveness, honesty, acceptance, fun, creativity, and relaxation. (Ephesians 3:14–17; Hebrews 3:4; Isaiah 32:18; Matthew 7:25; 12:25; Colossians 3:14; Psalm 91:1–2; 24:3–4; John 14:1–2; Deuteronomy 6:5–7)

Preparing Older Children for Purpose with Their New Sibling

The specific age—physical, intellectual, and emotional development—of older siblings helps guide the language and examples you use to talk about new or renewed purpose. The relationship of Joseph and his brothers (Genesis 37), for example, offers incredible teachable moments, but certain aspects of the story need to be discussed gently, sensitively, and with extensive explanation. Similarly, the stories of Cain and Abel and Jacob and Esau are cautionary tales of struggling sibling relationships. The accounts of Jacob and Esau and of Joseph and his brothers end in examples of forgiveness; the story of Cain and Abel requires deeper discussions of sibling struggles and jealousy.

Mary, Martha, and Lazarus are siblings who have some challenges but also love deeply and share affection, accountability, care, and faith in Jesus as their family purpose (Luke 10:38–42; John 11:1–44).

The older brother's and sister's role in protecting, providing for, and socializing their new sibling is immense. Similar to marriage, sibling relationships should be centered in love:

> Love is patient and kind; love does not envy or boast; it is not arrogant or rude. It does not insist on its own way; it is not irritable or resentful.
>
> (1 Corinthians 13:4–5)

What does it mean to have a new baby brother or sister in a Christian home? We can emulate what St. Paul says of love in the family. Specifically, we show love by giving younger siblings time to accomplish tasks that might seem simple to an older brother or sister. Siblings are kind to one another and interact with a patient, gentle, giving heart. Sibling love means we are not jealous of the time or energy parents need to spend with the baby, and we don't have to compete with the baby for parents' affection.

Love means we don't need to throw temper tantrums to get attention. Our life together in the family is much more pleasant when we resist acting naughty and do our best to obey our parents.

These behaviors take practice; parents and children alike are in a process of being healed by the Spirit to be more like Jesus. Parents and children alike express the fruit of the Spirit toward one another.

FAMILY WELLNESS IN THE WORLD

Outbreaks of viruses such as COVID-19 and influenza focus attention on the challenges and opportunities for the Christian family to be wellness leaders in a world that is shadowed by the darkness of infectious diseases and respiratory infections, along with their accompanying anxieties.

Coronavirus, the most recent, is not the first and will not be the last public health disaster to affect us as parents or touch the lives of our children. We have learned to stop the spread of these infections by practicing good health manners and, especially, "respiratory etiquette."

- Wash hands before eating, after using the bathroom, and after being in public spaces, such as the grocery story. Wash thoroughly with warm soapy water for at least twenty seconds. Include the spaces between fingers, under the fingernails, around the thumbs, and the back of the hands. You may also use 60-percent alcohol-based hand gel or disposable wipes.
- Cover the mouth and nose with tissue when coughing or sneezing, and dispose of tissues in the trash as soon as possible.
- Always wash hands after sneezing, blowing your nose, or coughing, and also after touching used handkerchiefs or tissues.
- Avoid touching face and mouth after direct contact with other individuals or surfaces that might not have been recently cleansed.
- Make every effort to stay home if you or a member of your household has a fever, sore throat, or a cough.
- See or telecommunicate with your health professional if you have a cough or fever. Follow the professional's instructions and take medications as prescribed. Get ample rest.
- If asked, use a face mask and gloves.
- Don't share eating utensils, beverage containers, food, and drink.
- Avoid sharing towels, toys, books, or anything else that might be contaminated with respiratory germs.

There may be times when your family is instructed to distance itself from others in the community. For the good of society and of your loved ones, comply. Use this valuable time of separation to gather around God's Word in devotions and stay connected to your faith family through live-streaming of worship or music. Build family relationships by conversation, playing games, completing jigsaw puzzles, or craft projects.

Stay connected with extended family and friends via phone calls and social media. Stay active by exercising. And explore opportunities to safely serve and care for the wellness of others.

RESOURCES

- Germs: Prevent Their Spread, www.doh.wa.gov (accessed 04-02-2020)
- Healthy Habits to Help Prevent Flu, www.cdc.gov (accessed 04-02-2020)

NOTES

1. Jacqueline Howard, "How Dad's Preconception Health Can Affect the Baby, Too," website of CNN Health (April 16, 2018), https://www.cnn.com/2018/04/16/health/dad-health-baby-preconception-study/index.html.
2. "Prescription Opioids During Pregnancy," marchofdimes.org (2019).

ADDITIONAL READING

- Guidelines to identify or manage lead exposure during pregnancy or breastfeeding, www.cdc.gov/nceh/lead/publications/LeadandPregnancy2010.pdf.
- "Alcohol Use in Pregnancy," CDC Report http://www.cdc.gov/NCBDDD/fasd/alcohol-use.html.
- "The Dangers of Secondhand Smoke," American Academy of Pediatrics (AAP), https://www.healthychildren.org/English/health-issues/conditions/tobacco/Pages/Dangers-of-Secondhand-Smoke.aspx.
- K. Mark, A. Desai, and M. Terplan, "Marijuana Use and Pregnancy: Prevalence, Associated Characteristics, and Birth Outcomes," *Archives of Women's Mental Health* 19 (1), 105–111.
- Cari Nierenberg, "Sleeping for Two: Sleep Changes during Pregnancy," *Live Science* (May 18, 2017), www.livescience.com.

CHAPTER 11

Wellness from Birth to 12 Months

The first twelve months are the most rapid growth period in the human life cycle. Baby's weight doubles in the first six months and triples by twelve months. Length increases by one inch per month during the first six months, then about a half inch per month over the next six months.

The most significant observation is that every child is an individual and grows at his or her own pace. There is a wide range of height, weight, and temperament. And parents can be assured that with few exceptions, it all is within healthy normal ranges.

MOVEMENT FOR BIRTH–12 MONTHS

The first twelve months of life are filled with rapidly transitioning movement activities, from nonspecific arm and leg movement to intentionally purposeful gross and fine motor function allowing mobility and self-feeding. Encouraging the building blocks of purposeful movement is essential.

Infants sleep most of the time, and they move during sleep. We want children to sleep on their back, which maintains clear airways to reduce the risks of sudden infant death syndrome (SIDS) or sudden unexpected death in infancy (SUDI). Restricting movement at bedtime by swaddling (wrapping a blanket snugly around the baby's body) to resemble life in the womb can be beneficial to help calm a baby. A swaddled child must be put on his back. At about 2 months, many babies begin trying to roll, so swaddling should be stopped at this point because there is increased risk of suffocation if the swaddled baby rolls onto her stomach and breathing is suppressed. It may also be harder for a swaddled baby to startle or arouse. It is important to talk with your pediatrician regarding swaddling and to learn how to properly swaddle your baby if you choose this practice. Absolutely do not leave blankets or pillows in the crib, as these may cause suffocation. Also, it is best for baby to sleep in his own crib, bassinet, or co-sleeper rather than in your bed, again as a precaution against suffocation.[1] In addition, do not place positioners, bumpers, or stuffed animals in the crib.

At about 1–2 months of age, babies should have short periods of tummy time so they can begin to build core, neck, and extremity strength to prepare them for sitting, crawling, and walking. For the baby's safety, she should not be allowed to nap or sleep while on her tummy, and parents and caregivers should remain awake and closely supervise her.

At around 6 months of age, children begin to sit upright for playtime and may safely begin self-feeding (see the section on weaning, beginning on page 98). This is also the time to encourage gross and fine motor movement in the hands so the child begins to grasp food and toys, which will end up in her mouth anyway—but that is good!

The American Academy of Pediatrics shares these guidelines for first-year activities:[2]

Milestones for Age 0–3 Months

- Lying on tummy, pushes up on arms and lifts and holds up head
- Moves fists from closed to open
- Brings hand to mouth
- Waves legs and arms off of surface when excited
- When lying on back, visually tracks toys and reaches up for items held above body
- Enjoys movement but calms with gentle touch or rocking
- Makes eye contact and turns to sounds or faces
- Cries differently for different needs
- Coos and smiles
- Sucks and swallows well for feeding, normally taking 2–6 ounces approximately six times per day

There are many additional milestones beyond movement regarding play and social skills, coordination, daily activities, and markers of self-expression, as well as warning signs for delayed development.[3] Talk with your baby's pediatrician for developmental milestones and to assess any delays. Take a list of your questions to your baby's scheduled appointments so you don't forget something you want to ask the doctor. Many communities have Parents as Teachers or similar programs that provide child-development assessment services at no or minimal cost; these can provide in-home evaluations of your child.

Motor Milestones for Age 4–6 Months

- Rolls from back to tummy and tummy to back
- Uses hands to support sitting
- Stands with support
- Reaches for toys on tummy with both hands, and exchanges toys from hand to hand on back
- Reaches with both hands to grab feet
- Brings hands and objects to mouth
- Shows interest and opens mouth to food[4]

Motor Milestones for Age 7–9 Months

- Sits without support and reaches for objects without flailing
- Moves from tummy to back to sitting
- Starts alternate arm and leg movement to lead to crawling or creeping
- Picks up small objects with thumbs and fingers
- Turns head to visually track objects when sitting
- Picks up head and pushes with elbows while on tummy
- Starts to imitate others' movements
- Turns pages of chunky book

Motor Milestones for Age 10–12 Months

- Pulls to stand and cruises along furniture
- Starts a few independent steps
- Moves in and out of positions to get various toys
- Claps hands
- Releases objects into a large container
- Maintains balance while sitting or throwing objects
- Uses thumb and forefinger to pick up objects (pincer grasp movement)
- Enjoys songs and music
- Can move to and away from objects in distance
- Starts with meaningful "mama" and "dada"
- Responds to simple commands of "come here" or "no"
- Starts to use simple hand movement to communicate (some parents introduce baby sign language to assist in communication as early as 6 months of age)[5]

It is worth restating that children may demonstrate advanced or delayed motor or communication skills in one or several of the markers noted for a specific age. There is significant variability. Discuss any questions with your pediatrician so that if there are delays, early intervention and enhancement can be given to help your child develop to his or her full potential.

Safe movement: As important as movement is in the first year of life, and as gratifying as it is for parents when their baby grows and develops, a word of caution regarding safe movement is in order. More than one million children die each year due to injuries, most of which are preventable. Children learn to move and move quickly. They can reach that hot cup of coffee, fall down a flight of stairs, or find an unsecured gun before you blink.

The greatest threat to infants and young children is automobile crashes. Be absolutely certain that your child's car seat is installed correctly, and make sure your child is secured in his car seat every time he is in the car.

Observing these additional guidelines will help you protect your baby's safety:

- Babyproof all closets, dressers, drawers, cabinets, bookshelves, and stairwells with babyproof locks, gates, and wall anchors.
- Install window guards and use babyproof doorknob covers.
- Use babyproof outlet covers in all floor-level electrical outlets.
- If you have a firearm in your home, secure it with extreme care.
- Be aware of any medications, including over-the-counter medications, and keep them well out of reach.
- Do not give the baby balloons, small items, or toys designed for older children.
- Keep candles and cigarettes completely away from the baby.
- Keep all appliances, tools, and other items designed for adult use out of reach or removed from the environment.
- Wrap and tie cords and cables for lamps, televisions, and other appliances so crawlers can't get tangled in them.
- Wrap and tie cords for window blinds and shades and keep them well out of reach. Don't overlook blinds and shades within reach of a toddler standing on the sofa, chair, or bed.
- Never carry your baby and hot liquids or sharp objects. You cannot handle both even if you think you are the world's best multitasker.
- Make sure your home has working fire and carbon monoxide monitors. Test alarms monthly.
- Never leave your infant unmonitored. He will put everything in his mouth, and he can manage to push his walker or jumper to the edge of every set of steps. Also never put your child in anything loose that could cover his face, restrict his neck, or block his airway.

There are lots of "nevers" and "alwayses," but during infancy you are the best assurance for your child's wellness through your constant care and leadership.

Vaccinations

The controversies, conspiracy theories, and social media debate regarding vaccinations continue to swirl in our culture. As a board-certified physician—and more important, as a parent and grandparent—I have heard most of these concerns; I have studied them and discussed them with medical colleagues and family, and I continue to hold one fundamental opinion and recommendation: vaccinations for preventable disease provide more wellness benefit than anything else a medical team can do to help you raise a healthy child. In the strongest terms I can state, I urge you to study this subject thoroughly, talk it over with your pediatrician, and make the most informed decision you can for your child. Here are a few informative articles:

- "Recommended Childhood and Adolescent Immunization Schedules," American Academy of Pediatrics Committee on Infectious Diseases, *Pediatrics* 143, no. 3 (March 2019)
- "For Parents: Vaccines for Your Children," Centers for Disease Control and Prevention, cdc.gov/vaccines/parents/index.html
- "Immunization in the United States: Recommendations, Barriers, and Measures to Improve Compliance," C. L. Ventola, *Pharmacy & Therapeutics* 4 (July 2016), 26–36

PLANT-BASED NUTRITION

Cow's milk is *numero uno* after one year of age. For the first year of life, however, the mother's own breast milk or a pediatrician-approved formula is a most nutritious avenue to provide a baby with food and drink. However, while I advocate breastfeeding, many mothers deal with extreme anxiety because they cannot breastfeed due to a host of issues (which I will address later). Please don't allow the issue of whether or not to breastfeed cause you—or your baby—undue stress and anxiety. Generations of us grew up on cow's milk, cereal, and formula. Although today physicians and nutritionists promote "healthier" avenues for nutrition, the fundamental fact is that we all need carbohydrates, fats, proteins, vitamins, and minerals to grow, and there are a variety of effective ways to accomplish that critical task.

God has created His children so magnificently that they are equipped for survival with a most beneficial energy and growth source—mother's milk. Although there are circumstances when there is insufficient breast milk to support all of a child's growth needs, science has shown that whenever possible, breastfeeding provides the finest form of nutrients for early life.

Myriad writings are available on the importance of breastfeeding. Leading child-care authorities, including the American Academy of Pediatrics, recommend the exclusive use of breastfeeding for approximately 6 months, to then be continued as solid foods are introduced, with breastfeeding continuing for a year or longer as mutually desired by mother and infant. Medical complications and contraindications for breastfeeding are rare. The American Academy of Pediatrics, World Health Organization, UNICEF, Centers for Disease Control, and US Surgeon General all support public policies that promote the health and economic benefits of breastfeeding.[6]

Need a bit more science? Breastfeeding augments the bond of mother and child through the release of prolactin and oxytocin, hormones that enhance feelings of peace, relaxation, and loving attachment between mother and baby. Breastfeeding also allows mothers to recover from childbirth more quickly, as the oxytocin acts to return the uterus to its regular size and minimize postpartum bleeding. There are reports that breastfeeding reduces the chance of breast and ovarian cancers, diabetes, rheumatoid arthritis, and heart disease in the mother's later life. Breastfeeding tends to delay the return of a mother's menstrual period, so if further pregnancy is not desired, additional measures are important to consider.[7]

There are also practical benefits to breastfeeding. For example, it costs less than formula and bottles, although nursing mothers do need to increase their consumption of calories. Your family is more mobile when you don't need to pack a bag of bottles and formula. Nighttime can be easier if you don't have to get up and warm a bottle; however, Daddy might need to get up and bring Baby from her crib to Mother's side. Dads also can help by positioning Mother with an extra pillow, providing her with a glass of cool water to keep her hydrated, putting on some relaxing music, rubbing her back, or adjusting the lighting in the room. Dads participate by being supportive of this most important part of parenting.

In addition to the nutritional importance of breastfeeding, there are significant bonding values.[8] A primary value of breastfeeding is that mothers receive a tremendous sense of maternal fulfillment and emotional and physical bonding with their baby, along with the knowledge that they are fulfilling their child's needs with everything God has supplied them in His marvelous creation.

However, mothers who do not breastfeed need not feel guilty. Today's infant formula is as nutritionally close to breast milk as is possible. Generally, formula isn't digested as quickly as breast milk, so formula-fed babies may not need to eat as often, especially in the first few months. Further, formula-fed babies are not affected by what their mother consumes. Breastfed babies may also need to have formulary supplements. Bottles and bottle nipples do need to be thoroughly cleaned. A variety of bottles and nipples are available to suit even the pickiest baby. Moms can share the work of keeping baby fed, and dads, grandparents, and others can experience the joy of snuggling with baby during feedings. And moms who work outside the home can do so without pumping and storing their breast milk.

Supplements, Iron, Adequate Calories, Foods to Avoid

What does all of this have to do with a plant slant to your diet as a parent? I urge a plant-based diet throughout this text, but I do not necessarily advocate a vegan diet to breastfeeding mothers, although that can be done safely. While a vegan diet is healthy, it may require supplemental vitamins and nutrients. A mother needs adequate vitamin B12 (from fresh fish and seafood, milk, cheese, eggs), calcium (milk, cheese, or yogurt), vitamin D (sunlight, salmon, orange juice, yogurt), protein (peanut butter, nuts, beans, and occasionally fish), iron (dark leafy greens, iron-fortified cereal, occasional meat), folic acid (spinach and other greens, citrus fruits, beans, and whole-grain breads), and zinc (mushrooms, cereals, seafood, dark chocolate—now we're talking!).

Your OB may suggest that you, as mother, take multivitamin supplements after your baby is born, and these are fine if they are of high quality. However, supplements are an addition to a healthy diet, not a substitute.

Iron. Iron in breast milk is sufficient for infants throughout the first 4–6 months as long as the mother is well nourished. In truth, a calorie-adequate, vitamin-adequate diet is more important for the mother's health. A breastfed child could be supported by a breastfeeding mother who eats predominantly junk foods; however, this is not in any way recommended.[9] In addition to fruits and vegetables, salmon (not more than two times per week to avoid excessive lead), seaweed, shellfish, and sardines are generally healthful foods. Small amounts of beef (once per week in 4- to 6-ounce servings), pork, and organically fed chicken can be healthy supplements and provide calories and iron.

Adequate Calories. A mother should be taking in about 300–500 calories more than her routine, nonnursing diet to maintain prepregnancy weight. That may translate to a diet of 2,000–2,500 calorics a day for a nursing mother's total intake. This is a general figure, and mothers may obsess over what is adequate. The rule of thumb is that you should eat when you are hungry and drink when you are thirsty.

The amount of dietary fat you ingest as a mother does not affect the amount of fat in your milk, but it can affect the *kinds* of fats (good vs. bad fats). There are really no foods you need to avoid just because you are breastfeeding. However, there may be foods to which your baby may have an adverse reaction. Pay attention to what you eat and avoid foods that seem to make your baby uncomfortable.

Foods to Avoid. It is always a good idea to limit or avoid caffeine, and it is also important to be careful with cow's milk and peanut proteins, which pass into mother's milk. Additionally, if you have a family history of food allergies, you may wish to limit or eliminate those foods.

Several foods seem to increase the amount of breast milk produced: oatmeal, carrots, spinach, nuts, garlic, and green papaya. Most plant foods are relatively low in calories, however, so it is important to eat adequate calories to meet both mother's and baby's daily needs. It is also important that both mother and child take adequate protein to support health.

It is best to avoid alcohol consumption during breastfeeding, as alcohol passes easily into breast milk and therefore to your baby. Alcohol may alter the taste of the milk and may actually decrease the amount of breast milk mothers produce. And it stays in the milk. If you really desire a glass of wine or beer, most evidence suggests that you may breastfeed four hours after your last drink. It is important to remember that it is not safe to try to care for your infant if you are intoxicated.[10]

That same caution applies to any drug ingested during breastfeeding. If necessary, use short-acting medications that are eliminated by your body quickly. Try to take medications just after a nursing session. Watch closely for any reactions your baby has, such as diarrhea, crying, loss of appetite, or skin rashes. You may even want to express and store your milk until you are sure the medication has cleared your body.

This pertains also to the use of birth control medications; these always should be discussed with your physician. There are less risky forms of birth control that may have fewer adverse effects than oral medications containing high doses of estrogen or progestin.

The same concern for your and your baby's health applies to the use of homeopathic and herbal medications. There is little medical research on using these supplements during nursing, so discuss honestly the use of these medicines with your doctor.

Introducing Your Breastfed Baby to the Bottle

Breastfeeding mothers may notice diminished milk production throughout the first year. They may also have to return to work, which will require pumping and storing milk or giving additional formulary products to provide adequate nutrition for their infant. There are healthful formula supplements that can then be added to the mother's milk supply. Consultation with your pediatrician is always strongly recommended to find the best option that agrees with your baby.

Expressing milk and storing it in sanitary conditions so it can be used are critical. Consider having your husband, a grandparent, or other close loved ones help introduce Baby to the bottle; your child may not be entirely happy if this change comes first from Mommy. Introduce the bottle about 1½–2 hours after breastfeeding so the baby is not ferociously hungry. You might try dripping a drop or two of milk from the nipple of the bottle onto the baby's lips or tongue and then gently introduce the nipple to the baby's mouth. This may take several attempts, so do not become frustrated yourself as your baby will pick up on your emotion.

There are a variety of bottle and nipple styles on the market, and you may have to try several to find just the right one; your baby can be extremely particular. Baby may even prefer a medicine cup or sippy cup to a bottle. Proceed with his or her preference and gradually create an acceptable pattern of feeding.

Immunity Value of Breastfeeding

Breastfeeding offers substantial benefits to your child's immune system. Your baby receives antibodies, immune factors, white blood cells to fight infection, and enzymes helpful for digestion. Breastfed babies tend to have far fewer ear infections, less diarrhea, less spitting-up and vomiting, and fewer urinary tract infections. It affords some protection from allergies that run in families, like eczema and asthma. Finally, children who breastfeed for as long as six months tend to have less likelihood of suffering acute leukemia, lymphoma, pneumonia, croup, or spinal meningitis, and, more important, far less chance of SIDS.[11]

Postpartum Depression and Breastfeeding

One additional topic worth discussing is the link between postpartum depression (PPD) and breastfeeding.[12] PPD occurs in approximately one in seven women and can occur anytime during the first year of your baby's life. A mother's mental health is paramount to the parenting of her child and the well-being of her family. Mothers suffering PPD are less likely to cuddle, read to, and interact with their baby. These deficiencies can pose a substantial detriment to a baby's development, sleep, and learning abilities. Your pediatrician is well trained to care for your child, but on occasion, along with your ob-gyn or primary care physician, he or she may be called upon to treat you as a mother. Your pediatrician is often the one to recognize PPD, as you are more likely see her or him than other medical personnel. The American Academy of Pediatrics urges pediatricians to screen mothers for PPD at their baby's 1-, 4-, and 6-month well-child check-ups.[13] All children need and deserve a healthy mom and dad. Tell loved ones your needs and seek help, please.[14]

Occasionally, breastfeeding can contribute to the mother's depression, and she may need to seek other forms of feeding. Mother's mental health care may include antidepressant medication and supportive counseling groups. Many medications for PPD are safe to use while breastfeeding, and this should be thoroughly discussed with doctors.

PPD can be severe enough to result in suicidal thoughts or actions. If the mother or a family member notes signs of suicidal intent, call 911 or 1-800-944-4773 *immediately* to be connected with professional help at once. Postpartum.net and ppd.com offer additional information and resources.

Formula Feeding

I have made a strong case for breastfeeding during the first twelve months of life. But there are circumstances when, due to the mother's health, infant's health, personal preference, or family and economic demands, formula feeding is the reasonable choice. Some of the same principles of breastfeeding apply:

- Offer 1–2 ounces of formula per feeding for the first few days.
- Awaken your baby for feeding if he is sleeping longer than 4–5 hours and begins to miss feedings.
- After a month, you should be offering 4–5 ounces per feeding about every 4 hours. By 6 months, your baby will require 6–8 ounces per feeding and at least 4–5 feeding sessions per day; she will let you know when she has had enough.

Formulas vary greatly, and you may need to try several to find one that agrees with your baby's digestive tract. Your best resource is your pediatrician coupled with trial and error. Formulas come in ready-to-feed, liquid concentrate, and powdered forms, and they are packaged in various sizes designed for convenience.

If your child appears to have lactose intolerance or an immunoglobulin E–associated allergy to cow's milk, other preparations such as soy-based formulas are available. Babies that have deficiencies such as iron may need a specific formula. The same guidelines apply to using formulas fortified with probiotics, the so-called "good bacteria." As always, check with the baby's doctor before use.

There are significant cost considerations with formula products. Take care to assure that you have a safe water supply. For feeding, formula should be warm rather than hot or cold (shake a few drops on the inside of your wrist). Formula is good at room temperature for only 1–2 hours after it is mixed (this varies by brand, so check the label). If it has not been given to an infant, it can be stored in the refrigerator for up to 24 hours so it is not contaminated. If the baby has had part of a bottle, any unused formula must be discarded within an hour, as bacteria are introduced during the feeding. Ready-to-use formula and formula prepared from concentrate should be covered, refrigerated, and discarded after 48 hours.

If using powdered formula, follow instructions exactly to avoid contamination with *Cronobacter*, a rare but serious illness linked to improper preparation (see the Additional Reading list at the end of this chapter).

Generally, babies don't need additional water besides their formula, and they never should be given sodas or artificially sweetened or high-concentrate sugar- or fructose-sweetened liquids, such as juice made from concentrate. Most important, as we mentioned before, every baby is unique. You and your baby will discover the pattern that works for both of you.

Although generations were raised on cow's milk, infants in their first year cannot digest cow's milk as completely or easily as breast milk or formula. Furthermore, cow's milk contains high concentrations of protein and minerals that can stress a newborn's kidneys, and cause fever, diarrhea, and heat stress. Cow's milk doesn't contain adequate iron, vitamin C, and other nutrients necessary for infants.

The general rule from pediatricians is that children should not receive any regular cow's milk for the first twelve months of life. You can safely introduce cow's milk to children older than 1 year. However, do not give your baby 1 percent or nonfat (skimmed) milk before his or her second birthday, as it has too high a concentration of protein and minerals (as a results of the skimming process), and children need the additional fats present in whole milk.

Bowel Movements and Urination: What's Normal and Healthy?

This section might better be named "The Scoop on Pee and Poop!" A good indication of your baby's hydration level is the number of times he urinates. Your baby may urinate 4–6 times per day. If he becomes feverish, his urine output may drop but still be in the acceptable range. Normally, infants should be have 6–8 wet diapers per 24 hours.

It is important to note if urination appears to be painful; it never should be, and if your baby appears uncomfortable, notify your pediatrician immediately. The baby may have an infection or urinary tract problems.

The urine should be light to dark yellow in color. If the urine appears pink, this may just be very concentrated urine, but monitor this closely. If this color persists, call the doctor, and if actual blood appears, notify the doctor immediately.

For the first few days after his birth, your baby's bowel movements are thick and black or dark green; this is called *meconium*, what the baby has ingested in the womb. Once the meconium has passed, the stools should turn yellow-green. If you are breastfeeding, the stools will be light mustard color and even have small seedlike particles. Stools may be very soft or loose and runny. If your baby is formula fed, the stools will tend to be firmer and tan or yellow, but they should not be firmer than peanut butter. If stools are harder, your baby may not be adequately hydrated. If they become very hard, especially after starting soft or solid foods, this may indicate that your baby is consuming too much cereal or cow's milk before the digestive tract is able to adequately digest these foods.

If your baby becomes constipated, you may observe a small streak of blood on the stool or diaper; the solution is to hydrate. However, if you see large amounts of blood, mucus, or water, or if your baby appears to have pain with bowel movements, call your doctor.

A breastfed baby may develop looser stools if the mother's diet changes. Clearly, make this judgment and, as a first step, assess your diet. Breastfed babies initially may have 6–8 bowel movements per day, but they may have only one bowel movement per week after a couple of months. Breast milk may leave very little residue. The key issues are (1) that bowel movements are no firmer than peanut butter and (2) that your baby is gaining weight regularly and nursing regularly.

Loose stools need not alarm you, but if diarrhea develops (very loose, watery stools, three or more times in one day), the baby may become dehydrated. And if fever accompanies the loose stools, call the doctor immediately.

Formula-fed babies should have at least one bowel movement a day. If they do not or if they appear to strain and be constipated, address this with your pediatrician.

If it seems like I am suggesting a lot of calls to your doctor, it's because responding to your questions and caring for your child is your pediatrician's job; it goes with the territory! Your child is the beneficiary when you and your doctor address a problem early on rather than letting the issue advance to the point that major intervention or even an ER visit is necessary.

A quick comment on baby wipes: don't flush them. They can wreak havoc on your plumbing system. Many wipes are not flushable anyway, so please read the labels. If a diaper is merely wet, wiping may not be necessary. Generally, you can reserve wipes for poop. You can also use a soft, washable washcloth or a quick dunk of baby's bottom in the sink or tub. Some babies, especially girls, may be sensitive to urine and may require a baby wipe with every diaper change. Let the day-care provider or other adult caring for the baby know so he or she can act accordingly. In any case, do not flush baby wipes!

Whenever your family ventures away from home, be prepared with a changing pad, wipes, diapers, a new outfit, or even an extra person to help. And be sure to cover the little guy, as baby boys come equipped with a multidirectional urinary apparatus that can surprise even the best-laid plans of mice and men (and women).

Baby-Led Weaning (BLW)

One of the major physical, behavioral, and social junctures in early life is the transition from breast or bottle to solid foods. Both the art and science of this transition have changed over the years, but there is one overwhelming assurance to parents: children are built to eat. Except in extraordinary circumstances, a child suckles without a lot of encouragement, right from the womb. And just as God has created us, we learn at the right time to eat the bounty of solid food resources that He has given to grow and sustain us. Our God is an awesome God!

The transition to solid food does, however, offer an opportunity for parents to lead children toward healthier eating behaviors than was popular in earlier generations. Merely look at the obesity rate in the United States, now exceeding 30 percent and accompanied by alarming rates of cancer, heart disease, diabetes, and inflammatory illness. The type, quality, and quantity of food consumption undoubtedly are keys to understanding and dealing with these trends. Data suggests that eating behavior has not merely physical but cognitive and emotional consequences as well.

Mealtime offers a magnificent place for spiritual growth within family life, which is often pulled by many adversarial forces.

In the last ten years, pediatricians and registered dietitians have been advocating BLW as a more appropriate process for making a healthier transition from milk to solid food. BLW not only makes sense medically but it also offers substantial benefits to behavioral and spiritual well-being for the family.[15]

In BLW, the weaning process is guided by the infant rather than determined by the parent. This represents a fundamental change in the medical community's principles of child feeding. Previously, parents determined what, when, and where food was offered to the child; BLW recommends that the child determine whether to eat a given food and how much of it to eat.

What is the philosophy behind this approach? By allowing the child the choice of eating and the quantity of consumption, a battle for control and wills is defused. The pressure to eat is removed. The spoonful of food swooping in circles, waiting to land in baby's mouth, is grounded. No more inappropriate bribes of getting a treat when they eat. And no more demands to clean a plate!

Key Parameters to Initiate BLW

- The child's physiological maturity helps guide the parent to the appropriate time to begin weaning. For most children, this is no earlier than 6 months of age. This is a recommendation from the World Health Organization and the American Academy of Pediatrics.[16] Children who were born prematurely, have developmental delays, are hypotonic, have certain genetic disorders, or have physical limitations (such as cleft palate) may need to delay until they mature further or the issue is corrected.
- The child should be able to sit upright and tilted forward to help prevent choking. (More about choking in a moment.)
- Most children's digestive tracts are not mature enough for solids before 6 months of age.
- Children should demonstrate the ability to reach out for objects and bring them to their mouth, bite, and chew (even without teeth). Generally, this starts around 6 months of age.
- Breast milk or formula can continue and may for some months remain the primary source of calories. Children will let you know when they prefer their calories from solids by their food consumption.

The key principle here is do *not* feed your baby. Let your little one pick the food up and eat it. This becomes an issue of trust and respect. Your child is the one to regulate his or her own intake, and God has composed a magnificently efficient eating, digesting, growing—and relational—little creation.

You might wonder how to actually begin BLW. First, serve meals in a relaxed atmosphere. Your child should not be tired and actually should not be really hungry. Second, include your baby at the dinner table when you are eating.

Begin the socialization process into the family around mealtimes. Start with a simple table prayer—"Come Lord Jesus, be our guest . . ." You might even help her bring her tiny hands together for prayer for just a moment and demonstrate your prayer posture for her to emulate.

You should place the high chair at the family table with the tray close to your baby's body. It is helpful to have a splat mat below because meals with a baby can get really messy. In addition to the high chair and the splat mat, it is useful for the baby to wear a sturdy pocket bib. Look for products that have bowls inset into the plastic pad. These are worth their modest price in terms of use and cleaning.

Place the food within reach on the tray or pad, and offer only two or three items at a time. Anything offered should be in finger or stick shape so it can be easily grasped.

It may be at 10 or 11 months before the thumb-forefinger pincer grasp is fully developed to allow more fine-motor movement, so your baby may clench the entire piece of food with a closed fist and just shovel it in.

A few simple and safe first food offerings include the following:

- Avocados
- Sweet potato fries
- Slightly cooked asparagus spears
- Half or quarter of a well-cooked meat ball (low in salt)
- Zucchini
- Kiwi slices
- Meat loaf in little chunks
- Ripe peach slices
- Cooked apples in very thin slices
- Previously frozen fruit (but no grapes, frozen or fresh, at this age)
- Pasta cooked to soft texture

Your baby will let you know when it's time to move along to other foods, so trust his palate. Start by offering solids at one meal a day. And you can offer your child water, perhaps in a little medicine cup or a sippy cup.

Patience is the key word. This type of feeding may take a long time. Be prepared to sit and be in a gentle, nonanxious environment around these important first meals together. It should be a time of fun and laughter.

It will definitely be messy. There may even be a few surprises when you change diapers later. Whole food may suddenly appear intermixed with more solid or unusually malodorous stool; that's perfectly normal.

Choking

Your baby has a gag reflex, so expect him to gag. It is part of the proces for the child to learn how to chew and swallow food. When children gag, they make noise. But when they choke, they make no noise and they appear to be in substantial distress—this is when we should immediately intervene. *All parents and day-care providers should know CPR.* Classes are readily available through your community's fire and police departments, hospitals, physician's offices, or the Red Cross.

Due to the risk of choking, there are several foods that really should be reserved for children over 3 years of age, including the following:

- Whole grapes and raisins
- Raw lettuce and other greens
- Nuts
- Thickly spread nut butter
- Popcorn (actually, wait until age 4)
- Seeds
- French bread
- Small pieces of raw carrots and celery

Use the "squish test": if you can't squish the food easily between your fingers, don't risk it in your child's mouth.

Food Allergies

Anyone who has spent time in a day-care center or school cafeteria has noticed the reserved seating for children with allergies. Our approach to food allergies is rapidly changing. Food allergy assessment and treatment should be done with your pediatrician's consultation. The most common known food allergens include the following:

- Peanuts
- Tree nuts
- Mixed nut butter
- Dairy
- Eggs
- Wheat
- Soy
- Fish
- Shellfish

A few allergy principles are worth noting. Potentially allergenic foods are being introduced to the diet in small quantities earlier in life and more often than in the past. Introduce only one new potential allergen at a time. Always have infant Benadryl on hand and predetermined dosing as discussed with your physician. For diagnosed and more substantial allergic reactions, your physician may also prescribe an epinephrine auto-injector (EpiPen) and will provide training for using it.

Importance of Iron-Rich Foods

Iron is a critical component of brain growth and red blood cell development. If babies do not receive adequate iron, the hemoglobin in their red blood cells cannot carry adequate oxygen to the body's organs and muscles. They may become anemic. Lack of iron may show itself in children who demonstrate slow weight gain, pale skin, lack of appetite, and irritability or fussiness. Interestingly, at 6 months, an infant actually needs more iron than an adult male. In later childhood, iron-deficient children may have shortened attention spans and poor academic performance.

Children are born with a reserve of iron from the mother's blood, and if they are breastfed or receiving iron-fortified formula, they should receive adequate iron. Iron-rich foods should be offered to children shortly after they begin eating solids and should be given approximately twice per day. There are two types of iron sources:

- Heme iron, found primarily in meat, tends to be more easily absorbed. Some great sources of heme iron are liver slices, well-cooked pork and beef, scrambled eggs, broiled or boiled chicken, chicken or turkey meatballs, salmon, tuna, shrimp (introduced carefully), and lamb.
- Nonheme iron comes from plants like legumes, vegetables, and cereals, so children can still get iron even if they are not eating meat.

It is important to pair iron-rich foods with vitamin C–rich foods for better absorption. (That's why meatballs are so well paired with tomato sauce.)

Purees

A logical transition from breast or bottle to solid foods can be achieved by including purees, such as hummus, guacamole, applesauce, yogurt, refried beans, tomato sauce, soups, and smoothies. Purees can be successfully used in BLW, but since self-feeding is encouraged, children need to be old enough to handle a spoon that is preloaded with the pureed food.

Foods to Avoid the First Year

There are a few foods that are best to avoid before age 1:

- Honey (because there is a botulism risk).
- Raw milk. Again, liquid cow's milk should be avoided before age 1. Fermented-milk products like cheese, yogurt, kefir, and cottage cheese have lower lactose content and might be tolerable in small amounts.
- Artificial sweeteners and sugar substitutes.
- Raw meat, raw fish, and raw eggs should be totally avoided until after age 5.
- Junk foods, highly processed foods, and gummy foods that are choking hazards should also be avoided completely.
- Salt (more than 400 milligrams per day); season foods with salt-free spices or herbs.
- High-fructose additives and refined sugar.

BLW and Child Care

Many mothers return to their jobs outside the home soon after childbirth, so it is necessary to plan feeding and nutrition with your baby's caregivers. To ensure consistency, prepare your baby's foods in the size and manner you select, making sure he has good pincer-grasp skills, and emphasize to your caregiver that your child should self-feed.

Teething

Teething can begin any time from 4 to 7 months of age. Usually, the two front upper or lower incisors will break through first, followed by first molars, then canines and eyeteeth.

Teething can be accompanied by significant gum discomfort, a low-grade fever, drooling, fussiness or irritability, and seeking cool or hard surfaces to chew. You may notice your baby chewing on the nipple of her bottle or putting her hands in her mouth. The safest and easiest therapy can be simply rubbing your clean fingers over your baby's gums. Hard rings can actually cause more harm than good as they may bruise her gums; frozen teethers can even cause frostbite. Consult your pediatrician or dentist for recommended teething toys, and if you allow your baby to have one, be very careful about the materials it is made of, as some may contain lead. Pain relievers applied to the gums often wash immediately away or can be harmful if they contain belladonna or benzocaine.

If your child is excessively miserable or has a temperature above 101 degrees Fahrenheit, suspect a cause other than teething and consult his doctor.

When you see or feel teeth, you should begin brushing them with a very soft brush and a tiny amount of fluoride toothpaste. You also can gently wipe the teeth and gums with a clean, soft washcloth.

Tooth decay is one of the most common chronic infectious illnesses of childhood. Excessive acid-producing bacteria are passed to the baby through saliva found on spoons, cups, and pacifiers. Foods with high sugar content exacerbate decay. The acids produced by bacteria cause the outer part of the tooth to dissolve. Probably the most destructive habit is to allow your baby to fall asleep with a bottle of formula, milk, juice, sugar water, or soft drinks. Reserve fluids like these for mealtimes and avoid soda and other sugary drinks completely.

As always, good oral care for you child begins with your own good oral care. Begin proper tooth and gum care in the prenatal period if you haven't already made it part of your wellness care.

American Sign Language (ASL) and Infants

Signing can be a wonderfully helpful communication skill for baby and parent and can begin at 4–6 months of age. Most likely you will note some frustration in your child's demeanor when he tries to let you know he is full or still hungry, especially when he is self-feeding. He may also want his milk or a drink of water to wash down those semisolids and clear his mouth. Or he simply wants more! You have likely already discovered certain inflections in your baby's grunts or cries, but those may not be specific enough to avoid frustration on both sides of the communication.

Some believe that children who learn to sign develop verbal language earlier and more rapidly because they have made the connection between language and needs. Early signing speeds up speech development, reduces frustration and anger, increases the child-parent bond, and improves self-esteem and confidence in your baby. Also, signing children are considered bilingual and are using both sides of the brain to communicate.[17]

Five simple signs will be most helpful, especially if you are pursuing baby-led weaning:

- *All finished* or *all done:* Hold both hands up and shake them. When your baby starts to throw more food off the table than is put in her mouth, it's a great time to ask if she's all finished. Be sure to give her some time to process the question before taking food away.
- *More:* Bring fingers to your thumbs on both hands, tap thumbs while keeping your hands in this position.
- *Milk:* Squeeze your hands like you are milking or on a cow.
- *Water:* Make a W with your fingers and bring it to your lips. This isn't exclusive to water you drink, so talk about water as it relates to a pool, rain, or in the bath.
- *Food or eat:* Pinch fingers to thumb and bring to your mouth. "It's time to eat" is a great way to talk about mealtime.

At 7–8 months, children will begin to be proficient with these simple communications and will link verbal sounds with their wants and needs. For hearing-abled children, it is also important to encourage both sound and movement mimicry.

REST FOR INFANTS

Sleep, glorious sleep! It is something all babies and parents need and parents often lack. Babies sleep much of the time but commonly awaken two or three times per night. Infants have shortened sleep cycles and will wake or stir every 40 minutes, but by 3–4 months, they should be settling into longer sleep times, perhaps as long as 4–5 hours. This is good news for the parents.

It is okay to have your baby sleep in your room if, when baby is sleeping, you, too, are able to rest. However, the room must be smoke-free, and baby should not sleep in the same bed as the parents, as this practice has been linked to infant death from smothering.

Good emotional attachments in infancy are important, so it is important not to let your baby cry for very long. When your baby awakens during the night, comfort your baby so she knows she isn't alone and so she can settle down enough to go back to sleep.

Many infants will sleep 14–16 hours a day for the first few weeks, but this is highly variable. However, by 3 months, they should be settling into longer sleep periods of 4–5 hours. Establishing a pattern of sleep and awake time is most important, and you can usually receive clues directly from your child. Yawning, jerky movements, fussing, rubbing the eyes, or clenching fists may be signs of tiredness. Your baby may not recognize the difference between night and day at first, so establishing a routine like low lights, soft music or a song, and gentle kisses may help the baby learn it is time for bed. Some babies are comforted by gentle massage in preparation for sleep. It's not too early to read a Bible story and to pray with your baby as part of your family's bedtime routine.

However, some babies are just tough to get settled. Here are a few suggestions to help from the HealthyWA website:[18]

- Swaddling in a thin cotton sheet or swaddling wrap specifically designed for this purpose may help. Some children really resist this, though, and need their hands free. Never place a swaddled child on his stomach. Most pediatricians suggest noting when the child is starting to roll onto his stomach from his back, and to stop swaddling at that point.[19] There are a variety of swaddling techniques to employ.[20, 21] Consult with your physician.

- When baby wakes during the night, hold her in your arms for 10 minutes or so and then try to place her back in her crib. If the infant cries when being transferred, you may try to just place your hand on her so she knows you are there; then gradually extend the time between touches.
- Play white noise or soft, melodious music to distract from other sounds.
- Provide a warm bath and finish with gentle massage using lotion or oil.
- Offer another small feeding so baby's tummy is full.
- Allow him to suck on a pacifier.
- For the first few weeks especially, use the Five *S*'s method of calming your baby: *swaddle* (wrap baby so his arms and legs are constricted as if he were still in your womb; keep his head unwrapped, of course); *side* (snuggle baby in your arms so he is positioned on his side); *sway* (hold the baby in your arms as you rock somewhat vigorously back and forth, much like a baby swing); *suck* (use her pacifier, as sucking is a way for babies to soothe themselves), and *shush* (make rhythmic *sh-sh-sh-sh-sh* sounds loud enough so baby hears only you, then gradually decrease your volume).
- It is critical for parents to take care of themselves. Take breaks when you can; put the cell phone on vibrate or silence; shut down the computer and tablet; turn off the TV.
- Ask family members for help, and connect with other parents who are going through the same experiences.

Are you taking time to think about your parenting? Use this precious pause to reflect and meditate on God's Word for you, and the incredible joy, even with the challenges, that this parent-child relationship is giving to you. Parenting is a wonderful gift. Just think of the joy your Creator has as He parents you, His child in His Son, Jesus.

FOCUS ON FAITH AND FAMILY

Baptismal counseling and follow-up should begin in the prenatal period or early in infancy, so meet with your pastor to discuss your baby's Baptism, to seek guidance on selecting godparents, and to be affirmed in your understanding of your own Baptism. Many parents find that planning their baby's Baptism provides an opportunity to review the gifts of Baptism as explained in Martin Luther's Small Catechism and to celebrate the Sacrament of water and Word in their own lives.

The first year of life, before and after your little one has been baptized, is the perfect time to affirm that he or she is a part not merely of an earthly family but of God's family. Baptism is only the opening verse of this lifelong grace-song. Our society is fraught with problems relating to the breakdown of family structure, family relationships, and home as the primary venue for faith formation. These first few months are prime time to place your energy in laying the groundwork for your family to be the best source for learning life together and learning faithfulness together.

Your local congregation supports the family beginning for your child at the baptismal font. Ben Freudenburg, division chair of the Family Life Program and emeritus professor of Family Life Studies at Concordia University, Ann Arbor (Michigan), uses the term "home-centered, church-supported" in his book *The Family-Friendly Church*[22] to describe the joint role of the home and the congregation in the faith formation process. The family has primary responsibility for nurturing the faith of the child, and the church provides support and training for the parents and their children through Word, Sacrament, and educational ministry. Freudenburg goes on to describe how this partnership works. It is always a both-and, with the home and church working together to create a rich environment for baptismal faith to grow into maturity that spans generations.

Having your child sit in her high chair at the dinner table allows you to teach her to bring her tiny hands together and learn the practice of regularly going to God in prayer. Reciting with children "Come Lord Jesus," "Bless us, O Lord, and these Thy gifts," or another traditional table prayer ushers them before God's throne of grace and mercy with you as part of

God's family.

Bringing infants to church may seem like a strenuous undertaking with all the preparation and literal ups and downs of a service; yet, verbally and nonverbally, you are saying to your infant that God's house is important to your family and is a part of your life. The presence and participation of even the youngest of children in God's sanctuary establishes them as a necessary part of the faith family.

Most members of your congregation will be delighted to see you and your baby at church; the next generation is a joyous reminder of God's master plan to further His Church and is a practical indication that your congregation is a thriving, growing, faithful community. Therefore, worship with the faith family opens lines of communication, support, accountability, and commitments that are meant to last into eternity. Ultimately, it is important to remember that the Holy Spirit works in the hearts of everyone present—even the preborn and newly born and distracted parent—to plant and nurture the seeds of faith in Christ Jesus as our Redeemer and Lord.

The simple fact is that even very young children see what parents do, what is important to us, and what we love. They follow our example.

> Train up a child in the way he should go; even when he is old he will not depart from it.
>
> (Proverbs 22:6)

In addition to bringing a sometimes-fussy little child into God's house, you are being faithful to the calling of the Christian parent. Remember the promise you and your congregation make when children are baptized, the responsibility to "pray for them, support them in their ongoing instruction and nurture in the Christian faith, and encourage them toward the faithful reception of the Lord's Supper. They are at all times to be examples to them of the holy life of faith in Christ and love for the neighbor."[23] In Baptism, parents, sponsors, and congregation members vow to raise our children according to God's will and Word.

The following suggestions can make worship more comfortable for your baby and easier for you so you can fully receive God's gifts:

- Remember this practical tip from Jesus' mom for dealing with a fussy baby in or out of church: swaddle. Babies love to be swaddled—that is, wrapped in a large, thin blanket—because it offers the same sense of security they experienced in the womb. "And she gave birth to her firstborn son and wrapped Him in swaddling cloths and laid Him in a manger" (Luke 2:7). This certainly suggests that Mary was an attentive and loving mother. Even the angels mention the swaddling cloths as a sign to the shepherds (Luke 2:12). It works well for all babies.
- Hold baby on her left side to help with digestion and colic.
- Rock your baby when you are standing.
- Avoid overfeeding.
- Make sure your baby doesn't need a diaper change.
- Consider using a pacifier.
- Mainly, be observant of the circumstances that always seem to produce distress and what works to help settle your baby's spirit.

When trying to calm your fussy baby (in church or out), consider these possibilities:

- Is she hungry?
- Is he hot or cold?
- Is she soiled or wet?
- Is he having gastroesophageal reflux, colicky, or experiencing other gastric discomfort?
- Is she feverish or congested?
- Is he overstimulated?
- Is she bored? If so, introduce movement or singing!

Fussy Babies and Parental Health

If your baby is fussy, and some are, be patient. It is completely normal for wonderful, loving parents to occasionally feel upset or frustrated (or even angry) with a crying baby. Take a deep breath and take a break by placing your baby in a safe place for a few moments. Listen to calming music. Pray. Call a friend. Run in place to burn energy.

Concern about not being able to calm their baby combined with simple fatigue can cause parents to feel anything but affectionate toward their child, but feelings of intense frustration and anger shouldn't be ignored. If you recognize that your emotions are exaggerated or uncontrollable when your baby is upset, seek help immediately. Call your doctor, your counselor, your mother. Many people experience postpartum symptoms, anxiety, depression, or uncontrolled anger; there is no shame in seeking medical intervention for these conditions.

PURPOSEFUL AND MISSIONAL LIVING

Can parents begin to instill meaning and purpose in the life of their very young child? Indeed they can, through action and example as well as verbal cues and guidance. As you give of your time—and for mothers, often this is seemingly *all* of your time—the loving attitude you display to them as you care for them has meaning and purpose. Your patience, tone of voice, and guidance show them that your purpose is to be there for them, to do for them when they can't master tasks themselves.

By 3–4 months of age, your child is starting to understand that he exists in this world and belongs with you. He is making eye contact, smiling to your face, and responding to your smiles—so smile a lot! Smiling gives him another healthy way to express himself other than crying. He will learn that when he grins, much more conversation comes his way. He is beginning to read your emotions and moods. His parents are the ones who are there and providing for his needs. He may not realize that you are a separate person until he is 7–8 months old. Your presence helps him understand that he is safe with you.

At first, though, your baby may actually smile past you and not make direct eye contact. This is a protective mechanism so that she is not overwhelmed. Gradually, however, she should begin holding your gaze and making eye contact. Your child is beginning to understand that relationships are rewarding and she is valuable; she actually is starting to develop some self-esteem.

Babies have personalities from the beginning. They can be calm and quiet or fussy and sensitive. Some sleep 14 hours a day and some sleep 10. Some sleep through storms, cell phone calls, conversations, and a blaring TV; others awaken with the slightest activity nearby. Both behaviors are normal and healthy. They are merely demonstrating early personality traits. Low birth weight or premature babies may be a bit less responsive at first and then later develop. Just be aware that your new baby quickly picks up your attitude, temperament, and leadership.

Grandparents and other relatives or friends who don't frequently see the child may not receive a warm smile at first. This is selective behavior; the baby is figuring out who's who in his world.

The earlier you incorporate verbal or sign language into routine activities, the fuller and more understandable life becomes to babies. Begin showing baby your tongue and speaking simple words like *mama* and *dada*. Repeat sounds your child makes so she begins to understand what sound she has made; this is early conversation. Repeat important words to her, such as her name, *bottle*, and *milk*. Sing familiar songs like "Jesus Loves Me" and "Children of the Heavenly Father." Say regular prayers at mealtime and bedtime. Gradually turn over age-appropriate activities and choices to your baby to help encourage and empower her with your loving guidance (as we discussed regarding baby-led weaning).

Read aloud from the beginning. Reading to your baby is a time for sharing and closeness and total focused attention. From six to twelve months, expect baby to try to put the book in his mouth; it means he's interested. He may bat, turn, or gum the pages. There are many, many books for babies made of durable materials such as cloth or thick board. (Be alert to the materials and ink, however, to be sure that the books are nontoxic.) Books for this age have big, colorful pages and familiar images. Some have only pictures; adults say the name of the item and point to it to help baby develop vocabulary and familiarity with things in his world. Others have simple text and illustrations. Read the same stories over and over, and change your inflection on occasion to emphasize the material. Once your child starts speaking, you will be amazed at how he mimics your voice.

This is a good time to catch any hearing difficulties that may be affecting the complex development of language and communication. Your pediatrician will do an initial hearing screening before your baby leaves the hospital after birth. Depending on that finding, further evaluation might be needed in the next few months. However, your observations about your child's response to sound, noise, and verbal communication are most important. Be assured that a potential hearing problem may be the result of easily correctable issues like fluid in the ear canal or a noisy testing environment.

Regarding electronics: more than 30 percent of infants and toddlers already have televisions in their bedrooms, and almost all of them are exposed to cell phones, from the birthing room (for photos and videos) to daily life with Mom and Dad. Children who have televisions in their rooms, who spend time looking at a small screen (such as a phone), or who often use a tablet tend to be overweight, get less sleep, and develop mental health problems as teenagers.[24] Parents have logical reasons for using small screens and televisions, but many health professionals recommend no screen time until children are at least 2 years old. For those families who choose to use them, we advocate moderation.

This family of God works and plays and worships together. As we've mentioned before, take your little one into God's house with you, to show her that she, too, is God's child, and begin introducing her by word and deed to what that means to her and for her. You are letting your baby know that he is important to you and to your family of faith. He has value and purpose in God's family. As often as possible, show and tell your baby that his purpose is to be a loving member of God's family and a loving member of your family.

NOTES

1. "Swaddling: Is It Safe?" www.healthychildren.org.
2. Growth-Developmental Baby Milestones, https://pathways.org/growth-development/baby/milestones
3. Ibid.
4. Ibid.
5. R. H. Thompson, N. M. Cotnoir-Bichelman, P. M. McKerchar, T. L. Tate, and K.A. Dancho, "Enhancing Early Communication through Infant Sign Training," *Journal of Applied Behavior Analysis* 40, no. 1 (Spring 2007),15–23.
6. "Breastfeeding for 6 Months," https://pediatrics.aappublications.org/cgi/doi/10.1542/p3ew.2011-3552.
7. "Birth Control and Breastfeeding," *American Association of Pediatrics* (AAP), https://www.healthychildren.org/English/ages-stages/baby/breastfeeding/Pages/Birth-Control-and-Breastfeeding.aspx.
8. P. Kim, R. Feldman, J. Swain, et al., "Breastfeeding, Brain Activation to Own Infant Cry, and Maternal Sensitivity," *Journal of Child Psychology and Psychiatry and Allied Disciplines* 52, no. 8 (August 2011), 907–915.
9. Kelly Bonyata, "How Does a Mother's Diet Affect Her Milk?" (April 2018), www.https://kellymom.com.
10. "Breastmilk and Your Diet," https://www.healthychildren.org/English/ages-stages/baby/breastfeeding/Pages/Breastmilk-And-Your-Diet.aspx (March 2020).
11. Tara Haelle, "Any Breastfeeding—Even If Combined with Formula—Cuts SIDS In Half," (October 31, 2017), https://www.forbes.com/sites/tarahaelle/2017/10/31/any-breastfeeding-even-partial-cuts-sids-risk-in-half/#43229bbe2519.
12. "Postpartum Depression Is One of the Most Common Medical Complications during and after Pregnancy," Sage Therapeutics, Inc. 11-18 MRC-PPD-00208, seeppd.com.
13. "Incorporating Recognition and Management of Perinatal and Postpartum Depression into Pediatric Practice," https://pediatriccs.aappublications.org/content/early/2010/10/25/ped.2010-2348.
14. "Medication Safety Tips for the Breastfeeding Mom," AAP, https://www.healthychildren.org/English/ages-stages/baby/breastfeeding/Pages/Medications-and-Breastfeeding.aspx.
15. I am most grateful to Diana K. Rice, RD, and Jessica Coll, RD (IBCLC), who provide Baby-Led Weaning workshops nationally, for their insights and guidance. For more information, visit www.diana@dianakrice.com and jessica@nutritionforbaby.com.
16. L. Fangupo et al., "A Baby-Led Approach to Eating Solids and Risk of Choking," *Pediatrics* 138, no. 4 (October 2016).
17. "Benefits of Sign Language for Young Children," www.educationplaycare.co/blog/sign-language-benefits-for-young-children.
18. "Sleep 0–3 months," Healthywa.wa.gov.au.
19. "New Crib Standards: What Parents Need to Know," https://nybirthingcenter.com/new-crib-safety-standards.
20. "Welcome to 7 Swaddles from ABC Doula Service," 7swaddles.com.
21. "How to Swaddle a Baby," slide show, mayoclinic.org.
22. Ben Freudenburg, www.concordiacenterforthefamily.org., personal communication; and Ben Freudenburg and Rick Lawrence, *The Family-Friendly Church* (Loveland, CO: Group Publishing, 1998).
23. *Lutheran Service Book*, "Holy Baptism" (St. Louis, MO: Concordia Publishing House 2006), 269.

24. "Healthy Digital Media Use Habits for Babies, Toddlers & Preschoolers," AAP, https://www.healthychildren.org/English/family-life/Media/Pages/Healthy-Digital-Media-Use-Habits-for-Babies-Toddlers-Preschoolers.aspx.

ADDITIONAL READING

Movement for Birth–12 Months

- "Rear-Facing Car Seats for Infants & Toddlers," American Academy of Pediatrics (AAP), https://www.healthychildren.org/English/safety-prevention/on-the-go/Pages/Rear-Facing-Car-Seats-for-Infants-Toddlers.aspx.
- "Burn Treatment & Prevention Tips for Families," AAP, https://www.healthychildren.org/English/health-issues/injuries-emergencies/Pages/Treating-and-Preventing-Burns.aspx.
- "Choking Hazards Parents of Young Children Should Know About," AAP, https://www.healthychildren.org/English/safety-prevention/at-home/Pages/Choking-Hazards-Parents-of-Young-Children-Should-Know-About.aspx.
- "Guns in the Home," (March 2020) https://www.healthychildren.org/English/safety-prevention/at-home/Pages/Handguns-in-the-Home.aspx.

Breastfeeding

- Anne Smith, "Think You Have to Have a Restricted Diet While Breastfeeding? Think Again!" *She Knows Pregnancy & Baby*, Pregnancyandbaby.com/baby/articles/937551/nutrition-exercise-and-weight-loss-while-breastfeeding.
- Drbrownsbaby.com (2019).
- "How a Healthy Diet Helps You Breastfeed," AAP, https://www.healthychildren.org/English/ages-stages/baby/breastfeeding/Pages/How-a-Healthy-Diet-Helps-You-Breastfeed.aspx.
- "Selecting a Caregiver Who Supports Breastfeeding," AAP, https://www.healthychildren.org/English/ages-stages/baby/breastfeeding/Pages/Selecting-a-Caregiver-Who-Supports-Breastfeeding.aspx.
- "Cronobacter Infection and Infants," Centers for Disease Control and Prevention, https://www.cdc.gov/features/ cronobacter/index.html.

Bowel Movements & Urination

- Regarding painful urination, see the AAP, https://www.healthychildren.org/English/tips-tools/symptoms-checker/Pages/symptomviewer.aspx.
- Regarding abdominal pain, see https://www.mayoclinic.org/symptom-checker/abdominal-pain-in-children-child/related-factors/itt-20009075.
- "Constipation in Children," AAP, https://www.healthychildren.org/English/health-issues/conditions/abdominal/Pages/Constipation.aspx.
- "Diarrhea in Breastfed Babies" and "Diarrhea in Formula-Fed Infants," AAP, https://www.healthychildren.org/English/tips-tools/symptom-checker/Pages/symptomviewer.aspx?symptom=Diarrhea.

Baby-Led Weaning (BLW)

- Gill Rapley and Tracey Murkett, *Baby-Led Weaning: The Essential Guide to Introducing Solid Foods—and Helping Your Baby to Grow Up a Happy and Confident Eater* (2010).
- Leslie Shilling and Wendy Jo Peterson, *Born to Eat: Whole, Healthy Foods from Baby's First Bite*, Kindle edition (New York: Skyhorse Publishing, Inc., 2017).

- Jessica Coll, registered dietitian and International Board Certified Lactation Consultant, Jessicacoll.com).

Purposeful and Missional Living

- "Responding to Your Baby's Cries," AAP, https://www.healthychildren.org/English/ages-stages/baby/crying-colic/Pages/Responding-to-Your-Babys-Cries.aspx.
- David Rueter, *Teaching the Faith at Home: What Does This Mean? How Is This Done?* (St. Louis: Concordia Publishing House, 2015).
- "Tips to Help Your Child Enjoy Reading Aloud," AAP, https://www.healthychildren.org/English/ages-stages/gradeschool/school/Pages/Help-Your-Child-Enjoy-Reading-Aloud-Tips-for-Parents.aspx.

CHAPTER 12

Early Childhood Wellness (Toddlers and Preschoolers)

As we read in the previous chapter, rapid and dramatic development occurs in the first twelve months of life (on average). The next four years bring significant developments as well, so here we divide early childhood into two growth periods: toddler (ages 1–2 years) and preschool (ages 3–5).

Wellness in Toddlers (Ages 1–2 Years)

Your child is leaving infancy and advancing toward preschool. Although the pace of physical growth and motor development may slow, you will begin to observe growth in emotional, intellectual, and social skills. This is also a most opportune time, with the power of the Holy Spirit, for building on the foundation of spiritual wellness. Always keep in mind that this is a time for your spiritual maturing as a parent-leader as well.

MOVEMENT IN TODDLERS

There are two simple words for children 1–2 years old—GO and PLAY! This is a time of continuous motion: running, jumping, climbing, and exploring God's marvelous creation. All of this going and playing (and that is exactly what is most important at this stage of life) is strengthening your child's body, mind, and spirit. Coordinating movements, connecting words to actions and ideas, and developing identity are the results according to God's design for human life. Most of this happens through play, so give your child plenty of time for movement. Support and encourage play with age-appropriate toys and books, with other children, and on his own.

One- and two-year-olds who have opportunities for group play are also preparing for preschool years. They are learning how to share, take turns, follow directions, and be a friend. Playgroup time allows them to separate from their parents and interact with other children. Their play also helps them learn about emotions like anger and fear.

Your parental role is to give your child safe items to play with: books, plastic tools and blocks, noisy pots and pans. Children this age are learning cause and effect, so you may pick up the same toy dozens of times as your toddler drops it from the high chair. Toys that encourage eye-hand coordination are engaging and instructive, so look for items that encourage little hands to open and close, zip, button, stack, turn, press, and slide.

Store items in a safe but accessible place and teach your toddler the importance of cleaning up after playtime. Also teach her to play courageously—she may fail, but she can try again and again until she masters a skill. Your child's play may be hard work for you, so if your 2-year-old tires you out, call a friend or grandparent to spare your energy and give you time to recharge.

Using cell phones, tablets, and television to occupy your toddler's time or "babysit" them is counterproductive and perhaps even harmful. The American Academy of Pediatrics urges that children under age 2 should not watch television at all. Small screens such as phones and tablets are linked to language delays. Rather, toddlers should play with other children, siblings, other family members, and with age-appropriate toys.

Toddlers should be active. Children who begin significant physical activity at early ages are less likely to be obese. (Pediatricians and educators are seeing increasing numbers of overweight and obese children entering our preschools.)

As children progress toward preschool years, they become more confident and in control of their body. Walking and running become smoother. They climb up and down stairs, scale furniture, kick or roll a ball, and seat themselves on a chair. Your parental task is to lead them safely through these remarkably skilled and coordinated activities, while realizing that their cognitive self-control and judgment may lag behind their motor skills.

You can help initiate the fun by rolling with them on the floor, giving them piggyback rides, leading or following them down small slides, and spotting them on floor-level balance beams.

Take your toddler outside whenever possible. He needs fresh air and sunlight. Some pediatric ophthalmologists are seeing increased numbers of young children with defective or weakened eye muscles that help focus near and far vision. They are also recognizing adverse effects of excessive blue light because children are looking at electronic screens rather than going out and experiencing outdoor recreation and sunlight.[1] You avoid these effects by spending time at a safe playground, joining a playgroup, taking your toddler to child-care centers, participating in toddler-related activities at community centers, going to story time at the library, and setting aside craft time and other structured learning opportunities at home. However, be alert to the long-term effects of bright sunlight on your child's eyes, and encourage her to wear sunglasses. And always apply sunblock before going outdoors.

Here are a few suggestions for you as a parent to encourage healthy playing:

- Make your own home a safe place by securing stairs, doors, closets, drawers, and stairways.
- Encourage playing with children close to your child's own age and monitor their play. Look for cooperation, leading and following, and solving problems together.
- Create safe play opportunities in your neighborhood park or open space and monitor this play. It's wise to visit a time or two beforehand to ensure that it is a safe environment for your child and others. Do you see fall risks? fire hazards? aggressive pets? If you note issues, seek the help of authorities to assure all children's safety there.
- Look for organized playgroups in your neighborhood, church, or preschool, and keep the number of children in the group small. Get to know the parents of the other children in the group, especially before you allow your child to visit at their home.

- Avoid toys and games that promote aggressive play.
- Have lots of items so everyone has access to playthings; conversely, let your child put his favorite things away so he doesn't have to share them.
- Don't overplan playtime activities; let some elements of spontaneity and creativity rule.

Aggression

Undoubtedly, you will observe cooperative, happy playing, but you may also see aggressive behavior. Aggression is common as children are trying to understand someone else's point of view or desires and are trying to understand themselves. When something upsetting occurs in the playgroup, intervene so no one is hurt. Defuse the aggression by diverting their attention. As appropriate, talk with the whole group about appropriate behavior, but keep the conversation short and to the point.

What if aggression is getting out of hand? Design the right amount of space for the number of children so they can move away from the fray as needed. Always respond to the situation in a positive manner; let the children know you are right there if they need your assistance in negotiating play. For example, say something like, "Maybe I can help count the number of blocks each of you will have so everyone gets an equal chance to play."

Try to redirect aggressive behavior like pushing, hitting, or grabbing others' toys by moving the children to an alternate activity. Say, "Maybe it is time to sit quietly by yourself with a book for a few minutes, rather than push each other over that toy."

Teach children to use civil words rather than physical responses, and teach them how words help solve problems. Say, "Everyone feels better when we ask for a toy rather than pull it away from our friend."

Preemptively address basic needs. For instance, make sure the room is not too hot or cold, that there is a snack and water if they are hungry or thirsty, and that there is a quiet place to rest if they are overwhelmed.

Games and Sports

As your child gets closer to preschool age, you may see play moving more into the realm of games and sports. Depending on individual physical development, this will be more successful for some children than others. Remember that your toddler's vision is not as mature as the rest of her body, so she may not yet be ready to follow a moving object like a ball, or she may have trouble determining how fast an object is coming toward her. It is not merely that her bones, muscles, and nerves are not yet fully developed, but also that her visual acuity and connection to physical reflex circuits are not fully developed. Opportunities like T-ball and soccer will start at around age 3–4, but toddlers-to-2s can use bigger and softer balls, which are ideal for advancing eye-hand coordination. And tumbling or rhythmic movement classes help build confidence. Check with your local YMCA, community center, campground, or dance studio to see what is available for young children.

PLANT-BASED NUTRITION FOR TODDLERS

You may observe a decrease in appetite after your child's first birthday. He may resist coming to the table for meals or take just a bite or two and then want to do something else. Your toddler may become very picky after having been "such a good eater." Should that be distressing? No; actually, it is normal. As his rate of growth begins to slow, his caloric needs begin to level. Your toddler will start to have food preferences, which will change from time to time. If you have introduced a variety of whole fruits and vegetables, his willingness to eat a variety of foods will continue.

These suggestions might help you deal with persnickety eaters:

- Make mealtime family time. Sit everyone together roughly on the same height level and legislate a "no cell phone, no TV zone" at the table.
- Serve the same meal to the entire family, but try to include at least one food choice you know your toddler enjoys. Provide balance and explain why you are serving a variety of foods.
- Do not bribe your toddler with food treats. Remember that children are also listening to their own bodies telling them when they

are full or hungry (recall baby-fed weaning). Your responsibility is to provide the food choices, and your child's job is to make choices.

- Try and try again with foods. Children have many more taste buds (10,000) than adults (about 5,000). Children taste food intensely, which is why you observe the facial contortions that often accompany a new taste. A child may have to taste something as many as ten times before it becomes an acceptable or desired taste.
- We all also have olfactory receptors in the nose that send messages to the brain that work with the taste buds to tell us what we are eating. When we get a cold, we may not be able to taste as clearly. Even then, stick to the "plant slant" principles. Continue to offer healthy fruits and vegetables and occasionally a small quantity of high-quality fish or lean meat if you wish.
- If you are not a strict vegetarian, you should offer a thoroughly deboned fish or a small serving of lean meat (2–4 ounces) about two times per week. Don't be afraid to introduce new spices and herbs and change flavors and textures.
- Make mealtime fun. Prepare food in interesting shapes amenable to being finger food. Cut food into bite-size chunks, but be sure the pieces are small enough to prevent choking, particularly since toddlers do not have fully developed teeth for complete and effective chewing.
- Your child's pediatrician may recommend dietary supplementation. If you are strictly vegan, it is a worthwhile discussion to have with your doctor or dietitian. Children can grow well on a strict vegan diet, but care must be taken to provide adequate vitamins so their blood, bone, organ, and brain development proceed appropriately.
- Many children require morning and afternoon snacks. Offer healthy fruits and vegetable-based foods that assist in reaching vitamin and other dietary goals. Avoid the highly processed foods and "store-boughts" that we know contribute to obesity and tooth decay.
- Offer fresh fruits prepared at home and absent of added sugars: apples, bananas, peaches, pears, and kiwi. Bite-size pieces of orange and grapefruit are good. Softer strawberries are often a favorite. You can give cherries, grapes, or plums after age 2, but they *must* be sliced or mashed, and they must be pitted. Do not give whole

grapes; cut them in half. Raisins and dried cranberries are tasty, but they may initially appear whole in the stool, so don't be alarmed. Try sliced avocado (yes, it is a fruit), which is less sweet on the palate and introduces wonderful fats.

- Be sure to brush your toddler's teeth and offer plenty of water to remove sticky dried foods from his teeth. Chewy, sticky foods (such as fruit snacks) lead to tooth decay.
- Just as in the first year of life, vegetables should be a snack staple. Well-cooked and diced carrots, cooked green beans, and steamed cauliflower and broccoli cut into small portions are tasty and nutritious. Yams and sweet potatoes well cooked and diced are terrific.
- You have avoided giving your child cow's milk during her first year of life, but now some dairy products are extremely beneficial for her. Consider cheese and yogurt, but limit very sweet dessert-style yogurts to small servings.
- Whole grains in the form of small pieces of whole wheat bread, pita or tortilla, graham crackers, and whole-grain dried cereals are good.
- Finally, lean proteins, such as deboned fish (fresh or canned tuna, salmon, sardines, and whitefish) and peanut butter or other nut butters are acceptable. Of course, if anyone in the home suffers from nut allergies, then nut butters must be avoided or given under the supervision of your pediatric allergist.
- Steamed and smashed edamame, chickpeas, hummus, hard-boiled eggs, and tofu cubes and dip can be wonderful sources of protein.

Remember these precautions when planning your toddler's meals and snacks:

- Big chunks of anything are a choking danger.
- Fruits and vegetables should be either cooked or cut into small pieces.
- Be extremely watchful when serving—or avoid altogether—excessively sticky foods, nuts, and popcorn, as they pose higher risks for choking.
- Be careful with any larger amount of peanut butter, not just because

of nut allergy fears but due to its thickness and the potential for choking as well.

- Recall that children younger than age 1 should not be given honey due to the Clostridium bacteria that can cause infant botulism. After age 2, however, your child should have an adequate digestive tract that allows the bacteria spores in honey to move through the body before they can cause any harm.[2]

There are many wonderful cookbooks that provide recipes that appeal to toddlers and preschoolers. You can find examples of dishes as well as average portion sizes for your child.[3]

Children of different sizes and activity levels have different caloric needs; on average, a 1- to 3-year-old will need about 40 calories for every inch of height. In other words, if your child is about 32 inches tall, she needs about 1,300 calories per day. Please consult one of the "Additional Reading" resources or talk with your pediatric dietitian for specific menus.

Toilet Training and Bedwetting

As we consider what helps our children grow, we understand that nutritional intake produces bodily wastes. Toilet training and bedwetting can be challenging and stressful for adult and toddler alike. Adults should understand that there are complex physical and mental abilities that allow us to use the toilet successfully, and there are a lot of emotions associated with this bodily function. This requires a sensitive, positive atmosphere, with no blaming and no teasing, both in your home and in your child's day-care environment. Some issues, such as prolonged bedwetting and constipation, may require medical assessment by your physician. Rather than an in-depth discussion of this topic here, I will refer you to wonderful articles that address it. (See the list of Additional Reading at the end of this chapter.)

REST IN TODDLERS

As the parent, you have a great deal to say about how much rest and sleep your child needs to be well. The challenges to accomplish this really begin in earnest in the toddler years. As the family's leader of wellness, it is your responsibility to help your children adopt healthy sleep habits and choices so they can grow into happy, healthy, and energetic teens and adults. You can begin by demonstrating your own healthy sleep habits to get adequate sleep, take appropriate rest periods during the day, and remove distractions from your rest areas.

Because your toddler's body is still growing, you need to incorporate dedicated times for rest so that all parts of her body, especially her brain, are restored and recuperate properly. Sleep-health discipline begins with establishing a healthy bedtime routine.

Children need more sleep than adults, but everyone needs adequate rest and sufficient sleep. The body has patterns, rhythms, and cycles of sleep that change through life. The patterns are regulated by light and dark. Your child's routine response pattern to light and dark should be established by 6 months of age, yet your toddler may still have trouble sleeping. What are a few of the issues disrupting her sleep?

- *Nightmares:* These occur late at night while she is dreaming and experiencing rapid eye movement (REM).
- *Night terrors:* These occur early in the night and may cause the child to scream out even though he is still asleep. Stress and lack of sleep can contribute to night terrors.
- *Insomnia:* This is trouble falling or staying asleep or early morning wakening.
- *Restless Leg Syndrome (RLS):* This is an overwhelming urge to move or jerk legs.
- *Sleep talking or sleepwalking:* Your child may laugh or cry out in her sleep, or get up and walk around. Up to 40 percent of 3- through 7-year-olds experience sleepwalking.
- *Snoring:* This is caused by a partial blockage in the airway, but 10–15 percent of children snore. It is worth an evaluation by your physician for correctable causes.
- *Sleep apnea:* Even children can develop sleep apnea when they have trouble breathing or their snoring is extremely loud. More distressing, their sleep may be interrupted by prolonged pauses in breath-

ing; these pauses can affect sleep and even affect heart function. Prompt and thorough evaluation is essential if you suspect sleep apnea.

Children who experience sleep difficulty may be prone to anxiety and depression, obesity, type 2 diabetes, and immune disorders. They may be twice as likely to have attention deficit hyperactivity disorder (ADHD).[4]

How can we help children sleep more effectively? Pediatricians suggest that everyone in the family—adults, teens, and younger children—have a set bedtime. Along with this, establish relaxing bedtime routines, including turning down the lights, playing soothing music, taking a warm bath, reducing the room temperature, reading a bedtime story, and saying bedtime prayers. Begin prayer time with a routine prayer, like "Now I Lay Me Down to Sleep." Gradually add spontaneous prayers for the child and other people: Mommy and Daddy, family and friends. Help your child begin to realize the importance of praying for their teachers and pastor.

Some children do well with sound machines that produce white noise. Others like bedtime companions like a doll or blanket (but only after 12 months of age, when choking and suffocating risks are diminished).

Do not allow caffeine (for anyone) for at least six hours before bedtime, and never put your child to sleep with a bottle, especially milk or sugared drinks; these increase the risks of choking, bacterial growth, and dental cavities.

This is a wonderful time to help your children begin to learn Christian hymns and songs. You can read with them stories about their Savior and the presence of God in their lives. Children respond extremely well to music and to people singing to them; their minds and their spirits readily absorb these messages.

Napping

Toddlers need a total of 12–14 hours of sleep each day, so if they are sleeping 12 hours at night, they may be getting adequate rest. Generally, most 2-year-olds can benefit from a 1- or 2-hour nap in the afternoon. By age 3, they may be getting enough sleep at night to cover their needs. This is an individual requirement, so judge your child's needs according to his emotions, moods, and physical activity.

All toddlers will benefit from some quiet time in the afternoon, whether it means a nap or just diminished activity. These siestas are wonderful times for both child and parent to restore body, mind, and spirit.

FAITH AND FAMILY IN THE TODDLER'S LIFE

At Christmas several years ago, my sister brought me a most special present. It was a vinyl disc home recording my parents had made when I was 2 years old, with my father leading me through the recitation of the Lord's Prayer and singing Lutheran liturgy. Hearing his voice drove home to me how the resonance of faith became so deeply anchored in my being, initially by rote memorization of the Word. It lives within me to this day, although I'm now a gray-haired grandpa.

It also reminds me that during these early years of life, we rapidly gain the ability to understand differences between right and wrong and acceptable and unacceptable behavior. Toddlers and preschoolers are able to learn healthy and unhealthy expressions of emotions and behaviors. Unhealthy expressions produce anxiety within us and others.

Dr. Kim Marxhausen, childhood education consultant, reminds us that a calm, nonanxious child is one who is encouraged rather than discouraged and who lives with hope and joy. She notes that healthy emotions grow right out of the Gospel:

- Calm comes from placing one's self in God's control.
- Hope comes from the forgiveness of sins.
- Joy flows abundantly when we see God's plan at work within us.[5]

So while we teach our children Bible stories and language (which we must), we also strive to build faith that doesn't merely lie on the surface of our children's beings, but is deeply embedded within the core of their mind, heart, and spirit. Christian parents hope to instill an abiding faith that remains for an earthly lifetime and into eternity. Abiding faith leads to healthy, Christlike conversation and interaction with the Creator and within our earthly family, as well as within us (self-talk).

One of the sentinel understandings of how we learn comes from the writings of Dorothy Sayers in her work *The Lost Tools of Learning*.[6] In this text, Dr. Sayers introduces the classical tools that originated in the Middle Ages that help children learn to communicate by first using grammar, then logic, and finally their own expression of what they want to communicate through their rhetoric. These communication tools correlate with a child's developmental age by recognizing milestones in brain physiology, physical development, and socialization skills.

Additionally, as Christian parents, we are teaching our children how to speak about and to God (spiritual grammar) and how they come to know their Creator. We want them to know, understand, and relate to their Creator the way Luther describes in his explanation of the First Commandment in the Small Catechism: "We are to fear, love, and trust in God above all things." We want their knowledge of God to be filled with awe and respect, and we want them to understand that God is rightfully angry at His people's disobedience. We also want them to come to God knowing that they can rely on Him to always hear and be with them. In short, we want their communication with God to be holy, reverent, and trusting.

Once the Holy Spirit instills spiritual grammar by rote (as we hear Bible stories and speak the verbiage of faith in daily devotions and during worship), He guides us toward learning how to love God through logic, through the exploration of our faith (asking questions and discussing faith topics), and through hearing and reading the Gospel. This generally doesn't happen to any extent until elementary or middle school years.

Finally, through the maturing work of the Spirit, your child can learn to place his trust in God and then share his faith through his own voice, which we might call rhetoric. His faith-filled voice becomes a communication tool for sharing the Gospel with others. While some children develop this very early in elementary school, it may take others until high school or later to find their Gospel voice. Regardless, we can trust that God the Holy Spirit will nurture your child's faith that you help instill at home when he is young.

Toddlers are on the ground floor of faith formation, learning words and stories received from God's Word. We are introducing children to the language of our faith, sharing with them the basic building blocks when we take them to church where they hear songs and hymns, prayers and confessions, and the Gospel of Jesus Christ preached in the sermon. We are teaching "Jesus Loves Me, This I Know" and "Children of the Heavenly Father." These expressions of Jesus' mercy and righteousness are the anchor of our hope. It is our vocation as parents to help our young ones learn the words of faith over and against the cacophony of sounds that fill the secular air spaces and that can clog their ears and heart with less than godly vibrations.

Safe Spaces for Toddler and Preschool Family Life and Faith Formation

In the noise instigated against faith and family by the devil, the world, and our own sinful flesh, some comments about the importance of safety within the Christian home and trust in God's provision and protection are in order.

Foremost, our children must feel that they live in a safe environment. Yet the headlines may cause us great heartache, and we and our children may feel the effects of tragedies of all kinds even though they happen in places far away. The world has always been dangerous, especially for vulnerable little ones. And in our world today, there are threats and risks outside our homes and even within them. The many instances of school shootings and stabbing violence keep senseless tragedies in our forethoughts. Yet our complete confidence is in our heavenly Father to guard our steps, so we pray to Him, "Let Your holy angel be with me" (SC, Luther's Morning and Evening Prayers). We take our responsibilities as parents seriously, so we take every measure to protect our children. Although most safety measures are simple, common-sense practices, here are a few safety tips worth remembering:

- Make sure your home is indeed safe. Install childproof locks on places that children should not access. This applies to any guns, knives of all kinds, power tools, cleaning supplies, appliances, and any toxic substances.

- Safeguard access to medications, open heating elements, stairways, roofs and balconies, chemicals (including laundry detergents), and any choking hazards. Explain to toddlers and preschoolers that you are doing these things for their safety.
- Secondhand smoke is quite dangerous for people of all ages, especially little ones with developing airways, eyes, and circulatory systems. Make every attempt to keep all forms of tobacco out of your home.
- Cover electrical outlets, secure cords and cables with childproof ties, and do not leave charging cables plugged in where your toddler can reach them (and put them in his mouth).
- Keep cords of blinds and shades well out of reach.
- Anchor bookshelves, dressers, and cabinets so curious climbers can't pull them over.
- Have a carefully planned escape strategy for any emergency. Rehearse with toddlers and older children how to get out of the home and where to go to wait for help. Have children test smoke detectors with you. Make sure they know which neighbor to go to for help.
- Teach your child to never, *ever* go back inside if the house is on fire.
- As they get to age 3, they should understand the basics of dialing 911, whether on landline or cell line, and teach them their street and address, which will be necessary for a cell line. Help your child understand that 911 is to be used only for threatening circumstances, and share with her what sort of situations would be emergencies.
- Teach your young child her first and last name and your first and last name. She will likely delight in knowing you as someone other than "Mommy" or "Daddy," and she may even call you by your first name to elicit a laugh. Should she become separated from you in a public place, however, knowing her name and yours will contribute to a quick reunion.
- Teach your child to be wary of people she doesn't know and to refuse the offer of gifts or treats from people outside of her immediate circle.
- Ahead of time, assign lines of communication and responsibilities to other family, neighbors, faith community, and medical care providers.

- If you haven't already done so, this is the time to identify legal guardians and make a will.

In addition to such practical physical matters, creating a safe home for your young child extends to protecting his mental and emotional health. Consider these topics:

- Be careful of the time and place you stream the daily news and social media into your home. Even very young children are listening, so be sensitive to words and visuals that may frighten them or cause them to worry.
- Be cognizant and sensitive to what your child is afraid of. Talk to him and ask open-ended questions. This is the time to clarify errors in his understanding so you can clean up misinformation and misconceptions. Assure your little one that he is safe at home, that you will take care of him, and that Jesus loves him.
- News of distressing events and tragedies must be communicated carefully. Young children are concrete thinkers until around age 5, so choose to tell them only the information that is pertinent to their immediate lives, and do not speak in metaphors or vague terms. When a loved one, a beloved pet, or a friend dies, for example, tell your young child that she will not see that person (or pet) again, and it's okay to be sad, but "we can always talk about the one we loved and remember happy times."
- Be honest and candid. You don't need to discuss the gory details with him, but you do need to let him know if something bad has happened and that feeling sad is okay.
- Emphasize to her the safety of her faith, that the knowledge and trust in God frees her to be bold, to try new things, and to enjoy the world. God is her "mighty fortress" and strength, an ever-present help for every need.

Make sure, from the earliest of ages, to let your child know that Jesus is real and present. Show him pictures of Jesus surrounded by children and Jesus as the Good Shepherd holding a lamb. Read illustrated Bible story books that teach about Jesus' life. Celebrate Jesus' birthday. Hang a cross in your child's room.

Although the concept of Jesus living in her heart is out of reach for children as young as 2 or 3, introduce it by showing photos of her Baptism and make the sign of the cross on her chest. Trust that the Holy Spirit is working in her life.

Spirit-Sculpting of Faith

An additional developmental process is occurring in toddlers. Not only are they learning faith-language, but they are also beginning to be shaped by self-regulation (self-limitation or self-control). They are learning to wait their turn and to share, among other interpersonal behaviors. While this is a natural cognitive process of the brain, Christian parents want the development of self-regulation to occur along with the creative and pruning hands of the Holy Spirit. In other words, even as your child is developing behavior characteristics that are turned inward on self, pray for the Spirit to be the sculptor and perfecter of your child's faith. I love the way Rev. Dr. Leopoldo Sanchez, professor of systematic theology at Concordia Seminary, St. Louis, Missouri, describes this work of sculpting: "Like the work of an artist who molds a lump of clay into its intended shape, the Spirit's sanctifying work lies in shaping people into the image of Christ."[7]

Use the following foundational statements and corresponding Bible passages as the basis for teaching your children about the fruit of the Spirit in the context of the Lutheran Wellness Wheel, beginning when they are toddlers and extending throughout your life together as a family. Memorize these Bible verses, as well as others you love, to build up a "Scripture memory bank" to call upon in days of trouble, days of celebration, and times of thanksgiving.

THE FRUIT OF THE SPIRIT AND THE LUTHERAN WELLNESS WHEEL

Love: Baptismal Well-Being

Love is the core of our identity as both a child of God and a child in our earthly family—love so profound that God "gave His only Son, that whoever believes in Him should not perish but have eternal life" (John 3:16). Love originated with our heavenly Father. Love is the deep attachment we have to our Creator that He breathes into our soul. It is the realization and acceptance that God loves us unconditionally, and it is the capacity He instills in us to fear, love, and trust in Him.

That same love is modeled when parents show their children care, acceptance, compassion, and security. Repeatedly showing and telling your child that you love him—and that Jesus loves him—assures your child of how special he is, in God's eyes and in yours. Such love includes plenty of affection, holding and hugging and cheek kissing, all the physical reminders of love, even in those moments when your child has strayed from the pleasantness mark. When he misbehaves (and he will), and if we still love him unconditionally, we will help him understand that there is a difference between our (and God's) dislike of poor behavior and our (and God's) unremitting love and esteem for him as a person. The Father loves us in this very manner, despite our sin, because of the sacrifice of His Son in our stead. Jesus is love.

> We love because He first loved us.
>
> (1 John 4:19)

Joy: Spiritual Well-Being

Joy comes from the heart of God. It is the exuberant delight we experience in our entire being (body, mind, and spirit) when we realize God's presence in our lives. That is why we can experience joy even in very difficult times. When we understand what God has done for us and how He cares for us, we feel joy. It comes about when family members work together to accomplish a task; everyone benefits and is joyful, glad, and satisfied. There is a difference between being joyful and feeling happy. Happiness is situationally dependent and temporary. However, joy is selfless and comes when we do things with and for others. Understanding joy in fulfilling tasks that bless others can become the anchor for pursuing the vocations to which the Lord calls us.

> Rejoice in hope, be patient in tribulation, be constant in prayer.
>
> (Romans 12:12)

> Rejoice in the Lord always; again I will say, rejoice.
>
> (Philippians 4:4)

Peace: Emotional Well-Being

When the Spirit gives us a sense of well-being that is grounded in a right relationship with God through Jesus, we experience a peace that passes all our understanding. We are in harmony with God's love. Christ's peace is available in times of calm or storm. Many of our anxieties flow from troubled relationships within and outside of our family and in our relationship with God. By turning our troubled relationships over to Jesus, through confession of our sins, the Holy Spirit is working within us to foster forgiveness and mercy, the same as we are given by Jesus' death on the cross. Similarly, under the Spirit's care, we work through our relational conflicts with others through careful listening and forgiving, through confessing, repenting, and asking for forgiveness. The Spirit works peace within our relationships. When we experience peace in our innermost being, we know the Holy Spirit is present. Long-lasting peace comes as a free gift from the one who defeated all anxiety and conflict, Jesus Christ. God invites us to turn our worries and concerns over to Him in Jesus' name, and to do so with thanksgiving in our hearts.

> Peace I leave with you; My peace I give to you. Not as the world gives do I give to you. Let not your hearts be troubled, neither let them be afraid.
>
> (John 14:27)

Patience: Relational Well-Being

Often we get upset or angry when we are faced with trouble, delay, or suffering. Sometimes it takes people time to do something that we might find easy. There are times we need to wait for something we really want. Occasionally, it is very important that we share things that are valuable to us. It is vital to take time to understand a situation by actively listening to others, understanding their perspective and viewpoint.

There is value in learning the discipline of waiting, even as a toddler or preschooler. Therefore, our Spirit-led response to trouble, delay, or suffering is patience, especially when situations are out of our control. Patience is a gift of the Spirit, who, despite our hurry, our self-focus, and lack of empathy for others, grants us peace, a nonanxious presence, and the ability to wait upon the Lord's time, answer, and will.

> The Lord is not slow to fulfill His promise as some count slowness, but is patient toward you, not wishing that any should perish, but that all should reach repentance.
>
> (2 Peter 3:9)

> But they who wait for the LORD shall renew their strength; they shall mount up with wings like eagles; they shall run and not be weary; they shall walk and not faint.
>
> (Isaiah 40:31)

Kindness: Intellectual Well-Being

When we treat others generously and considerately, and when we treat each person in our family as we would like to be treated, we exhibit tenderness, warmth, and concern for one another. We want to teach our children to show the same care to friends at the playground or preschool or work and play. We must be curious. We must continue to learn—learn about all God has done for us in Christ, all God sets before us in this world, and all those people God places within our daily path. Knowledge and understanding without judgment of one another contributes to stronger relationships, relationships where forgiveness flows more easily. Knowledge fosters the unconditional love that is characteristic of the presence of the Holy Spirit, a love in which forgiveness triumphs and where malice has no place, no place for a base of operations.

> Be kind to one another, tenderhearted, forgiving one another, as God in Christ forgave you.
>
> (Ephesians 4:32)

Goodness: Vocational Well-Being

Goodness is the very nature of God. Having good morals and living biblically and with integrity earns respect and trust as we deal with one another. We know we are unable to live perfectly because of sin, yet we know our Lord desires us to live according to His will and standards. The goodness with which we live does not earn God's favor; only Jesus has done that through His death on the cross. But with the Spirit's presence within us, we thankfully strive to follow God's commandments. Additionally, there may be times when we need to exhibit goodness by confronting or rebuking others when they do things that harm themselves or their neighbor. We do this, speaking truth according to God's Word, out of love for others, concern for their eternal salvation, and obedience to our Lord.

> Show yourself in all respects to be a model of good works, and in your teaching show integrity, dignity, and sound speech that cannot be condemned.
>
> (Titus 2:7–8)

Faithfulness: Financial Well-Being

We strive to take good care of everything we possess, and we are willing to share good things we have with others. All that we have belongs to God; we are merely (but importantly) stewards of our earthly possessions. Joyfully rather than begrudgingly, we are dedicated and committed stewards of the gifts and talents God gives us. With the Spirit's work in us, we are generous and look outside ourselves for chances to care for and serve others as the living out of our faithfulness to the One who died for us; we are committed to Christ.

> Each one must give as he has decided in his heart, not reluctantly or under compulsion, for God loves a cheerful giver.
>
> (2 Corinthians 9:7)

> But lay up for yourselves treasures in heaven, where neither moth nor rust destroys and where thieves do not break in and steal.
>
> (Matthew 6:20)

Gentleness: Vocational Well-Being

We are tenderhearted and mild-mannered, understanding and respectful to all with whom we come into contact, especially all of God's creatures we encounter in daily work or play. We are gentle and considerate with our friends (after all, a child's playmates are their workmates) so as not to hurt them or alarm them. We have reasonable expectations of one another, and we make gracious allowances for differences in passions, gifts, and abilities, all working together through the Holy Spirit to build up the Body of Christ. We are meek, but our meekness does not mean that we are weak. It shows that we are able to forgive others, correct others with kindness, live quietly with peace and tranquility, and serve one another with gentleness.

> Speak evil of no one, . . . avoid quarreling, . . . be gentle, and . . . show perfect courtesy toward all people.
>
> (Titus 3:2)

Self-Control: Physical Well-Being

Because of sin, we always live with a tension between satisfying our own desires (living for the satisfaction of ME) rather than living for the benefit of others (WE). Our natural self always wants to be in charge of all parts of our life rather than letting the Spirit rule in our hearts. For example, we try to play outside rather than watch TV or sit with our gaming system; we don't take things that belong to others; we eat fruits and vegetables because our parents explain why we need those foods to be healthy; we learn to go to bed around the same time each night and take our afternoon naps because rest restores us.

> Be sober-minded [self-controlled]; be watchful. Your adversary the devil prowls around like a roaring lion, seeking someone to devour.
>
> (1 Peter 5:8)

> For I do not do the good I want, but the evil I do not want is what I keep on doing.
>
> (Romans 7:19)

What are some practical ways to apply these fruitful principles to daily toddler life? Lutheran preschool director Kathy Greffet has these wonderful suggestions:

- At reading time, try to include at least one book that contains stories of Jesus' life and ministry.
- Draw pictures of things in Bible stories, such as the Garden of Eden, Noah's ark, the manger, Calvary.
- Consider gathering with other toddler parents and their children in the setting of your day care or preschool for a special event away from the commercialism of holidays. Gather with other Christian families to make connections.
- Keep a Bible among the other books in your home. Let your child see you read the Bible.
- Let your child see you pray about issues of importance to your personal or family life. Explain to him how your faith helps you navigate your own struggles and challenges.
- Make a point of asking your child for forgiveness when you have been cross or impatient with her.
- While many congregations may send children off to Sunday School during the worship service, keep your children with you in the service to emphasize that worshiping together is important to your family. It is something we *do* as a family.
- Be available to your child. Put down your cell phone, close your computer and tablet, and look your child right in the eyes. Dr. Marxhausen reminds us of three movements common among today's toddlers: pointing, pincer grasp, and the new one—swiping. Perhaps as Christian parents, we can teach our children to look at us face-to-face instead of looking at a screen and swiping.

PURPOSEFUL AND MISSIONAL LIVING IN TODDLERS

Can you begin to encourage purpose at the toddler stage in childhood development? Yes! Setting small, achievable, and age-appropriate goals gives your toddler direction and purpose. These targets give him a place to channel energy toward achievement and self-expression. Your toddler's ability to focus attention for longer periods of time develops gradually. However, if he lacks a sense of purpose, he may quickly become bored, directionless, or resentful.

Healthy self-esteem comes when a child discovers that she can achieve not only her own expectations but also the expectations of others who are foremost in her life—parents, grandparents, siblings, and day-care providers. The closer a child's self-perception is to how she would like to be perceived, the better she develops self-esteem.

Some of this self-esteem develops as a child feels secure within the family. It is also important for him to feel that he belongs to his playgroup and church and day care. It is critical that he feels as if he is a part of a group and not alone.

As the child begins to realize that she can feed herself, reach and grasp things she wants, and successfully communicate her wants and needs, she develops more confidence that she has personal strength and autonomy. She is encouraged when she tries, fails, tries again, and succeeds in achieving a goal.

Our parental role is to set appropriate expectations—not too high or too low. We should be careful not to be overly protective or solve every problem for our child. When he meets expectations, this should be verbally reinforced, such as saying, "Thank you for sharing your toys," or, "Thank you for being patient." If he doesn't meet expectations, we can offer correction by encouraging words such as "The toys still aren't put away. Would you do it right now so we can read a book?" or "No one likes to have their toy pulled away, so next time we will respect other children's things."

We also should keep our promises so our children trust us. We can build purpose by giving them opportunities to be trustworthy. Believe in your child and treat her as an honest person.

As you see their increasing ability to complete simple projects, toddlers can gradually be given additional small tasks without being constantly monitored. Assign tasks of meaning that contribute to the family good: let him help you set the table; work in the kitchen, adding ingredients, stirring or mixing with you at meal preparation; or feed the cat. As he accomplishes tasks, give him honest feedback that encourages him but also allows for small increments of improvement. Give lots of "attaboys" and "attagirls."

Children will make mistakes; they will fail at tasks. Our job is to help them understand that not achieving goals immediately is normal so they don't feel defeated. (We all can learn from our mistakes.) Parental guidance should be constructive, encouraging, and positive. Avoid words that cause guilt or shame. Rather, motivate them and provide them with realistic hope.[8]

Wellness in Preschoolers (3- to 5-Year-Olds)

Preschool children are just beginning to realize that there is a world beyond themselves, which had been their focus of self-preservation during infancy and the toddler years. They are naturally curious. They are beginning to push the boundaries beyond self and will start that process at home, where they feel safe with their parents and siblings. Many preschool teachers say that parents are often amazed at how well their preschooler is behaving at school compared to home: "Is that really my child?"

Jane Wilke, a respected Christian preschool educator, notes that preschool is the time when children begin to understand expectations. Therefore, she suggests, teachers and parents lead well when they use expectation terminology like "We take turns here at school," or "We wait patiently," or "We always say please and thank you."[9]

When a preschooler meets expectations, she should receive verbal reinforcement with a thank-you from the parent. When she doesn't meet expectations, the parent should have a quiet, firm, and brief conversation about how she could respond in a more appropriate fashion.

There will always be much to do at home (cooking, dishes, laundry) to interrupt the teaching of expectations of faith and purpose. But one activity that can easily be used as an effective vehicle to begin learning living skills is play. Play is how preschoolers prepare for school, for example, or how they learn about caring for the family pet.

Many mothers have established careers before having children. An increasing number of households depend on incomes from both parents, and these combined financial resources are critical to meeting the family's needs and desires. That necessitates daily child care, and for many families, that care is coupled with educational services in the form of preschools.

Church-run day-care centers and preschools are the largest component in the Christian school system. However, because there are many more public and nondenominational options, the growth rate in the number of Christian preschools is leveling off. And there are significant numbers of preschoolers being homeschooled, sometimes along with older siblings. (Much of what we discuss here is applicable to homeschooling.) Most day-care centers offer services for children beginning at the 6-month-old range to prekindergarten, or about 5 years of age.

There are three major ways preschools prepare children for the scholastic setting:

- First, they learn friendship and fellowship skills—how to get along.
- Second, they learn how to pay attention, feel comfortable being separated from their parents, and respect the authority of others besides their parents.
- Third, they begin to understand their emotions and how they can deal effectively with fear, anger, and frustration; they learn self-control.

Just as we discussed for toddlers, preschoolers need a safe setting with lots of options for both play and quiet time. We need to allow plenty of time for children to explore freely and safely. When we emphasize early reading interests and readiness, we help them expand language skills necessary for more advanced communication and conversation. In addition, we intentionally introduce a wider vocabulary of both secular and faith language. Use what you observe to guide your reading with your preschooler. Use situations that come up in his day where specific words and stories of the Bible can be applied. If she appears to make believe being a mom, share stories of families in the Scriptures. If we have a young child interested in sports, read something about the action figures of the Bible, like Joshua. Or if he likes specific food, explore books on growing and preparing meals, and include stories of the times Jesus used food in ministry (Luke 5:7–32; 7:36–50; 9:10–17). It is by God's beautiful design of His Word that the stories of faith can enter innumerable aspects of a young child's life experiences.

Preschoolers expend vast amounts of energy, so it is important for parents to judge their own needs for time, meals, and rest. Especially if you are homeschooling, make sure your own nutrition and rest needs are reinforced, perhaps with the help of other family members or sharing efforts with other homeschool parents. Seek services that are available in almost every community, congregation, and pediatrician's office. Find and use the village!

MOVEMENT IN PRESCHOOLERS

Although many topics of movement were addressed in the section about toddlers, what is significant here for parents of preschoolers is early interest in organized sports, dance, or gymnastics offered in your community.

Remember that visual maturity (and eye-hand coordination) may lag behind the development of other physical skills. Your child may have trouble focusing on moving objects or difficulty judging distances and speed. Be patient, encouraging, and realistic about your preschooler's interests and abilities. And keep in mind that most children will probably never appear in the Olympics or the X Games or on *The Wide World of Sports*, doing flips on the half-pipe or a triple Lutz-double loop.

Nevertheless, all children benefit from active play, improved physical function, and body image, and they learn important lessons about cooperation, communication, and responsibility by participating in team sports. This is a highly personal choice for the child, however. Sometimes the confusion and chaos of team sports is too much pressure for preschoolers, despite gentle coaching and encouragement. Be sensitive to your child's personality, emotional maturity, and interests, and if he or she doesn't want to play T-ball, for instance, then honor that desire.

One of the earliest activities for children requiring strength and coordination is simply riding a tricycle. This can begin at age 3. Then, between ages 4 and 7, most children learn to ride a bicycle. Like any physical activity, there are variations in the ages children learn these skills, and each proceeds at his or her own pace.

It is important to choose the right bike and correct bike size for your child.[10] He needs a bike that allows him to sit on the seat with both feet touching the ground. Be sure that when your son stands over a boy's bike, there are just a few inches between the bar and the groin.

Using a bike with training wheels or even without pedals (called a balance bike) allows the child to experience and learn some balance before proceeding to a larger bike.

Always insist that your child wear a well-fitting helmet. Parents should also wear helmets when biking to set a solid example and for their own protection. It helps for children to wear clothing that is tightly fitted around the ankle to avoid catching pant legs, and it is helpful to wear bright-colored clothing for safety. To keep your child's bicycling experience as safe and comfortable as possible, observe the following:

- Shoes should fit well, be tied securely, and have closed toes. Flip-flops are not safe for bike riding at any time.
- Knee and elbow pads are helpful for beginners.
- All bikes should have good reflectors, although young children should not ride at dusk or after dark.
- Teach children safety rules of the road and how to ride courteously so as not to injure others.
- Children should dismount when crossing roads, and observe all stop signs.
- Bike riders of any age should not wear headphones or use a cell phone.

Another must for preschoolers is learning to swim. The number of injuries and drownings in this age group is frightening, so swimming ability and water safety can begin during the latter part of infancy (older than 6 months). However, the American Academy of Pediatrics states that children are developmentally ready for formal swim lessons by age 4.[11]

Although you may have the skill to teach your child safe swimming techniques on your own, virtually every community center and athletic club with a pool has early-age swimming instruction with qualified teachers. They also have safety services as a part of their offerings.

Even if your child does not learn swimming techniques, she must learn to float and kick. Then if she accidentally falls into water over her head, she will know to hold her breath until her head is above water, to look for the edge of the pool or lakeshore, and to kick until she can safely get out of the water.

The following suggestions will help to safeguard your child when he or she is near the water:

- Reinforce to your child that murky or cloudy water is not safe unless an adult is with him. Lakes and ponds may be safe for swimming but not for solo swimmers.
- Teach your child that the beach is different from the pool. You may feel safe letting her swim in a neighborhood pool, but rivers and the ocean have active, sometimes hidden currents that can rapidly sweep her away. A fun day at the beach includes a life vest.
- It is most important to emphasize, whether you are teaching swimming on your own in the backyard pool or doing so through formal training, that your child requires an adult's direct supervision anytime he is in or near water.
- Make every effort to safe-proof your home pool, and apply the same precaution to neighbors' pools, public pools, and hotel pools.
- Emphasize to your preschooler that he or she is absolutely not to go swimming alone, that she must ask permission before getting into any pool (even shallow kiddie pools), and that she must wear flotation aids until further notice.

Although there may be other sports available for preschoolers in your community, the most common is soccer. At first, soccer reassembles "herd-ball" as the children cluster chaotically around the ball no matter where it is on the field. This relatively safe team sport benefits even preschoolers because it reinforces important life skills such as following directions and cooperating.

The soccer field is a great place to show your child unconditional love, patience, and self-control. It is a place to observe and appreciate physical, emotional, and even spiritual progress and growth. We strive to teach our athletes to play fair and to demonstrate good sportsmanship. But in addition to teaching children about being on a team, of utmost importance is reminding parents to be good sports. Parents' actions speak as loudly as their boisterous words, especially if they are unkind. The soccer field can be an especially appropriate place for parents and children to remember the fruit of the Spirit as they interact with friends, neighbors, and referees.

You may have particular interest in sharing your love for sports like golf, racquet sports, gymnastics, or skiing. Volunteer coaching can be rewarding for adults and is certainly helpful to children. Volunteers should always have team members' best interests at heart, and they should understand that although some members of the team will be better than others, all should be treated fairly and respectfully. People who choose to coach children's sports should do so safely, under good supervision, and with love for the sport rather than a "winning at all costs" attitude, especially with children at these tender ages.

PLANT-BASED NUTRITION FOR PRESCHOOLERS

Preschooler growth and appetites come in spurts. You may notice that your child has suddenly outgrown her clothes and shoes. She may eat ravenously one day and show no interest in food the next. This behavior may raise parental alarm—but it's normal. The most important consideration for parents is to offer a selection of healthy options so the child gets what she needs to grow well. As with toddlers, offering multiple types of fruit and vegetables is important to reinforce when children may start to be exposed to other families' eating habits.

All preschoolers need a well-rounded diet, comprised of the following:

- *Fiber:* It can be a struggle to move children from starch-based fiber products like macaroni and cheese, French fries, and chicken nuggets toward plant-based fiber like fresh fruits, fresh vegetables, whole grains, and beans. Nuts are also great as long as there are no nut allergies. These preferred fiber foods help protect against atherosclerosis, diabetes, and constipation. A good rule of thumb is to "Eat Five"—that is, try to get a minimum of five servings of fruits and vegetables daily.

- *Calcium:* The body needs calcium to build strong bones and teeth. Cow's milk can be safely consumed after age 1, and milk does remain the best source of calcium. Lactose-free milk products like soy milk, sardines, calcium-fortified orange juice, tofu, cereal and oatmeal do have excellent quantities of calcium.
- *Protein:* Preschoolers need about 1–1.5 grams of protein for every 2 pounds of body weight. So a typical 40-pound child needs about 18 grams of protein daily. This is contained in two 8-ounce cups of milk. Eggs, almonds (if not an allergy risk), oats, cottage cheese, Greek yogurt, and broccoli are also wonderful sources of protein. For snacks, trail mix, veggies with yogurt dip, tuna, hard-boiled eggs, and peanut butter on celery sticks all are terrific. Again, make sure that food allergies are monitored. If your child is not gaining weight or height adequately, consider that he might not getting adequate protein.

Encourage your child to plan and cook meals with you and even go to the produce aisle or farmers market to see the varieties of food available. Invite him to pick the fruits and vegetables for the meal so he can take ownership. You may want to foster budding little chefs, as they can stir, count, and measure with you. This is an important preamble to their entrance into the preschool era.

FAMILY WELLNESS IN THE WORLD

Outbreaks of viruses such as COVID-19 and influenza focus attention on the challenges and opportunities for the Christian family to be wellness leaders in a world that is shadowed by the darkness of infectious diseases and respiratory infections, along with their accompanying anxieties.

Coronavirus, the most recent, is not the first and will not be the last public health disaster to affect us as parents or touch the lives of our children. We have learned to stop the spread of these infections by practicing good health manners and, especially, "respiratory etiquette."

- Wash hands before eating, after using the bathroom, and after being in public spaces, such as the grocery story. Wash thoroughly with warm soapy water for at least twenty seconds. Include the spaces between fingers, under the fingernails, around the thumbs, and the back of the hands. You may also use 60 percent alcohol-based hand gel or disposable wipes.
- Cover the mouth and nose with tissue when coughing or sneezing, and dispose of tissues in the trash as soon as possible.
- Always wash hands after sneezing, blowing your nose, or coughing, and also after touching used handkerchiefs or tissues.
- Avoid touching face and mouth after direct contact with other individuals or surfaces that might not have been recently cleansed.
- Make every effort to stay home if you or a member of your household has a fever, sore throat, or a cough.
- See or telecommunicate with your health professional if you have a cough or fever. Follow their instructions and take medications they prescribe. Get ample rest.
- If asked, use a face mask and gloves.
- Don't share eating utensils, beverage containers, food, and drink.
- Avoid sharing towels, toys, books, or anything else that might be contaminated with respiratory germs.

There may be times when your family is instructed to distance itself from others in the community. For the good of society and of your loved ones, comply. Use this valuable time of separation to gather around God's Word in devotions and stay connected to your faith family through live-streaming of worship or music. Build family relationships by conversation, playing games, completing jigsaw puzzles, or craft projects. Stay connected with extended family and friends via phone calls and social media. Stay active by exercising. And explore opportunities to safely serve and care for the wellness of others.

RESOURCES

- Germs: Prevent Their Spread, www.doh.wa.gov (accessed 04-02-2020)
- Healthy Habits to Help Prevent Flu, www.cdc.gov (accessed 04-02-2020)

DENTAL CARE IN CHILDREN

It is important to reinforce the importance of oral health for your child. For perspective, dental disease (caries and cavities) is five times more common than asthma or allergic illnesses in children, and 50 percent of children have one or more cavities before they go to kindergarten. Furthermore, cavities in baby teeth are not harmless; they can lead to difficulties in permanent teeth.

In infant and toddler years, especially if your child is obtaining significant nutrition from milk products via a bottle, you need to be aware that tooth decay and gum disease can begin any time they have prolonged exposure to milk or sugary liquids, including juices. Perhaps they are ingesting these liquids only at nap time or bedtime. Front teeth especially are bathed in these liquids, so children can develop bottlemouth syndrome. This is characterized by sore red gums and mouth and teeth that are discolored or have excessive deposits. Sadly, if untreated, this can lead to tooth decay, pain, and infection. Complications may require oral surgery under general anesthetic. Ask your child's pediatrician about any concerns and a referral to a pediatric dentist if necessary.

One of the easiest ways to prevent bottlemouth is to never let your child fall asleep with a bottle in her mouth. You can also give your child water to rinse off sugary substances after meals and snacks.

As we noted earlier, in infancy you can use a soft washcloth to wipe your baby's gums after feeding. For children under age 3, use a soft toothbrush smeared with about a rice-grain-amount of toothpaste with fluoride. Brush morning and evening.

Children ages 3–6 can apply a pea-sized amount of fluoride toothpaste and learn to brush up and down, back and forth, and with circular motions. Teach your preschooler to be thorough on each tooth, including the hidden teeth in the back of the mouth.[12]

Here are a few brushing tips:

- Teach your children to brush after meals, especially breakfast and supper or before bedtime.
- Children should brush for at least two minutes. Make it fun; sing a

song or set a timer. There are new brushes that play music or light up for the recommended duration.

- Check their brushing and praise if they do well. Encourage and correct if they miss spots. Pay attention to the back or biting teeth as well as the smile teeth.
- Let your children choose the toothpaste or brush that appeals to them.

Fluoride is a mineral that is added to the water supply in most communities. It strengthens tooth enamel and reduces the ability of plaque-forming bacteria to make an acid environment in the mouth. Using fluoride is a safe and well-documented means of preventing tooth decay.[13] Check with your community to see if fluoride is added to the water; if not, use toothpaste with fluoride, or add foods that are loaded with calcium and vitamin D. Your dentist may also administer a fluoride treatment to your child's teeth.

A healthy, plant-based diet rather than sugar-laden foods is critical to dental health. However, dried fruit, such as raisins and chewy snacks made from concentrated juice, sticks to the teeth and in between teeth and should be avoided entirely.

It is recommended that babies see a dentist within six months of the first tooth's emergence. The pediatric dentist will determine the frequency of follow-up visits. At a minimum, parents should establish a dental home by the time their baby reaches her first birthday. Everyone in the family should receive regular professional dental care throughout life.

While children should floss with parental help during ages 2–6, by the time your kids are in the 7- to 10-year-old range, they should be taught and encouraged to add flossing to their brushing regimen on their own.

While we are focused on infants, parents of toddlers and preschoolers should be aware of these two important dental maladies:

Tongue-tie is a restriction of the undersurface of the tongue due to a stringlike frenulum attaching the tongue to the lower surface of the mouth. It affects up to 10 percent of the population. It can lead to breastfeeding attachment struggles or, later in childhood, to speech difficulties or poor oral health. It is easy to fix by simply severing the connecting tissue; done by the pediatrician or ENT doctor, this procedure doesn't require general anesthesia. Afterward, the area under the tongue needs to be swept back and forth with your finger for about two weeks so the tissue does not reattach.

Bruxism, or tooth grinding, is common in toddlers and preschoolers. It usually goes away by age 6, although some children continue until they are teenagers. The cause is usually pain from earaches or teething or from improper teeth alignment. Stress and anxiety can aggravate the condition but usually are not the cause. Although it generally does not lead to permanent problems, check with your child's dentist if you are concerned.

Additional Dental Health Challenges

Dental anesthesia: Options for sedation and pain control to make dental procedures painless range from injected lidocaine and inhaled nitrous oxide ("laughing gas") to general anesthesia, where the patient is completely asleep and pain-free. Please ask lots of questions about the various needs for sedation, and be very comfortable about who is providing this service to your child.[14]

Mouth guards: These are a must for all sports and many recreational activities. They help cushion blows to the mouth and lower face and help reduce the risk of broken teeth, and tongue, lip, and jaw injuries. They usually cover the upper teeth but some also offer protection to the lower teeth. Generally, they are somewhat molded to the mouth by placing them in warm water to soften and then inserting them into the mouth and biting down. They can also be custom-fitted by your dentist and will fit precisely. If your child is wearing dental braces, he should obtain specially fitted guards through his orthodontist. Have your child keep the mouth guard clean by washing it in warm soapy water or by brushing with his toothbrush and paste.

Tooth whitening: Over-the-counter tooth-whitening products like strips, trays, and gels have exploded in popularity, especially among teenage girls, so you may also face this subject with your teen. Teeth should not be bleached until all the baby teeth have fallen out (often in late elementary or even early high school). If your child desires this treatment, you as the parent should read the product labels first. Dark teeth can be caused by an injury, decay, cavities, or darkly colored liquids like some juices and coffee. Discuss this with your dentist and follow the dentist's guidance.

Braces: The topic of orthodontic and endodontic care can fill an entire book. Work closely with your dentist, who will likely have working relationships with highly qualified and board-certified orthodontists (for braces), endodontists (for gums), and periodontists (for bone and teeth ligaments) to provide high-quality care. Wearing braces is almost a rite of passage for many children, but the resulting cosmetic and medical benefits, once the course and follow-up care are completed, are worth the cost, effort, awkwardness, and self-consciousness.

REST FOR PRESCHOOLERS

Some preschool children may no longer be napping, but many still like that afternoon quiet time and sleep. Preschoolers still require 10–13 hours of sleep daily (including naps). When children lack sleep for any length of time, they are far more prone to a variety of health issues, especially obesity, depression, headaches, poor concentration, hypertension, and reduced immune response. Children getting enough sleep show far better memory and attention-related behavior, perform better in school, and are happier and healthier overall.[15]

One way to see if your child is getting adequate rest is to ask her preschool teacher if your child is paying attention and is generally getting along with others. If she is cranky or whiney, or falls asleep at school, she is either ill or is likely not getting enough sleep at night.

Just as we have emphasized for toddlers, preschoolers respond well to routine bedtime activities: avoid caffeinated beverages and sugar-heavy snacks, brush teeth, wash face and hands, use the toilet, read a book, and say bedtime prayers. Encourage physical activity during the day, but reduce activity before bedtime. Monitor closely screen time and electronics in the bedroom. All screens ought to be turned off at least an hour before bedtime (a rule that would benefit all members of the family, as adult sleep cycles are affected by blue light as well).

Be aware of sleep problems as described for toddlers. Watch for night terrors, nightmares, snoring, or sleep apnea breathing issues.

Also think about sleep issues if your child is demonstrating learning issues or misbehaving during the day. Some preschool children may still exhibit separation anxiety, especially when parents go out in the evening and the child is left with a babysitter, or if there is tension in the home. Take time to introduce your preschooler to the sitter if he or she is new. Or allow the sitter to introduce a new toy or new activity, such as a simple craft; then say goodbye and promptly leave. Always be honest with your child and let him know you are going to leave but you will see him when he awakens in the morning or when you return after your activity.

Divorce and Sleep

In our country, over one million children a year experience divorce. This may create substantial separation anxiety, and sleep can be further complicated by different bedtime routines between households. Often, though, when the change in schedule involves regular, recurrent weekend or holiday periods, children have an easier time adjusting. In any case, a frank discussion of parenting parameters can be extremely beneficial for your child's mental and physical health.

On occasion, however, you may observe a regression to younger behavior, such as thumb sucking, bedwetting, or interrupted sleep. This may be a signal that more attention needs to be paid to routine on the parents' part or that some professional counseling for the child (perhaps to include joint-parenting counseling) might be necessary. Work together as parents to duplicate favorite toys or music or books, and work closely with your pediatrician and lawyers to place the child's welfare foremost in everyone's thoughts and actions.[16]

FAITH AND FAMILY FOCUS IN PRESCHOOLERS

The assurance of safety and love remains a necessity for preschoolers just as for toddlers. It is likely that preschoolers will be spending more time away from their parents, often in large blocks of time, if they are in a day-care setting with preschool educational components.

Whether you're preschooling at home or away, faith formation is a necessary component of the curriculum at a Christian Day School and includes reading Bible story books, prayers, and devotions.

Prayers: Most often, the early portal into prayer is through the fixed prayers of our faith, such as the Lord's Prayer, common table prayers, and bedtime prayers. Repetition is important, and you may notice your toddler and preschooler speaking the words of the prayers along with you or echoing your "amen."

Spontaneous prayer can be taught by modeling for them how to begin: "Dear God," "Dear Heavenly Father," or "Dear Jesus." You can then teach the closing "in Jesus' name," "for Jesus' sake," or just "Amen." Listen as your children fill in the middle of their spontaneous prayers, as they may reveal troubling or joyful parts of their lives. You can also guide your children in praying for pastors, teachers, brothers and sisters, or other special people in their lives.

Devotions: It is helpful to have four components to family devotions: (1) a reading from God's Word, (2) portions of Luther's Small Catechism or the catechism of your faith community, (3) a hymn, and (4) life application. You can also include a simple question for discussion.

Many resources are available from Christian publishers. Look for children's devotionals, illustrated Bibles, catechisms, and hymnals. Familiarizing your children with the books they will use during formal religious instruction (such as the catechism) and the hymnal they see in worship will anchor them in faith traditions, reinforce faith language, and teach them that God's Word is the center of the Christian's life. Additionally, there are many wonderful visuals like Advent wreaths and Christmas decorations that can be used as teaching aids. Daily family devotionals, Bible reading plans, and seasonal or themed devotionals are readily available online as well, but be aware that not all of these materials will be consistent with the teaching of your church. Ask your pastor if you want particular guidance.

Luther's Small Catechism was written—and is still used—for the primary purpose of teaching the Six Chief Parts of the faith in the home. Luther's simple explanations of the Commandments, the Apostles' Creed, the Lord's Prayer, Baptism, Holy Communion, and Confession may be beyond the reach of your preschooler, but he or she will soon learn to recognize the words and will internalize the concepts. Reviewing these faith basics is always beneficial to parents as well.

Christian preschools: The number of Christian preschools and day cares grew exponentially over the last two or three decades, but more and more private and public organizations are offering options for families.

There are many well-established and comprehensive resources to help parents who choose to homeschool. Many communities offer homeschool co-ops or groups to share educational responsibilities. Many online communities and social media groups offer support to parents as well. I recommend that you spend significant time exploring possibilities and checking with fellow homeschooling parents about their preferred resources.

If you are looking for a preschool program outside your home, understand that preschool programs are regulated by your state's department of education. They must meet requirements for academics, space, student-teacher ratio, accessibility, safety, public health codes, cleanliness, creative play resources, and more. Your decision should include careful assessment of all of these requirements as well as faith-based curriculum and teachers consistent with your faith and confessions.

Here are a few tips for considering a preschool:

- Although you may observe lots of children playing with blocks and crayons and running with lots of energy and vibrancy, talk with the teacher in the room to understand the purposeful strategies and skills he or she employs to help children learn. Look for children's opportunities to exercise choice.
- Take the opportunity to study the certifications of the teaching staff. States have varying educational requirements for preschool teachers and helpers; many require only that teachers hold an associate's degree in child development. The value of having a bache-

lor's degree is unclear. However, a variety of continuing education programs in preschool care are available, according to Deborah Stipek,[17] professor and former dean of Stanford University's Graduate School of Education.

- Look at the art projects lining the school walls. If all the pictures are of exactly the same yellow flower, for example, that may be a sign that the teachers are largely directing activities rather than allowing the children to choose subject matter and engage in creative expression.[18]
- Know the number of children being supervised in any given classroom. Usually state law requires one adult for every eight preschoolers and one certified teacher for every twenty. Other adults may be assistants, aides, or helpers and may have tasks that are important but not directly related to teaching: supervising recess or snack time, helping children to and from the bus, helping with coats and with trips to the bathroom.
- Make more than one visit to observe the learning environment. The school's open house will not show a typical day, and the teacher may be too busy to answer specific questions.
- Know where bathrooms are and make a trip there yourself to see if they are in easy view and accessible. Know the protocol for children making trips to the bathroom, and review it with your child.
- Observe to see how children safely move around the classroom. The room should have furniture with rounded corners; clean, covered sockets; and all cleaning supplies safely stored. Toys and books should be within students' easy reach so they don't always have to ask for assistance. It is productive to have different sections in the room for different activities: blocks here, dress-up clothes there, toy stoves and kitchen items in another spot. A room that is organized gives teachers clear sight lines.
- The classroom should include toys that encourage pretend play. Toddlers and preschoolers love pretending. Imaginative play encourages the development of language, social, emotional, thinking, and behavior skills.
- The school should ensure that children are screened for special needs and should use assessment tools that give teachers regular

information about children's progress in different domains, including early math, language, and literacy skills, as well as self-regulation and social-emotional development. Then, teachers should use the information to adjust and individualize learning opportunities to meet children's individual needs.[19]

- You should be able to observe teachers approaching children at their level and making good eye-to-eye contact so strong bonds of trust with the teacher can develop. This facilitates learning.
- There absolutely should be no yelling and no harmful physical contact. Look for the ways teachers healthily support children to resolve conflicts in the classroom.
- Christian parents will want to evaluate the preschool's programs, materials, and teaching philosophy to be sure that the parents' and family's faith confessions are being taught and followed in the school setting. This is not to say that a Christian school outside of your family's faith tradition shouldn't be an option for you. However, your child's school should support your vocation as your child's first faith teacher as much as possible.

You are entrusting to the preschool a significant amount of your child's time and educational foundation to supplement what you are providing at home. It is worth a day or more of observation, along with recommendations from your pastor and other parents, when you choose the preschool that is best for your child.

PURPOSEFUL AND MISSIONAL LIVING IN PRESCHOOLERS

Commonly, preschool is the age when many children are introduced to formal education. They learn critical social skills like standing in line, listening, paying attention, and cooperating. Preschool is the bridge between life as a baby and life as a child, and it supports them in their vocation as student, which will continue for at least fifteen more years.

A great number of resources to aid in teaching the faith are available to Christian parents. These include teacher guides, flash cards, finger puppets, music, books, internet programming to introduce words and phrases, and age-appropriate and understandable Bibles.

Educational resources for preschoolers generally use purposeful play to help children make meaning out of their experiences and interactions with other children and adults. They allow children to explore hands-on interactions with materials to develop answers to their budding questions. They encourage questioning strategies to help children learn. Preschoolers are starting to formulate questions that help them learn to make decisions and that help them see the consequences of their choices.

Resources that communicate Christian values help children begin to understand that their choices should be made with an understanding of right and wrong, of truth or fabrication, and the effects of their choices on others. When they use these resources, parents are helping children develop self-awareness and empathy for others. They are learning how to cope with relational stresses in a healthy manner.

It is important, therefore, to talk with children in words that help them understand the question, "Do you have a purpose (reason) for being in this family, or school, or on this playground today?" This topic may be a challenge for a preschooler to grasp, but to ask "What is important to you? What matters to you? What do you want to do today as you play?" is something they can intellectually and emotionally begin to deal with in preschool.

Christian parents are tasked with the faith development of every child in their home. The ideal situation is one where their children are nurtured and taught in a Christian school. Yet many parents cannot ensure that their children have the benefit of Christian Day School and must rely on public education. We are blessed that public schools in the United States are childcentric and are free. Yet we must recognize that when public school is the only option, our children will be exposed to secular thinking. We should therefore have significant concern about education programs that defy the Scriptures, and we must be prepared to refute nonbiblical teaching in a way that does not confuse our children or turn them against educators. This can be tricky, but you know your child best and with the help of the Holy Spirit, you will find the words to assure her of God's glory, provision, and promise.

The first conflict you may encounter is the early teaching of evolution and the survival of the fittest as a basic child-rearing philosophy. Some environments propose that we should emphasize opportunities to have our child succeed in all aspects of life over and against other children. This represents the ME posture for education, sports, and social advancement.

Counterculturally, we want our children to learn to steward their gifts and talents to the best of their ability and to the glory of God. We want to teach them to purpose their lives in healthy relationships, with their energy and efforts aimed at lifting up their neighbor in need. We want compassionate and empathetic kids.

One of the critical messages to instill in the life of young Christians is the understanding that "it's not all about you." Much of their first two to three years of life have focused on getting their particular wants and needs satisfied. This is a natural growth process, of course. But as they begin to interact increasingly with other children and a wider array of adults, they will notice that there may be joy and satisfaction in helping another person. Four- and five-year-olds can be given "chores." When children help out with the needs of the family, they develop a sense of service, first to their family and later to others. They can see the benefit that their service provides for others, and they can develop pride in their purpose.

To merely force a child to help in the family doesn't develop a sense of mission. The task has to be important enough to be meaningful to the child. This often requires that the task has a level of interest or energy for the child. The care of a pet, for example, may ignite a sense of joyful purpose, and the child can feel the cause and effect of his or her pet care, whether that pet is a fish, turtle, gerbil, dog, cat, or even a horse.

One of the strongest realizations of purpose in young children occurs when they are invited to serve like their most important model—you—serves. When your child sees that Mom and Dad serve others at church, school, home, or in their community and appear to experience joy and fulfillment through that service, he or she begins to grasp an understanding of the importance of living outside one's self.

Preschoolers can also learn about purpose through all of the wonderful Bible stories parents and teachers share with them. How does God use His children to create change and betterment in the world? How does Jesus heal people's diseases, comfort their sorrows, or show compassion? How can Jesus use you as His child in the home and in the world?

Instilling a sense and value of living with a purpose that is bound deeply in our relationship with Jesus anchors the health and wellness of your child to the arms of the Good Shepherd, the Great Physician, the Servant King. May the Holy Spirit guide and support you in your efforts.

NOTES

1. "Effects of Excessive Screen Time on Your Kids' Eyes," www.myopiainstitute.com/eye-care/video.
2. Madhushree Desiraju, "Can I Feed My Baby Honey?" (October 2018) https://kidshealth.org/en/parents/honey-botulism.html?WT.ac=ctg.
3. Leslie Shilling and Mary Jo Peterson, *Born to Eat: Whole, Healthy Foods from Baby's First Bite*, Kindle edition (New York: Skyhorse Publishing, Inc., 2017).
4. "ADHD and Sleep and Sleep Disorders-CHADD," https://chadd.org/about-adhd/adhd-and-sleep-disorders.
5. Kim Marxhausen, Comments at the LCMS Missouri District Preschool Conference, 2019. kim@marxhausen.net.
6. Dorothy L. Sayers, *The Lost Tools of Learning* (CrossReach Publications, 1947; reprinted independly, 2016).
7. Leopoldo Sanchez, *Sculptor Spirit: Models of Sanctification from Spirit Christology* (Downers Grove, IL: InterVarsity Press, 2019).
8. "Helping Your Child Develop a Healthy Sense of Self Esteem," American Academy of Pediatrics (AAP), https://www.healthychildren.org/English/ages-stages/gradeschool/Pages/Helping-Your-Child-Develop-A-Healthy-Sense-of-Self-Esteem.aspx.
9. Jane Wilke, author and Lutheran preschool director, personal communication March 2019.
10. "Choosing the Right Size Bicycle," AAP, https://www.healthychildren.org/English/safety-prevention/at-play/Pages/Choosing-the-Right-Size-Bicycle.aspx.
11. Vincent Jannelli, "When to Start Swimming Lessons for Kids," https://www.verywellfamily.com/swim-lessons-for-kids-2632446.
12. "Toothbrushing Tips for Young Children," AAP, https://www.healthychildren.org/English/healthy-living/oral-health/Pages/Toothbrushing-Tips-for-Young-Children.aspx.
13. "Water Fluoridation," (March 2020) https://www.healthychildren.org/English/healthy-living/oral-health/Pages/Water-Fluoridation.aspx.
14. http://www.mouthhealhty.org/media/MouthHealthy/Files/AZ/Anesthesia-and-Sedation-Questions-to-ask-for-your-child.pdf?la=en
15. "Sleep and Mental Health," https://www.health.harvard.edu/newsletter_article/Sleep-and-mental-health.
16. "How To Support Children after Their Parents Separate or Divorce," AAP, https://www.healthychildren.org/English/healthy-living/emotional-wellness/building-resilience/Pages/How-to-Support-Children-after-Parents-Separate-or-Divorce.aspx.

17. Deborah Stipek, featured, "Tools for Parents: What to Look For in a Preschool Program," (May 2019) https://esource.org/2013/tools-for-parents-what-to-look-for-in-a-preschool-program/3962.
18. Ibid. and personal communication with Deborah Stipek.
19. Ibid.

ADDITIONAL READING

- "10 Tips to Prevent Aggressive Toddler Behavior," American Academy of Pediatrics (AAP), https://www.healthychildren.org/English/ages-stages/toddler/Pages/Aggressive-Behavior.aspx.
- "Winning the Food Fights," AAP, https://www.healthychildren.org/English/ages-stages/toddler/nutrition/Pages/Winning-the-Food-Fights.aspx.
- "5 Great Reasons to Cook with Your Kids," AAP, https://www.healthychildren.org/English/healthy-living/nutrition/Pages/Cooking-With-Your-Children.aspx.
- "Anemia and Children and Teens: Parent FAQs," AAP, https://www.healthychildren.org/English/health-issues/conditions/chronic/Pages/Anemia-and-Your-Child.aspx.
- "Choosing Healthy Snacks for Kids," AAP, https://www.healthychildren.org/English/healthy-living/nutrition/Pages/Choosing-Healthy-Snacks-for-Children.aspx.
- "Sample Menu for a Two-Year-Old," AAP, https://www.healthychildren.org/English/ages-stages/toddler/nutrition/Pages/Sample-One-Day-Menu-for-a-Two-Year-Old.aspx.
- "How to Get Your Child to Eat More Fruits and Veggies," AAP, https://www.healthychildren.org/English/healthy-living/nutrition/Pages/How-to-Get-Your-Child-to-Eat-More-Fruits-and-Veggies.aspx.
- "Kids Need Fiber: Here's Why and How," AAP, https://www.healthychildren.org /English/healthy-living/nutrition/Pages/Kids-Need-Fiber-Heres-Why-and-How.aspx
- Amy Warren Hilliker, *Little One, God Made You* (Grand Rapids, MI: Zonderkidz, 2004).
- One in Christ, Preschool A and Preschool B curricula, Concordia Publishing House.
- "Bedwetting," AAP, https://www.healthychildren.org/English/ages-stages/toddler/toilet-training/Pages/Bedwetting.aspx.
- "Regression re: Bedwetting," AAP, https://www.healthychildren.org/English/ages-stages/toddler/toilet-training/Pages/Regression.aspx.
- "Develop Good Sleep Habits," AAP, (March 2020) https://www.healthychildren.org/English/healthy-living/sleep/Pages/default.aspx.

CHAPTER 13

Early Elementary Wellness

(Kindergarten-Grade 3)

In many ways, the educational system in this country has moved kindergarten from a gentle, preparatory introduction to social, emotional, and educational interaction to the standard all-day launch pad for formal, structured learning.

It is clear is that among the many families who choose outside-the-home formal education, most elect—by choice or necessity—to place their children in full-day kindergarten (about 80 percent of all kindergartens today), a daily regimen that will follow the child throughout his educational career.[1] Most children, although not all, will adjust well to being away from parents for six-plus hours a day. Others may struggle with this separation and need more attention from parents and educators to make the transition.

I group formal education into three developmental categories that are acceptable to many physicians and educators:

- Early Elementary—Kindergarten to Grade 3
- Late Elementary—Grades 4–8
- High School—Grades 9–12

Some educators classify grades 5–8 as middle school years due to the physiological, emotional, and behavioral changes accompanying those students. Legitimate points can support their case. For the purposes of our discussion, however, I use the designations above.

CRUCIAL FIRST STEPS (KINDERGARTEN–GRADE 3)

Many elementary educators believe that the groundwork laid in kindergarten through third grade determines subsequent educational success for children, particularly the ability to read and comprehend. Related to this, the recently reauthorized Federal Elementary and Secondary School Act requires annual testing of children in grades 3–8. That means that those test results heavily influence the assessment of a school's quality and performance. But testing formats are not as reliable for evaluating children younger than grade 3, which means that children (and school programs) in this age range who might benefit from preventative measures and early intervention might not be identified. Also, because schools' ratings and funding may be dependent on high test scores, administrators, educators, and resources focus on the later elementary grades (with their readily evident test scores), even though resources for early grades may produce pronounced long-term benefits to students.[2] Political power struggles regarding elementary education at the federal and state levels dramatically affect where policy and dollars go within the K–12 spectrum. However, regardless of the public policy controversies that trickle down to affect our children, parents have primary control and responsibility to foster wellness in the five arenas of health behavior addressed in this text. Let's examine the possibilities.

MOVEMENT FOR EARLY ELEMENTARY STUDENTS

No doubt you have you heard another parent say something like this: "Honestly, my kids are allergic to exercise; I can't get them off their tablet or smartphones, or away from their video games!" This observation correlates closely with the fact that nearly one-third of our elementary population is overweight or obese.[3] Obesity is at epidemic proportions in the United States, and it will translate into dramatic increases in chronic, life-shortening illnesses like diabetes, heart disease, hypertension, cancer, and orthopedic disease.

As a parent-leader, maintaining an active lifestyle yourself, including a healthy weight, should be the starting point for the wellness care for your family. Our parenting goal is to establish and maintain lifelong fitness for our families. Opportunities to play with your children, for instance, will provide health benefits for everyone. Children who are more fit tend to develop a larger hippocampus (memory center)[4] in the brain and appear to have better concentration in school.

Incorporating regular exercise also gives parents and schools the opportunity to educate children about the importance of connecting physical activity to good eating habits. We know that good nutrition helps to diminish illness, improve focus, and help emotional life. Yet with educational money shortages, formal physical education programming in schools and even some nutritional programming may be susceptible to funding cuts. This makes it all the more important that we continue this emphasis in the home.[5]

The daily recommendation for physical activity, primarily in the form of play, for children in the early elementary grades is at least 60 minutes per day; the time can be broken into shorter blocks of 15–20 minutes. The activity should be vigorous enough to make children breathe hard and perspire. A good rule of thumb is that the exercise should be intense enough that it is hard to talk with someone while in motion. Simple activities like bicycling or running are very effective, as are jumping rope, walking, and playing kickball.

Dance is a wonderful physical activity for girls and boys. Again, it can be formalized into classes and lessons, but it can be just as effective to put on music and allow your child to move legs and arms, hands and feet. You can assist by dancing with him, and you can help guide the music selection or discover what "moves" him.

Some board games encourage activity; Twister is one that comes to mind. Any toy store will have additional suggestions, or you can visit an online source.[6] And some video games encourage physical activity in the form of dance, golf, baseball, bowling, and more.

Weight training is not recommended for children in this age group. Effective weight training that helps rather than harms bones, muscles, and ligaments requires that the lifter have correct form and move the weights in an efficient and safe manner. Lifters need proper posture, balance, control, and coordination—a level of control that doesn't develop until a child is at least 7–8 years old. They also need to be able to pay attention, stay focused, and be very open to instruction.[7]

Some families and some children will be interested in formalized sports, perhaps a school, church, or community soccer, baseball, swimming, or basketball program. If this is important to your family and, most important, of interest to your child, seek those opportunities but keep them in perspective. Balancing sports with other aspects of the young child's life is important to his overall emotional well-being.

Remember that even if your child does not want to participate in formal sports, it still is important that he or she is physically active. This may require more input and involvement from you as a parent, but the benefit to your child and to you is definitely worth the effort. You can help encourage movement in these ways:

- Consider activities like walking, bicycling, swimming, gardening—anything that gets your child outside.
- Buddy up with other less active kids, but make sure to be an encourager.
- Engage your child with pet care, such as going with you to walk the dog, or playing with the cat.
- Play simple games like tag, hide-and-seek, and red light, green light.
- Use workout or dance videos in your home and invite your child to join you.
- Encourage stair walking whenever the opportunity arises.
- Look for YMCAs or Boys and Girls Clubs, scouting, and church youth activities.

PLANT-BASED NUTRITION FOR EARLY ELEMENTARY STUDENTS

If you have introduced a predominantly plant-based diet to your child as a toddler, he or she will likely continue to enjoy and select more whole-food, plant-based options. It is not uncommon for any 6- or 7-year-old to suddenly decide to be predominantly vegetarian once he begins to appreciate animals and the origins of his food.[8] He can get plenty of protein from rice, beans, milk, peanut butter, and eggs. Young children who are learning about the global nature of our food supply may become interested in where their food comes from.

When children start school, they may be exposed to new food choices. This may include more foods like sugar-filled snacks and chips. Packing your child's lunch can help regulate some of this exposure, but it is important to try to guide her choices. For example, encourage her to drink water throughout the day and to choose water over sweetened beverages. You can add a bit of lemon, lime, or cucumber to her water to enhance the taste.

Remind your child that fruits and vegetables are great sources of flavor as well as necessary fiber. Fiber helps make us full and keeps our digestive tract moving and healthy. For this age, we encourage at least five servings of fiber with 5 or more grams of fiber in each serving. Check the nutritional facts of the foods you eat; packaging and online sources provide extensive nutritional information for almost all foods.

Not all fiber is the same. Choose whole grains like whole wheat, brown rice, buckwheat, oatmeal, whole oats, whole rye, and wild rice, again understanding fiber content by reading labels.

Although you will model good nutrition at home, if your family eats at fast-food restaurants on occasion, you can help your child learn good food choices by taking a few simple measures:

- Look up menus online before going to the restaurant.
- Pay attention to serving sizes, especially for early elementary students.
- Avoid sugary drinks; encourage water or unsweetened decaf tea.
- Avoid caffeinated beverages in any form.
- Choose baked or grilled items over fried and breaded foods.
- Watch salt content.
- Go light on sauces like mayonnaise, ketchup, and ranch dressing.
- Skip the cheese, please.

- Look for fruit or veggie options or salad with low-calorie dressings (as long as they aren't loaded with artificial sweeteners).

How does this look in reality? Choose the burger without the fat-laden additives. Order the pizza with a whole grain or cauliflower crust, and try to get your kids to enjoy vegetable toppings rather than sausage, bacon, or pepperoni. Grab a nonfat frozen yogurt rather than a loaded shake or ice-cream sundae. Avoid soda.

Is it easy? Not really, but it is worth the effort!

Here are a few additional tips for predominantly eating at home:

- Keep a prewashed bag of salad in the refrigerator.
- Keep fruit snacks readily visible and prewashed; prepare low-fat dips.
- Try to offer colorful fruits and vegetables daily: at least one green and one yellow or orange.
- Offer vegetarian spaghetti or chili and soups.
- Put a fruit or veggie in every lunch you send to school.
- Eat fruits and vegetables yourself—you're the best model your child can have.

For your own reference, an average-size early elementary student needs about 1,200–1,400 calories per day, based on energy levels.[9]

A comment about fat in the diet is in order, especially because of increasing heart disease, cancer, and obesity in our country. We must have fat in our diet. We need good fats for energy and we need important fatty acids to clot our blood, absorb vitamins, and sustain metabolism. Saturated fats, which are the basis of many health problems, are solid at room temperature. They are the common fats found in fatty meats like beef, pork, lamb, ham, and bacon. They are also found in whole milk, ice cream and cheese. They harm us by building up fatty, atherosclerotic plaques in our arteries, especially in the heart. Saturated fats produce high cholesterol levels in people with an inherited tendency toward high cholesterol, and this includes many Americans.[10]

Rather than a diet high in fat-laden red meat and milk products, encourage your children to eat fish, skinless turkey and chicken, or very lean meat. Serve broiled, baked, or roasted meat rather than fried. Encourage low-fat dairy products and unsaturated fat oils, such as olive oil. As a guideline, your child's diet should have less than 30 percent of its calories from fats, with 10 percent or less containing saturated fat. Try to use unsaturated fats, which are liquid at room temperature, such as olive oil, soybean-based oil, sunflower oil, canola oil, corn oil, and safflower oil. Also try to limit the total amount of fatty food consumed by everyone in your family.[11]

Sugar in the elementary school diet should be carefully monitored. While sugars supply plenty of calories, they are often empty calories because they do little other than supply energy. The real problem is that children tend to consume sugar calories at the expense of other foods. They may choose cakes and candy over fruit and vegetables, or soda over milk or water. It's important to monitor sugar intake; too much can often reveal itself in overstimulated behavior and dental decay, and can contribute to long-term health problems.

While not as great a cause for concern as fat and sugar, salt must also be monitored. While salt enhances the taste of food, it also may lead to high blood pressure over time. In fact, more than 25 percent of adults are treated for high blood pressure. Salt is an acquired taste, so diminishing reliance on salt by cooking with less salt and substituting other seasonings can have lifelong benefits. Try cooking with herbs or lemon juice as a salt substitute. Don't set a salt shaker on the dinner table. And remember that there are high quantities of salt in processed foods like canned vegetables, processed cheese, salad dressing, chips, and pickles. Use these packaged foods sparingly.

REST FOR EARLY ELEMENTARY STUDENTS

The American Academy of Pediatrics supports sleep guidelines for 5- to 8-year-olds that range between 10 and 13 hours of sleep in 24 hours, including naps.[12] Parents feel and perform better with adequate sleep, and children also enjoy improved mental, social, and emotional function if they get adequate rest. Just as your child benefited greatly from routine sleep and nap times from infancy through preschool, your early elementary child will demonstrate less irritability, less difficulty concentrating, less obesity, hypertension, headaches, and depression, and better immunity, behavior, and memory if he has proper rest.[13]

Follow the general rules for sleep time mentioned earlier: keep bedrooms cool (62–65 degrees Fahrenheit), dark, and safe (no burning candles or fireplaces); and consider adding soothing smells like lavender, rose, or chamomile. Two hours or so before bedtime, offer a very light, low-calorie snack, such as a slice of fruit or whole-grain cracker or toast, seeds, or nuts.

Stay consistent with your family's bedtime routine: brush teeth, read a book, ban electronics, and dim or turn off lights. (Again, your children are well served if you keep all screens, cell phones, and electronic tablets out of the bedroom. Smartphones and e-readers of all kinds emit blue light. Blue light has a short wavelength that affects melatonin; it disrupts sleep patterns. Blue light tricks the brain into thinking it is daytime, making us more alert rather than appropriately sleepy.) Also let your children learn to tidy up their room before bed and assemble things they need for the next day. Mornings will be so much smoother.

Melatonin is a natural hormone produced in the pineal gland of the brain and it affects alertness. Melatonin is sold without a prescription as a sleep aid, but it is not regulated by the Food and Drug Administration. It is not a sleeping pill and should be given to children only after a full discussion with your pediatrician. Your doctor may suggest melatonin as a short-term supplement for rest, but only while you are simultaneously trying to establish a good bedtime routine for sleep. Be cautious and careful with melatonin, and always be working with your doctor.[14]

As with toddlers and preschoolers, be aware of alterations in your early elementary child's normal sleep patterns or habits. If your child has difficulty falling or staying asleep, snores loudly or irregularly with long pauses in breathing, or wakes with night terrors, address these problems immediately with your health care provider. Furthermore, if you find your child sleeping or zoning out during the day while in school or at home, this might be a sign of poor nighttime rest.[15]

Naps for early elementary students should be limited to no more than 45 minutes so as to not disrupt their nighttime sleep patterns.

Meditation

A rest option for early elementary students is deep breathing with mental resting or reflecting, sometimes called *meditation*. Meditation in a variety of forms has been used throughout the ages to deal with the challenges of the world. Just as athletes do different exercises to build strength and energy, our body and mind can benefit from different forms of rest. We live in an extremely stressful time, and the anxiety and busyness that accompany it clearly interfere with physical, mental, and spiritual wellness.

Many schools are incorporating meditation at the start of the school day, and some scientific evidence suggests that students who meditate are less anxious, more focused, and able to perform better in the classroom.[16]

For Christians, meditation sometimes bears a negative connotation as being a component of non-Christian religions. Meditation certainly is a part of those traditions. But quieting the body and mind through deep breathing also can accompany rest for Christians, and it can accompany prayer. One use, even for younger children, is encouraging a quiet time to focus or meditate on the Holy Scriptures, the Lord's Prayer, the creeds, or parts of Luther's Small Catechism. (See "Meditating on God's Word," *The Lutheran Study Bible* [Concordia Publishing House, 2009], 289.)

Children may have difficulty sitting still to just breathe for any length of time. However, they can develop patterns to close their eyes, breathe (5-count in, 5-count out), or just sit quietly, perhaps placing themselves mentally at the foot of the cross or in the arms of the Good Shepherd, as they listen, hear, pray, and inwardly digest God's Word. Soothing music played quietly can also be helpful.[17]

Studies in school settings are demonstrating substantial improvement in behavior and attention, sleep and eating disorders in children who meditate for 3–10 minutes, usually twice per day.[18]

Deep breathing or physical and mental downshifting can have health benefits in a number of settings. For example, incorporating deep breathing in their bedtime routine helps children slow down mentally and physically. We can teach children to take a few deep breaths before beginning to take a test or answering tough test questions, or when they feel themselves becoming agitated. It helps to do deep breathing with others, including classmates, parents, and teachers.

FOCUS ON FAITH AND FAMILY FOR EARLY ELEMENTARY STUDENTS

No better example of the importance of faith and family can be found than allowing your children to see you read the Bible, especially as they begin to read on their own. Respectfully bow your head and pray, and include them in the things in life that bring you joy, as well as times when you feel worried, anxious, or tense.

Christian preschool director Kathy Greffet states it succinctly: "I try to engage them in the Bible stories that evoke my surprise, vulnerabilities, or fears. And then I try to show them how I use my faith to navigate my life. Model prayer," says Ms. Greffet. "That may mean praying with them or praying for them in their presence so they understand how easy and how valuable it is to converse with God."

Memorizing Bible verses is of great value to the Christian home and something the entire family can do. Most Christian Day Schools will use one or more verses for memory weekly. If your child attends a Christian Day School, take time to memorize the week's passage with her, and discuss what the verse means during your family's daily devotions. Keep verses visible by writing them on index cards and putting them in places that are often seen, such as the refrigerator door or the bathroom mirror.

Cindy Koch, referenced earlier, is a key writer for 1517 The Legacy Project.[19] She suggests that a sentinel part of parenting, especially in early elementary years, is to give our children spiritual grammar, the communication tools for a lifelong conversation with God and with their loved ones. Anchor them in the fear, love, and trust of God. For early childhood students, that translates into making the stories and the words of our faith indwelling in what I would call your child's "spiritual DNA." "K–3rd graders respond to praise," observes Ms. Koch. She suggests positive reinforcement to give your children incentive to memorize Bible passages or parts of the Small Catechism. Make memory work fun. It might be something as simple as stickers or stars on paper or lots of "attaboys" and "attagirls."

While mealtime remains the most opportune time to gather the family in conversation and open sharing, a second valuable opportunity comes at bedtime. Encourage your child to talk about his day, share his frustrations and happiness. Ask about an occurrence where God worked in his life that day. Ask, "Do you think you see a place where Jesus was with you or someone else today?" Answer this question yourself, and point your child to evidence of Christ at work through His Gospel.

Many congregations commemorate the day of a child's Baptism with a baptismal candle and a small cloth representing the "robe of righteousness" Christ places on him or her. Celebrating your child's baptismal birthday regularly brings forward the importance of Baptism in the daily life of the Christian child and family. Light that candle on good days but especially on tough days in your child's life to remind her that she is safe in God's arms.

Regular participation in the Divine Service and in Sunday School is a critical family faith activity. Children should accompany their parents to worship services, follow the order of service, and use a hymnal. Pre- and emerging readers can follow along, with Mom or Dad pointing to the words. They can stand and sit at appropriate times, join other children at the front of the church during the children's talk (if that is part of the service), and put an offering in the collection plate. They will also enjoy participating in Sunday School with others their age (and parents can take advantage of that period to engage in adult Sunday School or Bible study). Vacation Bible School is designed especially for children and offers an engaging, rewarding variety of activities and learning.

Early in your child's grade school years, your family may face potential conflicts between worship/Sunday School and sporting activities. You fulfill your God-given vocation as parent by prioritizing your faith and family values so you do not often face this issue. When you surround your family with families of similar faith traditions so that other children are not faced with these troublesome choices, you can all mutually care for and support one another.

The amount of influence from media is staggering. The information barrage comes at your family space from all angles and all modes. Parents have the primary responsibility for annotating what your children read or watch or listen to on a daily basis. Be aware of the use of electronics that are connected to the internet, such as cell phones and tablets that can be easily accessed by the youngest of elementary school students. Many schools have tablets and laptops for research and homework. While all schools that use these devices have policies and restrict access, parents should take time to be absolutely certain about what sort of media their children can search by these means and how much time they will be spending on these devices.

Be aware of the content of the music your child is listening to and often mimicking. The lyrics of much current popular music include substantial negative and derogatory self-talk. Children are memorizing the words, assimilating the language, and often taking on the sentiments and attitudes expressed in the lyrics. Take the time to really listen to what your child is absorbing, and help him or her make good choices. This doesn't mean that your youngster should be listening only to Bach arias and Handel chorales; delightful Christian music is readily available on almost every community's airways or through streaming services. However, frank conversations about the appropriateness of contemporary entertainment media must begin as early as possible in the family, school, and church community. Outstanding resources are available that bring Christ-centered guidance to the home and school; a quick internet search will reveal the options.

Finally, as input from media is constant for your child, you might find yourself dealing with questions flowing directly from today's news: "How could Jesus let something bad happen to a little child?" It is a common concern that your child may struggle to express and you stumble to explain. You may have dealt with this faith challenge already and have worked out an answer. Don't hesitate to call on your pastor, deaconess, or Christian teacher if you face this question. Remind your child that children do not face these fears alone; that their parents and pastor and teachers are all there for their care and safety. Make sure your youngster understands that God knows our hurts, angers, and pains (Hebrews

4:15). Remind him that God understands his fears and needs and that God is with him, always, working for good to come from all tragedies (Romans 8:28). Urge your child to continue to lift all her worries and concerns to God in prayer (John 9:31; 1 Peter 3:12). You cannot reinforce this truth too much or too often.

PURPOSEFUL AND MISSIONAL LIVING FOR EARLY ELEMENTARY STUDENTS

The early elementary years introduce an expanding educational and social effort to encourage purpose, especially when we look at both secular education through social studies and the entire curriculum in Christian Day Schools.

In our public school systems, social sciences curricula are aimed at advancing the democratic ideals of liberty and justice for all. In recent years, however, an estimated 44 percent of school districts have reduced time for social sciences.[20, 21] Nevertheless, social sciences educators emphasize four core social disciplines: civics, economics, geography, and history.[22] Awareness of these disciplines begins as social and physiological development among kindergarten and first-grade children who begin to differentiate what happens in the past, present, and future. They begin to understand the difference between events happening at home, at school, and in their community. Children begin to comprehend that there are costs associated with consuming things, buying things, and experiencing things. They learn how to take responsibility for their actions. Children become more self-sufficient; they can determine when and how to get to the bathroom, among other destinations. These are all social science accomplishments.

Many families choose to—or must—utilize public education, yet they truly desire to encourage faith principles and purposeful, missional living in their children. Setting aside daily "purpose pause points" like breakfast time, devotional time, during or after the evening meal, or before bed offers opportunities to discuss what has happened and what has been learned at school that day. Parents can prompt discussion by gently exploring relational triumphs or struggles that may have arisen at school or playtime. Discussions of possible service projects in home, school, or community can stimulate excitement and encourage skills or gifts your child might have to practice: generosity, goodness, kindness, and other fruit of the Spirit. Ask to be introduced to your child's friends and offer opportunities for your child to interact with her classmates within your own home as a place of comfort and safety. This can demonstrate in a visible manner your family's value of living a life of acceptance, equality, and justice for each of God's creatures.

With the multiethnic, multiracial, multireligious, and multicultural mix found in so many classrooms and within our democratic society, understanding equality and the way diverse people can live life together can be daunting. We want our children to be able to live with one another with respect and social empathy. We want them to be good citizens in our nation, which is a fulfillment of the vocation of citizen. We also want them to understand what is needed to form effective relationships with others, to institutions in our nation, and to the environment we are all called to steward. Good relational skills help us make rational decisions individually and collectively for the good of all.

Ever since sin entered the world, society has existed in a time of turbulent change. It may be in the social setting that the Gospel voice will help our young students make God-pleasing decisions and understand and learn to live with integrity as they deal with the consequences of their choices.

Christian elementary education is guided by a commitment to know Jesus as Savior and Lord. Students are taught to live and relate to one another and to the world with Christ-inspired and patterned character. Therefore, they are taught to not merely serve God but to become leaders, movers, and shakers within the church and the world. They are guided by a partnership among their parents, teachers, and pastors to grow in their faith and in their understanding of God's Word. As their faith is strengthened by the power of the Holy Spirit to develop servant hearts, they are encouraged to discover and develop their spiritual gifts and their talents to glorify God and care for one another. Through service, they find purpose and mission in living.

Christian education frames the subjects of civics, economics, geography, sociology, and history not only in the setting of secular society but also from the perspective of the family of God. Christians are called for the purpose of glorifying God in all thoughts, words, and deeds and of focusing energy and attitude outward into care for other people and all of God's creation. These are sacred purposes because the opportunity to live out these callings is won by Christ's death and resurrection; our good works in Jesus' name are sanctified.

To accomplish these goals, Christian elementary education strives to produce a safe and secure learning setting and excellence in academic instruction. It develops integrity, compassion, courage, responsibility, prayer and worship life, loving relationships, and repeated opportunities to encounter and interact with others who know Jesus. That interaction occurs in the Divine Service, in the classroom, on the sports field, and in the home. These value-added efforts are led by the faculty, school staff, clergy, and fellow parents, and are meant to support the Christian parenting of purpose within the student's family. In the same manner, the Christian home is meant to encourage the prayer, worship, Word and Sacrament, praise, evangelism, counseling, service, and care-purposed ministries of the Christian congregation.

NOTES

1. Brian D. Ray, "Homeschooling Growing: Multiple Data Points Show Increase 2012 to 2016 and Later" (blog), NHERI (April 20, 2018), nheri.org/homeschool-population-size-growing/.
2. "Don't Forget the Early Elementary Years," www.usnews.com/opinion/articles/2016-10-06/early-elementary-education-years-are-important-for-public-policy.
3. "Obesity Facts/Healthy Schools," Centers for Disease Control and Prevention, https://www.cdc.gov.healthschools/childhood-obesity-facts.
4. J. Firth, B. Stubbs, P. Ward, et al., "Effect of Aerobic Exercise on Hippocampal Volume in Humans: A Systematic Review and Meta-Analysis," *NeuroImage* (published online ahead of print: November 4, 2017).
5. "Young Children Need Physical Education," https://blog.schoolspecialty.com/young-children-need-physical-education.
6. "5 Healthy Goals," *Healthy Kids, Healthy Future*, Nemours Children's Health System, https://healthykidshealthyfuture.org/5-healthy-goals/get-kids-moving/classroom-activities
7. Paul R. Stricker, "Weight Training: Risk of Injury," (updated Nov. 2, 2009) www.healthychildren.org.
8. "Vegetarian Diets for Children," American Academy of Pediatricians (AAP), https://www.healthychildren.org/English/ages-stages/gradeschool/nutrition/Pages/Vegetarian-Diet-for-Children.aspx.
9. "What Is the Recommended Caloric Intake for Children?" https://healthfully.com/2434-what-is-the-recommended-caloric-intake-for-chidlren.html.

10. "How to Reduce Fat and Cholesterol in Your Child's Diet," AAP, https://www.healthychildren.org/English/ages-stages/gradeschool/nutrition/Pages/How-to-Reduce-Fat-and-Cholesterol-in-Your-Childs-Diet.aspx.

11. Ibid.

12. S. Paruthi et al., "Recommended Amount of Sleep for Pediatric Populations: A Consensus Statement of the American Academy of Sleep Medicine," *Journal of Clinical Sleep Medicine,* (May 25, 2016) pii:jc-00158-16. PubMe PMID: 27250809.

13. "Sleep Tips for Your Family's Mental Health," AAP, https://www.healthychildren.org/English/healthy-living/sleep/Pages/Sleep-and-Mental-Health.aspx.

14. Melatonin: What You Need to Know, National Center for Complementary and Integrative Health, https://nccih.nih.gov/health/melatonin.

15. "Noisy Breathing in Children," AAP, https://www.healthychildren.org/English/health-issues/conditions/ear-nose-throat/Pages/Noisy-Breathing-in-Children.aspx.

16. Alice G. Walton, "Science Shows Meditation Benefits Children's Brains and Behavior," *Forbes,* (Oct. 18, 2016, accessed Jan. 13, 2020) www.forbes.com/sites/alicegwalton/2016/10/18/the-many-benefits-of-meditation-for-children/#477a7e03dbe3.

17. John D. Eckrich, "Word-Saturated Meditative Prayer" in *Resilient Aging and Wellness* (n.p., Tenth Power Publishing, 2018), 203–209.

18. Jane Case Smith, Julie Shupe Sines, and Maryanna Klatt, "Perceptions of Children Who Participated in a School-Based Yoga Program," *Journal of Occupational Therapy, Schools, and Early Intervention* 3, no. 3 (Taylor & Francis Group 2010), 226–238.

19. Cindy Koch,www.cindykochwrites.com.

20. P. G. Fichett and T. L. Heafner, "A National Perspective on the Effects of High-Stakes Testing and Standardization on Elementary Social Studies Marginalization," *Theory & Research in Social Education* 38, no.1 (2010), 114–213.

21. K. A. O'Connor, T. Heafner, and E. Groce, "Advocating for Social Studies: Documenting the Decline and Doing Something about It," *Social Education* 71, no. 5 (2007), 255–260.

22. "Powerful, Purposeful Pedagogy in Elementary School Social Studies" (2017), www.socialstudies.org.positions/powerfulandpurposeful.

ADDITIONAL READING

- "Healthy Sleep Habits: How Many Hours Does Your Child Need?" AAP, https://www.healthychildren.org/English/healthy-living/sleep/Pages/Healthy-Sleep-Habits-How-Many-Hours-Does-Your-Child-Need.aspx.
- John Eckrich, "Word-Saturated Meditative Prayer" in *Resilient Aging and Wellness* (n.p., Tenth Power Publishing, 2018), 203–209.
- "Helping Children Handle Stress," AAP, https://www.healthychildren.org/English/healthy-living/emotional-wellness/Pages/Helping-Children-Handle-Stress.aspx.

CHAPTER 14

Late Elementary Wellness
(Grades 4-8)

School lessons begin to get longer and the subjects wider and more complex as children enter grade 4 and progress through 8. Some children will have the maturity and attention span to learn well with these longer and more diverse subjects. Others may need shorter lessons and more frequent breaks to succeed in learning. In some school districts, children may move from the elementary school building to a middle school and junior high that can include fifth through ninth grades. Students will mingle, at least for a few minutes a day, with others of varying ages. As with younger age groups, these 9- to 14-year-olds are unique and develop along individual paths that are still within typical ranges.

Having become accustomed to studying core subjects, specific interests may drive learning. Many educational systems begin special opportunities to dig deeper into STEM classes—science, technology, engineering, and mathematics. Also, children are entering a time of logic-driven learning.[1] They begin to develop questions regarding how things work and why things happen. This pertains to their spiritual maturity as well, as late elementary students, in preparation for confirmation, have questions about their faith.

At this point, students may begin to explore the local, school, or parish library at the direction of teachers, pastors, or directors of Christian education (DCEs). More likely, they will seek answers on the internet about places, people, prominent events, or inventions and science. They may also explore social and cultural trends that they see prominently displayed in media and by peers (who are influenced by media)—videos, video games, entertainers, sports, or whatever is interesting to them.

Their learning styles need to be acknowledged, as does the growth in their bodies and minds as they enter puberty. It is a time to connect with them about what they are experiencing by having frequent and in-depth one-to-one conversations. Spend as much time with your child as possible so she can access your wealth of knowledge and experience to give context to what she is seeing and experiencing. Assure your child that you love him, care about him, and provide care for him. Although she is establishing her own boundaries and separating from you (individuating), at this age she wants stability, security, and unconditional love from her parents. Keep communication open so your child feels comfortable coming to you with questions and so he trusts you for a loving response.

Children in this age range are especially sensitive, even if they don't show it. They can quickly become disenchanted with the adults in their lives and will quickly learn to find other sources of information, explanation, and acceptance. Some of those sources definitely don't have their best interests in mind. Let's look at how the five wellness behaviors can be helpful at these ages.

MOVEMENT FOR LATE ELEMENTARY STUDENTS

It is important to remember why exercise matters, especially for children in the late elementary years. Weight control is, of course, a major concern for everyone, but there are a few other reasons why physical activity in these middle years is so critical:

- It builds strong bones, muscles, and joints.
- It decreases total body fat.
- It enhances flexibility.
- It reduces the potential for developing heart disease, hypertension, and diabetes.
- It builds energy.
- It helps deal with stress.
- It promotes self-esteem and confidence.
- It enhances social acceptance.
- It helps build friendships.
- It adds substantially to concentration.
- It promotes rest.

Always be aware of what programs for physical activity are offered in the school setting. This could come in the form of physical education (PE), recess, or organized sports. Be an advocate for continuing to include exercise in every school day, as this is often an activity on the chopping block due to diminished school funding resources and the increased variety of elective courses.

Your child's body composition and flexibility should be reviewed and monitored for his or her own health. Children and teens are different from adults in body composition and flexibility. Profound physical, emotional, and mental changes take place in children 10–14 years of age. Your child will be cognizant of many of these changes and oblivious to others; regardless, the rapid growth will affect his or her relationships and responses.

Because of size, weight, and body composition, boys and girls can play together until about the third grade. After that it is probably a good idea to start separating boys and girls, especially for contact sports, because of the disparity in physical size and emotional maturity. It is not uncommon to see a significantly larger girl in height and weight facing off against a much smaller boy of the same age in the early elementary grades. Girls' bodies generally carry more body fat than boys in these early years. Girls begin puberty around age 11½, but it can begin as early as 8 or as late as 14. Once girls enter puberty, their bodies begin to store more body fat. Boys' bodies, on the other hand, are influenced by increasing levels of testosterone in puberty and begin to add muscle mass. Boys begin puberty around age 13½. These physiological changes are important in that they affect performance in athletic endeavors.

At the outset of puberty, both girls and boys go through the *adolescent growth spurt* (AGS). The AGS quickly changes height and weight and therefore changes the body's center of gravity. The brain has to adjust to a different angle of observation, so the child may appear a bit clumsy. This can really throw off an athlete participating in balance sports like figure skating, diving, or gymnastics. Longer arms and legs can affect the ability to connect ball with bat, ball with basket, puck with stick, and ball with racket or lacrosse stick.

Furthermore, at the ends of the bones, where softer cartilage grows and eventually turns into bone, there is a section of cartilage called the *growth plate*. It is more delicate than other tissue during the growth period, so injury to the growth plate can affect the bone's ability to grow in length and strength. The growth plate can be injured by overuse or by direct trauma or fracture. Overuse must be avoided at all costs.

Another common injury in preteens is a strain or tear of the *anterior cruciate ligament* (ACL), one of the main ligaments that stabilizes the knee. According to the American Academy of Pediatrics, ACL injuries increase in 12- and 13-year-old girls and in boys ages 14–16.[2]

There is an increased tendency for children in middle school and junior high to specialize in one sport, often as part of a select team. These are highly competitive and sought-after positions that include tryouts, cuts, and intensive training commitments. The American Academy of Pediatrics recommends avoiding specializing in one sport before puberty.[3] Overtraining can result in short- and long-term physical injuries; the pressure to perform and the lack of downtime can contribute to emotional burnout. Parents must carefully weigh the positive and negative effects; in any case, parents are encouraged to promote physical activity for their children because of the overwhelming health benefits.

Children are more flexible than adults, but their flexibility diminishes during the rapid growth they experience in puberty. A significant risk for injury can occur when bones are growing more rapidly than the tendons and muscles can stretch to keep up with the bony growth. So in puberty, boys grow muscles, lose body fat, and lose flexibility. Girls' muscles and ligaments can tighten during the growth of puberty, but increased production of estrogen usually allows girls to regain and improve flexibility as their growth rate starts to slow. Be aware of flexibility issues, especially early in high school. Students taking part in sports will benefit from careful attention to flexibility.

PLANT-BASED NUTRITION FOR LATE ELEMENTARY STUDENTS

If you wander through your child's school cafeteria, you will notice a toxic nutritional environment. Even if reasonably healthy meals are available through school meal supplement programs, there are usually vending machines that stand as barriers against healthy eating.

American children (as well as those throughout the rest of the developed world) consume nearly 90 percent of their daily calories from processed foods and animal products.[4] That means that most kids are consuming fewer than 10 percent of their calories from whole-plant foods. Again, there are clear medical indications that most of the chronic diseases that limit the quality and quantity of life—obesity, diabetes, hypertension, and heart disease, and probably multiple forms of cancer—begin in these early years. To reiterate, the most powerful influence on your child's dietary habits are *your* dietary habits. There is no substitute for eating at least one family meal together each day, where you have control over what is put on the table. Involve everyone in the family in the cooking and cleanup to give them ownership in the meal. Serve more vegetables and fruits in interesting ways. Outlaw soda (even diet soda). In fact, the best way to not serve unhealthy food is to not bring it into your home in the first place. As before, also ban phones, TVs, tablets, and gaming devices during meals and replace them all with conversation.

Here are a few tips for healthy eating with preteens:

- Limit sweet drinks to one per day. Offer fruit- or vegetable-based drinks, milk, or water rather than sugary, high-fructose, or artificially sweetened beverages.
- Serve whole-plant foods: broccoli, cauliflower, green beans, peas, corn, and greens such as kale and spinach. Serve fresh fruit, such as an apple, orange, banana, berries, pineapple, or watermelon, for dessert.
- When introducing new foods or new combinations, establish a rule that everyone try just one bite to discover something new. Tastes change over time, and taste buds take years to adjust to new flavors. Therefore, give children time to get used to new foods. If their response is negative, try again in a couple of months.
- Serve everyone the same food. If parents are eating stir-fry, don't place pizza or chicken nuggets in front of the children. This just reinforces picky eating.

- Experiment with recipes. It is easy to serve the same things each week because you know "at least they'll eat it!" Try ethnic foods, different preparation techniques, sauces, and marinades.
- Do not reward trying new foods with sweets or desserts. Eating healthy is not a punishment; eating healthy food is a huge value in itself.
- Prepare food more interestingly. Cut food in unusual shapes or add some interesting sauces.
- Roast or puree foods; changing the texture can enhance their appeal.

REST IN LATE ELEMENTARY STUDENTS

Most 4th- through 6th-graders need 9–12 hours of sleep, and children in grades 7–8 need at least 8–10 hours, depending on the onset of puberty. They are probably not interested in naps, except on weekends, but if they doze for 20–30 minutes after school and it doesn't disrupt their nighttime sleep, that is just fine.

The most important challenge for parents is to set a good example for their children by making sufficient sleep a family priority. It is good for everyone to have fairly established patterns and to avoid excessive sugary food, caffeine, and blue light exposure for an hour or two before bedtime. If you are pulling all-nighters to get your work done, you are not setting a good example. If your child finds you vegging out on a tablet or phone well into the night, that's not good modeling.

It is important to continue to keep to a regular schedule for all family activities: eat at roughly the same time; awaken at the same time; allow family conversation and playtime somewhere in the evening.

Especially when your child is in junior high, try to sit with him at bedtime; hear his prayers and pray with him. Talk about his day and let him unload his burdens so he does not carry them into sleep. Share a devotion or Bible reading and reflect on how it applies to his day and yours.

Weekend routines might be a bit less regimented than school nights. However, it is a good idea to keep wake-up time within an hour of the weekday time. Sleeping too long can disrupt a vulnerable child out of her sleep phase or the periods she wakes and sleeps. She may have trouble resuming school day schedules, and this can affect school performance.

Monitor your child for sleep disorders, heavy snoring, irregular breathing, and anything else that might suggest sleep apnea. If you suspect that, discuss it with your pediatrician.

Curfews and Overnights

The older your child is, the more likely he or she will spend recreational time away from you. Children need to be gradually introduced to situations where their standards of behavior and codes of conduct will be tested. Therefore, it is critical to establish and reinforce expectations before children reach this stage so they are equipped to make decisions that respect your guidelines and honor their Lord.

Before your child reaches junior high, you will want to consider with your spouse how you will handle curfew, particularly on school nights. Social activities without his parents and with his peers are opportunities for your child to develop emotional maturity and personal responsibility. Yet parents must set and keep clear expectations. For example, you must know who he is with and where he is at all times. Determine a time for him to be home and explain that you expect him to let you know if he cannot honor that. Is he cooperating with your rules? Such ground rules maintain his safety, reinforce your authority as his parents, and modulate your flexibility for future curfews. These often-stressful topics are as much about relational living and respect within the family as they are about rest for both anxious parents and active, independent-minded teens.

Staying overnight at a friend's house (or having overnight guests in your home) will increase in middle school. Knowing the other child, her parents, and where she lives will set your mind at ease, so do not hesitate to ask. Familiarize yourself with the other family's standards for conduct and lifestyle. Are they careful about the movies and video games their children consume? Is their home a safe environment? Will they be home while your child is there or will the children be supervised by an older sibling or babysitter? Will the other family honor your expectations for meals (no soda, for instance) and for a reasonable bedtime? It is important to reinforce the importance of adequate sleep if it is on a school night, if the child is scheduled for sporting activities the next day, or if she is expected in church with the family.

FOCUS ON FAITH AND FAMILY FOR LATE ELEMENTARY STUDENTS

These grades not only transition from acquiring the building blocks of communication—the grammar—but they also now expand to the development of logic, thought, and conversation. It is the same for spiritual development.

Children in the late elementary grades begin a time of questioning Bible stories, biblical truths, the whys of faith, and the meaning of relationships. This, then, is the perfect time for the formulations and instructions in preparation for confirmation and reception of the Lord's Supper. In many faith communities, those are now separate experiences, with entrance to Holy Communion offered at younger ages. In any case, it is important for young people to express questions to gain a deeper insight into the mysteries of our faith and how they come to know God through the fear, love, and trust of the Holy Trinity. And it is important to seek answers to those questions in the Scriptures and in the Confessions of our faith—the interpretation and practical application of the Scriptures. These young people are building a spiritual conversation with God.

Late elementary students are also furthering conversation with their family, and it is a time for more-specific conversation about faith and its application to daily life. They begin to question the dictums and family rules they have been taught from infancy, as well as some of the behavioral guidelines of how to play, share, and get along with others. Physiological changes, growing awareness of the world, and continuing individuation cause tweens and teens to question those relationships and rules, especially when they see others who don't seem to follow the same set of moral guidelines or who present a different set of facts and call those facts truth.

This can be a difficult and confusing time for your child; so who better than his parent to closely walk with him through this period of uncertainty? The assurance that you love him and want him in your home and life and also that his Savior, Jesus, loves him enough to give His life for him should be an ongoing theme. You may feel ill equipped for these conversations, but your honesty will reinforce that trait in your child. Parents can determine to learn along with their children; they can recommit to Sunday School (for example) or study the catechism along with children who are preparing for confirmation. Here also, the faith family can be your ally, whether that family comes to your child through Christian Day School, weekday after-school religion classes, Sunday School, or confirmation instruction. Through the power of the Holy Spirit, your pastor and church staff of youth ministers, DCEs, and other Christian parents all make up the critical faith village to guide and nurture your child in faith.

Author Cindy Koch reminds us that sometimes these logical conversations can be very difficult. Children were born into the same sin as their parents and every generation before them. By nature, they want to talk and think only about how the world affects them (ME), not others (WE), Ms. Koch says. For example, discussing with your elementary child how her actions can hurt others can be not only tough but also noisy and disturbing for both parent and child. This is where, Ms. Koch says, time and conversation around and in the Bible can quiet the din of Satan's battle for our hearts. Don't be fooled; the devil and his colleagues are close at hand in these circumstances; it is only the armor of God that guards our souls:

> Put on the whole armor of God, that you may be able to stand against the schemes of the devil. For we do not wrestle against flesh and blood, but against the rulers, against the authorities, against the cosmic powers over this present darkness, against the spiritual forces of evil in the heavenly places. Therefore, take up the whole armor of God, that you may be able to withstand in the evil day, and having done all, to stand firm. . . . In all circumstances take up the shield of faith, with which you can extinguish all the flaming darts of the evil one; and take the helmet of salvation, and the sword of the Spirit, which is the word of God, praying at all times in the Spirit, with all prayer and supplication.
>
> (Ephesians 6:11–13, 16–18)

This "home-centered, church-supported" role is critical to faith formation, notes Rebecca Duport, assistant professor and director of the DCE program at Concordia University, Irvine (California). Parents cannot drop off their kids at the church front door and delegate the responsibility for faith development to the pastors and Sunday School teachers. Ms. Duport says, "A family has more influence on a young person's growth in faith than anything that happens in a congregation or ministry."[5] By God's design, the parent is the family leader. Parents are with their child more than anyone else. Their bonds of trust and love develop first and deepest, and even into middle school and junior high; family bonds should be greater than any others. Their leadership needs to be more prominent than anyone else's.

Who is teaching confirmation class in your congregation? Is it the pastor or DCE alone, or are you also being involved as your child's most important influencer? Are your children asking life's tough questions of you, of Google and Siri, or of their friends? Parents serve their children best when they take time to wrestle with questions early and often.

If they are not already established in the family routine, these parent-led initiatives are beneficial:

- Continue—or begin—family devotions.
- Pray regularly together, especially at meals and bedtime.
- Regularly attend worship and Sunday School as a family.
- Participate in service projects in the church and community.

In addition, beginning with your own work, social, and leisure time, help your child to not overschedule life. Reserve regular, dedicated time for family fun, including family vacation time, if possible.

Whether both parents are in the home or the household is led by a single parent, be intentional about finding "dad focused" faith activities. The Scriptures actually give fathers the responsibility for faith formation:

> Fathers, do not provoke your children to anger, but bring them up in the discipline and instruction of the Lord.
> (Ephesians 6:4)

And Martin Luther wrote the Small Catechism for fathers to use in teaching the faith at home, presenting each of the Six Chief Parts "as the head of the family should teach it in a simple way to his household."

Look for opportunities in your congregation, school, or community for parent-and-child communication classes. Later, in junior high and high school, look for parent-and-child sex education classes, workshops, or retreats.

Finally, consult with your pastor to see how parents can participate in confirmation classes.

All of these activities are focused not just on building faith but also on strengthening the bond of your family.

One additional topic of importance regarding faith and family bonds is sex education. A discussion of the topics and conversations critical for parents and teens regarding sex will be covered in the next chapter under "Focus on Faith and Family for High Schoolers" (pp. 202–210). However, the reality is that these conversations should begin at elementary school age. While there are wonderful sex-ed curricula in both public and parochial/private schools, there is nothing as important to a child as a heart-to-heart series of talks about sex with a compassionate parent.[6] Please spend time reviewing this section in preparation for that all-important conversation with your child.

PURPOSEFUL AND MISSIONAL LIVING IN LATE ELEMENTARY STUDENTS

Purposeful and missional life will flow from parents and children who are intentionally living life together, intentionally honoring the vocations God has given them. Look at and talk about family service projects as opportunities to live faithfully:

> And Jesus came and said to them, "All authority in heaven and on earth has been given to Me. Go therefore and make disciples of all nations, baptizing them in the name of the Father and of the Son and of the Holy Spirit, teaching them to observe all that I have commanded you. And behold, I am with you always, to

> the end of the age."
> (Matthew 28:18–20)

There are two important messages in this passage for your child. First, because he is baptized in the name of the triune God, Jesus is reflected in everything he does and says. He should trust Jesus' divinity and be unafraid to live boldly when he lives according to His Word. Second, even as a young person, he is a disciple and missionary. The way he communicates and interacts with others and the decisions and choices he makes to move, eat, rest, and reflect life in his family, with his peers, and in the community shows Jesus to others.

You as his parent do not expect perfection from him. You know he isn't perfect. There will be times when he doesn't reflect Jesus very well, just as there are times when you don't. Those are learning opportunities for you both.

Mistakes, sins, disappointments, and failures provide openings for talking about the love, mercy, and forgiveness that is ours because of Jesus. We show one another the same love, mercy, and forgiveness that our Redeemer shows us.

These moments are also prime time for encouraging learning from our actions and resolving to improve. Repentance is recognizing times of failure, asking for forgiveness, and then Spirit-led changing direction to live the humble servant life of a disciple of Christ. By the working of the Holy Spirit, we can achieve the repentance to which we are called because Jesus is continuously transforming us. We confess this each time we say the Apostles' Creed: "I believe in the Holy Spirit, the holy Christian church, the communion of saints, the forgiveness of sins, the resurrection of the body, and the life everlasting. Amen."

Living purposefully also means your child should begin to understand how she can become a leader. Christian leadership begins by understanding whose we are: children of God, created in His image. Therefore, we continue to celebrate baptismal birthdays and the heritage of being a child of God into eternity. It encompasses the full knowledge of our worth and worthiness in Jesus because we are loved and forgiven. We can live boldly in the confidence that we acquire by our knowledge of

Christ's Gospel as revealed in God's Holy Word. Part of our vocation as parents and as children is pointing others to Jesus.

The same academic pursuits of learning purpose and democratic principles of living, discussed in the chapter on early elementary grades, apply to this age group but with deeper dives into the subjects of civics, economics, geography, and history. The coursework in the late elementary grades expands the worldview and global connectiveness to discuss justice and equality for all. Late elementary students will be involved in innovative and expansive learning projects that examine social justice. In their schoolwork and by their conversation with us, our children can teach us increased sensitivities regarding equality. That is missional, purposeful living at its best.

NOTES

1. Dorothy L. Sayers, *The Lost Tools of Learning* (CrossReach Publications, 1947; reprinted independently, 2016).
2. "ACL Injuries in Young Athletes," (March 2020) https://www.healthychildren.org/English/health-issues/injuries-emergencies/sports-injuries/Pages/ACL-Injuries.aspx.
3. "Intensive Training and Sports Specialization in Young Children," *Pediatrics* 106, no. 1 (July 2000), 154–57, /https://doi.org/10.1542/peds.106.1.154.
4. Emily Honeycutt, "How to Teach Kids to Eat and Love Healthy, Plant-Powered Foods (From a Mother Who Knows)," https://www.awaken.com/2017/07/how-to-teach-kids-to-eat-and-love-healthy-plant-powered-foods-from-a-mother-who-knows/.
5. Rebecca Duport, Assistant Professor/Director DCE Program, Concordia University, Irvine, CA, Best Practices Presentation, Phoenix, AZ (2019).
6. https://www.cdc.gov/healthyyouth/protective/factsheets/father_influence.htm.

ADDITIONAL READING

- "Preventing Overuse Injuries in Young Athletes," American Association of Pediatrics (AAP), https://www.healthychildren.org/English/health-issues/injuries-emergencies/sports-injuries/Pages/Preventing-Overuse-Injuries.aspx.
- "Sleep Tips for Your Family's Mental Health," AAP, https://www.healthychildren.org/English/healthy-living/sleep/Pages/Sleep-and-Mental-Health.aspx.

CHAPTER 15

High School Wellness

Traditionally, high school encompasses 9th–12th grades, and that is the designation I am using here, while fully acknowledging that there are variations within that range. Often middle school and junior high school span fifth through ninth grades with high school consuming three years.

In any case, high school is preparatory school, whether that is laying groundwork for college, a trade, the military, or life in general. It is an important transitional time to adulthood, not just physically but intellectually, emotionally, relationally, vocationally, financially, and, not least, spiritually.

In Sayers's learning model,[1] high school is the time for rhetoric: the period of life when teenagers get to express publicly all they have learned, reasoned through, and wrestled with in their first 13–14 years of development. It may be a time of great rebellion for some as they try to find their own voice. Or it may be a time of pain or great shame if they are not happy with who they perceive themselves to be, their self-esteem, or their security about whether they are valued by family, friends, or their Creator. Sometimes that uncertainty leads to attempts to soothe their pain by self-medication or destructive behavior.

Alternatively, the teen years can be a time of substantial maturity, a blossoming into adulthood with expressions of confidence, boldness, and clarity of purpose. It may be the entry point to answering callings into vocations, services, and a deepening faith.

We parents hope high school is a time of physical, cognitive, and spiritual well-being. Our robust desire, as Christian parents, is for our children to live with love, purpose, and servant hearts. However, our child's high school years may challenge us more than any other time in their lives thus far. And for that, we must parent with the indwelling of the Holy Spirit; that is, with confidence that our Lord creates and sustains faith in us and in our children, guiding and preserving us throughout this life and into eternity.

Let's look at our five areas of wellness behavior, keeping foremost in our minds and hearts a prayer for the armor of God to clothe our children into eternity by the Spirit of the living Christ.

MOVEMENT FOR HIGH SCHOOLERS

There is no scarcity of physical activities available to high schoolers. Often, the more direct question is how to move their interest from online videos and electronic games to fitness and movement. Hopefully, your encouragement has begun at a young age so interest and participation in physical activity is a habit and lifestyle choice. The following recommendations apply, whether your child is into physical fitness or is just gaining a new interest in being physically active:

- Begin with a conversation with a physician, either pediatrician or family practitioner or internist. Not only can doctors check core organs, vital signs, and chemistries, but they also may be able to share insights as to the most appropriate sport or activity suitable for your child's abilities.
- Focus on an activity that your child enjoys. It is important to assess this with your child periodically. It is not uncommon for a youngster who has played ball since first grade to get burned out. He may be afraid to raise this issue with his parents as he sees them take pleasure and pride in his accomplishments. Our children often misinterpret our behaviors, so have regular heart-to-heart conversations with your teen.
- Make sure the sport and the level of that sport are truly age appropriate; this pertains particularly to weight lifting and long-distance running, but all sports, played with intensity, pose injury risks.
- Provide a safe environment, safe equipment, and trustworthy instructors.
- Turn off the TV and electronic games; that goes for you as well as your child. In fact, children who see their parents being active in

exercise regimens or in sports are far more likely to have an interest in and participate in sports themselves. Participate in a shared sport like golf, tennis, or bicycling.

- Make time for physical activity. Don't overschedule your child with academics, but allow time for activities outside of school that encourage movement.
- Continue to remind your child to pay attention to her body. Encourage her to tell you if something hurts so you can get it checked out. As important as it is to strengthen muscles and ligaments, it is equally important to allow them to rest and restore. Be aware of what injuries are common in the particular sport your child is playing.
- As we will explore in the next section, always complement movement with proper nutrition, hydration, stretching, and rest.
- Most important, *be a role model!*

Sportsmanship: Parents can model this aspect of athletics clearly and emphatically. The media is filled with examples of parents acting out against referees, coaches, their own child, and their child's opponents with verbal abuse and even physical violence. You want to build more than muscles and talent in your child; you want to instill character, self-esteem, and self-discipline. That's impossible to do if you are screaming from the stands, enraged and running onto the field, or criticizing after the game. You want your child to learn teamwork and sportsmanship, which includes the ability to handle adversity and learn from setbacks.

How do you help build these important characteristics in your child?

- Begin by being there; attend her events as often as possible and smile and cheer.
- Spend some one-on-one time with her, helping her improve her skills.
- Be encouraging rather than criticizing his miscues. When your child constantly gets negative feedback from peers, coaches, or his own parents, it is tough for him to feel good about himself.
- Make sure he knows that you love him unconditionally.

- Set realistic expectations.
- Put your child's interests and wishes ahead of your own. Respect her parameters.

Weight: Monitor your child's weight for excessive gain or loss, and consult with his pediatrician if you have questions. It is worth comment that too many athletes, dancers, and cheerleaders develop anorexia or bulimia, or use performance-enhancing drugs. They risk lifelong disabilities and even death from these conditions. If you suspect any body- or mind-altering behaviors, contact your physician, coaches, or school counselors, and pastoral care team. Develop a well-thought-out plan to approach your child, and then enter a Christ-centered, gentle, concerned conversation with him, followed by appropriate action as necessary.

Safety: Parents are their child's best advocates for safe environments so injuries are avoided and bullying and abuse can be prevented.

Adequate equipment and instruction in using it must be a focus for every coach, volunteer, and participant. This includes ensuring safe travel to and from practices and games.

Make yourself aware of the coaches' backgrounds, qualifications, and certifications. Explore how and why your child's coach was hired for the team. Even volunteers should be fully vetted, a process that includes a background check and drug screen.

Review the safety policies of your sports association and your school, including the safety guidelines for classrooms, boards, committees, and organizations. Staff members should have completed training that includes hostile environment, bullying, and other harassment-related topics. Be sure every organization your child is involved with complies with all recommended best practices for reporting situations so that any suspicious behavior by players or coaches is dealt with immediately and appropriately.

This should include clear guidelines that prohibit hidden emails or personal conversations between adults and student athletes. Any one-on-one training should be in a public, highly visible space.

Parents should be apprised of all details of any team travel plans.

There should be outstanding safety and security measures in place at all facilities where children compete, with appropriate locker-room and bathroom facilities.

If your child discloses inappropriate behavior, believe him. It is not your child's responsibility to determine if his impressions are founded in truth.

It is your and your community's responsibility to be aware of child advocacy services that ensure safety. Most communities have SAFE-CARE Providers or legal child advocacy centers who have trained interviewers. Know how to seek them out should you need them.

Basic Core Strength

Whether your child chooses to pursue formal sports or just wants to stay fit, there is great benefit in exercise that strengthens the muscles of the abdomen, hips, and pelvis that support the spine—what is commonly referred to as *core strength*. Enhancing core muscles is important to all sports and is also critical to proper posture and body alignment of the spine, shoulders, and hips. It is important when working on core muscles to maintain regular breathing during these exercises, which commonly require contracting (holding) muscles in one position for prolonged periods of time and through one or more movements. Otherwise, holding your breath might harmfully increase blood pressure.

Four basic exercises that are easy to incorporate and that provide great benefit are:

Kegels: This involves tightening the same muscles that stop the flow of urine. You contract or draw in the abdomen just below the belly button and pull up or tighten the pelvic muscles as you inhale and exhale normally. You may sit, stand, or lie down.

Bridge and Knee Extension: Lie on your back with knees bent, feet flat, thighs parallel, and both hands on the floor with palms facing the floor. Next, lift your buttocks one or two inches off the floor and hold this position for five seconds, then lower buttocks. Next, slowly lift and straighten a knee with thighs kept stable. Hold this for five seconds. Lower the leg to the floor and repeat on the other side. Begin with three repetitions and gradually increase to ten.

The Clam: Lie on your left side with head resting on left arm and right arm resting at your side. Place your body in a slight fetal position. Then open and close your knees, trying carefully to keep your pelvis, low back, and shoulders still. Repeat this ten times; then flip to the other side and repeat the movement ten times

The Superman: Lie face down on the floor with arms and legs fully extended in the flying Superman pose. Lift right arm and left leg as you tighten abdominal muscles. Hold for two or three seconds and then relax and return limbs to the floor. Lift left arm and right leg, taking them through the same poses. Work up to ten repetitions on both sides

An internet search for core exercises will reveal videos and descriptions that will guide you in learning proper technique.

Choosing and Evaluating Sports Programs

When children are ready, willing, and able to participate in formalized sports, parents should consider a few issues.

First, be aware that girls have just as many opportunities as boys, with well-funded, well-coached teams in a myriad of sports.

Second, not all children have the fitness, coordination, or stamina to participate in every sport. Their desire and physical capabilities may or may not be similar to yours as a parent. They may not have inherited your basketball gene. If your child suffers a negative sports experience, she may be burdened by stress and frustration, the opposite of what you wish for your child.

Third, make sure both you and your child have a fairly clear sense of objectives for participating in a sport. Few good grade-school athletes are great in high school. Out of 7.3 million high school athletes, only 2 percent receive an athletic scholarship for college.[2] And only 1 in 6,600 high school football players ever gets into the NFL. Be real, but don't be discouraged. Participating in sports has benefits well beyond a career goal.

Finally, if your child just wants to have fun or just play with friends, so be it. If winning is highest on your or your child's list, your priorities may be out of line. Winning is great and adds excitement and joy. Contrary to "play of the week" videos, however, building lasting experiences and memories around a sport and developing skills to carry into the rest of your child's life are far more meaningful outcomes.

PLANT-BASED NUTRITION FOR HIGH SCHOOLERS

High school students often are faced with the temptations of sugary, salty, and fried foods on drive-through menus that are a staple of our society. They can easily consume a full day's recommended calories (or more) with fast-food meals. "I'll have a loaded burger, large fries with extra ketchup and salt, and a shake"—or, in a health-conscious teen, "Make that a diet soda." Then there's pizza.

There are exceptions to this scenario, of course, and if you've raised a teen who reads labels, chooses fruits and veggies with low-calorie dips, and carries healthy snacks—you're fortunate! You can remind your teen that the school cafeteria and most fast-food restaurants offer a veggie selection or salad bar, broiled chicken, a fried fish sandwich, and (increasingly) plant-based options.

It is hard to maneuver around the cost and convenience of our national nutritional habits. Parents must find a balance between what is affordable and what is nutritious.

By the time your child has reached high school, his dietary desires have been established. Just as at younger ages, he needs nutrients to match his increased growth and development due to puberty and to accommodate the energy requirements of his activity level.

This includes plenty of energy foods, protein, calcium, and iron.

Carbohydrates: Fruits, vegetables, and milk provide great simple carbs, but complex carbohydrates add fiber that is important for aiding sugar absorption and bowel activity. Complex carbs include whole grains, legumes, unsweetened cereals, and starchy vegetables. An average teenage boy uses 2,000 calories per day, and if he is athletic, he may need up to 2,800. Average girls need 1,600–2,200 calories per day.

Protein: On average, your teenager will require 45–60 grams of protein each day. This is needed for growth and muscle strength. Meat and fish are ready sources of adequate protein. However, she can obtain just as much protein from vegetables, including beans, legumes, peanut butter, roasted nuts (almonds, walnuts), sunflower seeds, and soy products.

Iron: Iron is needed for oxygenation of muscles, brain, and the immune system. A teen boy needs about 11 milligrams per day of iron. A teen girl requires at least 15 milligrams per day because of menstruation. Green leafy vegetables, lean meat, nuts, and whole grains are great sources of iron.

Calcium: We need calcium for strong, well-developed bones and teeth. A teenager needs at least 1,200 milligrams per day of calcium from dairy products, cereals, and green leafy vegetables. It is also important to reduce the intake of sugary foods and drinks, such as soda, which leach calcium from bones.

Vitamins and Minerals: These are important for your teen's immunity and protect against anemia, vision disturbances, and muscle weakness. Most foods in our country are fortified, but your physician may recommend dietary supplements. Foods like milk, cheese, yogurt, eggs, carrots, peaches, mangoes, kiwi, strawberries, spinach, salmon, tuna, and oranges all are great sources of vitamins and minerals. Think smoothies! Slip in some spinach or kale for a kick. Avocados, bananas, beans, and peas are also flavorful additions.

Not only do you want to place good nutrient sources before your teen at home, but you also want to encourage good plant-based choices when she is not directly in your care. You can support this by using mealtime to discuss rather than debate food. Try to keep nutrition from being a power issue or legalistic, but present it as a topic near and dear to your heart. Being careful about your child's nutrition is a way to fulfill your vocation as her parent. Being a good steward of her body is a way to honor God, who gave us our bodies.

Don't be afraid to try new recipes and involve your teen in cooking. In fact, assign one family meal or more per week to your teen to choose, buy, and prepare. Shop with him to help him assess nutritional values and the economics of feeding a family. Emphasize colorful food choices. This also allows you to teach the negative effects of junk food. Show how to read labels, and stock your home with healthy choices. Explore spices, condiments, and sauces. (Incidentally, these activities will show your teen that math and science learned in school have practical applications in daily life.)

If you or your spouse has health concerns such as hypertension, diabetes, or heart disease, or if a member of your household has food sensitivities, talk with your teen and tell her that you want to help reduce her own risks through eating a plant-based diet.

REST IN HIGH SCHOOLERS

Teens need 9–10 hours of sleep to function at their best. Does that surprise you? It may, since we often find our high school students burning the midnight oil as much or more than their parents do, yet they still have to wake up in time to go to school. The result of long-term lack of sleep may cause symptoms we see so often in teens: poor concentration, irritability, headaches, slipping memory, depression, hypertension, and obesity. Susceptibility to viruses may also be a sign that your teen needs more rest. During your parent-teacher conferences, if your teen's teacher notes that your teen appears to "zone out" repeatedly in class, consider that she may be lacking sleep. Remember, too, that with the weight gain that sometimes accompanies puberty, your child might be more susceptible to sleep apnea and might require testing. Be suspicious if you hear loud snoring or stalled breathing with long spells when he doesn't seem to be breathing at all.

Be aware that teens require more sleep; their brains are still developing, and they periodically experience growth spurts requiring more rest and energy.[3] Furthermore, sleep-wake cycles begin to shift to two hours later than in grade school. Some educators are advocating that middle and high schools shift their school start times back to 8:30 a.m. or later, although there is significant resistance to that in some communities. Parent organizations can work closely with school boards to assure a start time that has proven efficacy.[4]

At home, you can provide an adequate bedroom and monitor your teen's use of electronic, audio, and viewing devices in the bedroom. Encourage physical activity during the day with plenty of fresh air. Also help your teen find balance among homework, sports, and other activities. Give your teenager time to wind down for an hour or two before bedtime.

Curfews: A significant vulnerability for parents and their children may occur when they begin to deal with curfews. By now, you will have assessed your child's responsibility at overnights in grade school and her accountability at keeping you informed about where and who she is with.

The first question your teen will ask is, "How late can I stay out?" Parents may choose a consistent time at a given age or may have a flexible curfew depending on the circumstances. An advantage of having a flexible time is that it encourages your teen to demonstrate responsibility in exchange for expanded privileges. Clearly, in the last year or two of high school, with your teen facing increasing school, social, and volunteer commitments, flexibility may help him prepare for decision-making in the years ahead when he is on his own. Regardless, whatever the agreed-upon curfew is, establish and communicate the ramifications of missing it. (Naturally, if an emergency arises, communication is critical on your responsible child's part. Everyone has access to a cell phone these days.)

A good way to choose a curfew is to ask your teen what time he thinks is reasonable. Remind him that the purpose of curfew is to keep him healthy and safe. You, your spouse, and your teen should discuss together your individual comfort levels in choosing a curfew, and keep it within the context of the event, the people he will be with, and your community's parameters.

It becomes increasingly important for parents of teens to know the families of their friends. If your teen is staying overnight, know the family she is staying with and make sure you discuss safety issues and behavior expectations. Teens face many temptations, and even the most confident teen may give in if she is encouraged. It can't be said enough that before your teen is in a tempting situation, she should know how best to handle drugs, guns, alcohol, and pressure to have sex.

Here are a few other rules to put in place:

- No matter what time your child arrives home, enforce the "check-in rule." Have him tell you good night face-to-face. That can help you assess alcohol or drug consumption. It will also give you the opportunity to hear about his evening out and to tell him you are glad he is safe at home.
- You, your spouse, and your teen need to be respectful of one another's freedoms and responsibilities within the family. Therefore, spell out the expectations and consequences of the curfew and stick to them. If she misses curfew, assure her that you were worried but now are relieved that she is home, and you will talk with her in the morning. For either of you to blow up late at night is a recipe for a disaster. The next morning, then, assure her that privileges will be rolled back as a result of breaking the curfew. A similar rollback can be put in place if her schoolwork deteriorates because of her social life. Grounding as the response to the first offense is usually counterproductive, but it may be necessary if disrespecting the curfew becomes frequent.

The bottom line for parent and teen to acknowledge is that curfews are in place to help protect her health and maintain her safety. Curfews allow the teen to express self-control and management of time. The child's responsibility may lead to flexibility, but failing to obey curfews will result in consequences and loss of privileges.

Rest through deep breathing: As discussed in the previous chapter, slow, controlled breathing practices are useful to help deal with anxiety. Periodic pause points in the day to sit, breathe, and use guided meditation or scripturally centered meditation are excellent ways to incorporate rest within the waking hours of daily life. Periods of fasting from social media and texting, shutting off the phone, or just spending alone time are helpful ways to let the teenage body rest and recuperate from a bombardment of stimulants. Helping your teen learn to replace negative self-talk (such as accusatory or derogatory internal conversation) with positive and affirming words from the Scriptures or solid and sensitive Christian writings has great benefit.

God modeled rest in His creative process (Genesis 2:2–3). Christ rested alone to be with His Father, and He spent time away from the busyness of ministry to be with friends, talk, and pray (Mark 1:35; 6:31–32). So should we. These biblical examples give us a model and are for our benefit, regardless our age but especially during the frenetic teenage years.

FOCUS ON FAITH AND FAMILY FOR HIGH SCHOOLERS

It is critical that teens be surrounded by caring, compassionate, faith-filled, and accountable adults. Late elementary and high school students are transitioning from the grammar and logic of their spiritual journey to the full rhetoric and self-expression of their faith. They have learned faith basics; and they have questioned the logic of the tenets of their faith as they prepared for confirmation. From Baptism onward, with the partnership of parents and faith leaders and the work of the Holy Spirit, teens are growing in understanding their identity as children of God, made in His image and redeemed by the blood of Christ. As they are being matured in their faith by the Holy Spirit, they become aware that the full expression of their faith means their personal identity must diminish and their new identity in Christ must increase. They are called to put off selfishness and put on selflessness. From the voice of John the Baptist at the river's edge:

> He must increase, but I must decrease.
>
> (John 3:30)

One expression of how our identity in Christ increases is in the way we use our body, mind, and spirit; the way we steward self and all the gifts God has given us to His glory and for the good of His people. This includes the responsibility for decisions regarding sexual activity, drug use, smoking, submitting to the influence of electronic communication devices, and bullying.

Teen Sexuality

For parents and children junior high or older, one of the most anxiety-producing conversations is "the sex talk." Parents are hesitant to converse for a host of reasons, including feeling unqualified, feeling awkward, distress they recall from their own discussion with their parents, or missteps in their own life. Teens are at an even higher state of discomfort. They may feel self-conscious about the intimate topic or about their own fears and misunderstandings about what is happening to their bodies and emotions. They may feel as if the conversation is unnecessary because they are loaded with a host of "everyone knows *that*" street knowledge.

Parents, be encouraged to bring this important conversation to the level of just that—factual knowledge and compassionate communication. But be not deceived; your children are learning about sex on a daily basis from their phones, tablets, media of all varieties, and their peers. They may know more about the variety of sexual behaviors, topics, pleasures, and pitfalls than you do. That said, *you*, Mom and Dad, are the most important sources of information, attitude, values, understanding, comfort, and security in their lives, especially regarding sex.[5] In fact, there is good evidence that closeness with parents may be the best predictor of conservative sexual behavior.[6]

How do you begin this conversation? One way is to take advantage of teachable moments:

- Your teen spending increasing time with a boyfriend or girlfriend
- A situation your teen's friend or acquaintance is going through
- News stories on topics like rape or unwanted pregnancy
- Celebrity coverage on body shape or size or glorification of image
- Adoption
- Coming out or transgender issues
- The music and videos your children are consuming

You can begin with a simple comment: "You know, I remember having a discussion about sex with my father [mother] and how uncomfortable I was; I felt so embarrassed. Maybe you are as well. But it would be a good time for us to talk about this subject."

Always remember to end this segue with these words: "You know God loves you and I love you and will always love you no matter what." Is that corny? No; it is absolutely essential.

To help you prepare for your conversation, here are some facts to anchor your comments:

- The average age for first-time sexual intercourse among American teens is 18.[7, 8]
- There are 52 teen pregnancies per 1,000 teens and 14 abortions per 1,000 teens yearly in the US
- Teen sexual activity is not only a moral and spiritual threat but also a physical danger: sexually transmitted infections (STIs) are being treated at record levels of 8,000 teens per day.[9]
- Young people with firm religious beliefs are less likely—but not absolutely unlikely—to engage in sexual activity than their peers.[10]
- A strong relationship with compassionate parents strongly influences sexual behavior, as we noted above.[11]

What to say specifically is determined by your actual conversations. Be confident that you will have the right words at the right time. Pray for God's guidance. Trust yourself. And equip yourself by knowing themes to continually reinforce as your child deals with his or her sexuality:

- *Creation:* Sex is a part of being a human created by God. It is good when it functions the way God designed it. God intended marital sex to be a blessing to His people (Matthew 19:4–5).
- *Sexual desires:* Our physical, mental, and emotional responses to sexual urges are a normal part of who we are created to be; therefore, sex talk should be factual but should always include talk about values and boundaries.
- *Questioning your feelings:* It is normal for each of us to have questions about sex. Therefore, as parents, it is far better to provide children with healthful, scriptural, and well-educated facts rather than have them obtain their knowledge from media or peers who do not necessarily have their best interests at heart.
- *Sexual responsibility:* Each of us, young and old, has responsibility for and authority over our sexual behavior; we must never relinquish that control to others. No one should pressure your son or daughter to have sex. Empower your teen with self-esteem and values to make choices with healthy outcomes. Help your teens to reason through their decisions about sex, especially those that could potentially lead to pregnancy or disease. Remember to share with

them the consequences beyond the physical: distrust and the effect on their relationship with you, their parents, and with God.

- *Respect:* The Bible makes it clear that respect is important in all relationships (Ephesians 4:2–3; Hebrews 10:24–25). God's Word informs us that He created us to enjoy fulfilling sexual relations within marriage (1 Thessalonians 4:3). As parents, we should emphasize that waiting until marriage brings great blessings and benefits to the marital relationship. Casual and impersonal sex without emotional connection and commitment diminishes the importance of physical intimacy, a devaluation of sex that can last a lifetime and certainly carries into a subsequent marriage. Remember as well that romantic relationships are often short-lived (weeks for young adolescents; months for middle adolescents; years, perhaps, for older teens and young adults). With lack of permanence, there may be wild swings in emotions, especially if your teen is going through his or her first serious relationship.
- *Body image:* Body image involves our perception of our physical self: how we see ourselves, how we think others see us, and how we feel about ourselves. It includes how we think about ourselves and how we behave to preserve or alter our body and thoughts. Overeating, undereating, and purging may be physical responses to emotions related to self-image. Obesity, anorexia, and bulimia disorders can be as deadly as any illness. Social media is a marketing tool for all sorts of dietary, cosmetic, clothing, and exercise trends. We know that frequent social network use increases body dissatisfaction.[12] So be aware that teens may use software or apps to digitally alter or enhance their image, leading to a misrepresentation of themselves and perhaps indicating a concern about self-perception or emotional well-being. There are parental measures that help, including frank discussions among the entire family, involvement of school counselors and athletic coaches, and online positive body resources such as Project HEAL, Dove Campaign for Real Beauty, Eating Disorder HOPE, and Love Is Louder. Be aware body image is an issue for both boys and girls. An emphasis on good general health including exercise, plant-based diet, rest, closeness to family, and faith is imperative.
- *Friendship:* It is important for our children to be able to develop friendships with the opposite sex without having sexual relations,

especially in a culture dominated by increasing equality in sports, education, activities, and work. Christian parents strive to teach their children to respect and honor everyone they relate to wherever they are (1 Corinthians 7:3–4). Friendship (connectedness) is a predictor of long-term relationships because it involves trust, respect, communication, conflict resolution, and accountability.[13]

- *Sexual identity:* It is also normal for children to wrestle with the topic of sexual identity, including lesbian, gay, bisexual, transgender, queer, intersexual, and asexual (LGBTQIA) issues—if not for him- or herself, than as the friend of someone who is questioning. Whether or not they agree with you, your children will benefit by clearly knowing your values and your views on these subjects. Suicide rates for kids who suffer bullying because they struggle with gender identity are substantially higher compared with the general population. LGBTQIA children who are rejected by their family have five times the suicide attempt rate as heterosexual children.[14] As much as possible, it is important to clarify fact and truth as you formulate your own opinion. Do not sacrifice the channels of open communication and conversation. There are many resources to help both parent and child if you or your family are struggling with sexual identity issues.[15, 16, 17, 18]
- *Abstinence/birth control:* Be honest with your children about the risks of pregnancy, the limits of different forms of birth control if that topic is raised, and the short- and long-term consequences of sexually transmitted disease and infection. It is important to talk about abstaining from sex before marriage and the spiritual and personal values of this practice. It is the only form of birth control that has a 100 percent guarantee of avoiding pregnancy and disease. Unfortunately, research shows that children who receive abstinence-only sex education are no more likely to refrain from sex than teens who receive no sex ed at all.[19] Your relationship with your teen, your own behaviors, and your perspective are critical. Consult with your health-care provider during regular well-child visits to discuss the variety of means available for preventing pregnancy and disease. That way you are sure to provide the most up-to-date facts for your teen. Even if he or she is practicing abstinence, being well-informed can help your child be an invaluable resource for his or her peers.

- *Sexting:* This is the transmission or receiving of sexually explicit messages, photos, videos, or other media, most often using cell phones but also tablets and computers. It leads to enormous personal relational disasters and legal risks. For example, explicit photos of a person under age 18 are considered child pornography. Sending or receiving them is a crime. Remind your child that she has the right, self-worth, and moral responsibility to say no to both sex and sexting (Matthew 5:27–30).
- *Sexual language:* Use age-appropriate words for body parts and functions rather than playful or distracting words or slang. This is important, especially for younger children who are learning about themselves. Using correct terminology serves to honor our bodies and conveys dignity.
- *Masturbation:* Discussions on this subject are often avoided due to misinformation and embarrassment. Talking about masturbation with your teen needs to be accompanied by a discussion of pornography. Please read the comments on pornography in "The Influence of Media and Electronic Communication" (p. 212).
    - Masturbation is sinful, and it is a sin against the vocation of marriage. To use sex out of the context of marital relations is to misuse it. We abuse our vocation when we use it selfishly. One of the greatest gifts of our faith community is teaching and leading lives of sexual integrity. Here is what the Scriptures teach us:
    - Jesus warns that whoever looks lustfully at a woman has already committed adultery in his heart (Matthew 5:28), and such inordinate desires are clearly called sin by the Lord (v. 27).
    - St. Paul reminds us that there must not be even a hint of sexual immorality in our lives (Ephesians 5:3). It is doubtful that anyone could masturbate without sexual thoughts or mental images.
    - It contradicts the purpose of sexuality laid out in the Bible, such as being intimate with one's spouse (Genesis 2:18, 24) and procreation (1:28).
    - Masturbation in childhood can be a form of temporary experimentation. Parents should help their child to know that God warns us about the voluntary indulgence of sexual fantasies because they may endanger our faith, spiritual, and

relational life. As a child grows into maturity, their youthful fantasies and lusts are to be left behind (2 Timothy 2:22). Furthermore, masturbation often carries an inherent sense of guilt and shame. The guilt may be obvious, but the helplessness to stop may lead to great shame. It can become addictive and difficult to stop.

- Here is where we need God's help! Christian pastors are ready to offer Christ's forgiveness, and those Christian pastors, physicians, parents, and counselors can remind your child of the power of the Holy Spirit to help them lead a decent, chaste, and upright life. They can share with your child the joys of remaining faithful to what God teaches in His Word about the gift of sexuality.[20]

- *Oral or anal sex:* All sexual behaviors carry risk of disease and infection; these practices are especially prominent ways to spread STIs and human papilloma virus (HPV). The Centers for Disease Control and Prevention recommend all children, beginning at age 11, be vaccinated against HPV. Guided by your physician, this vaccination is an opportune time to begin speaking in earnest to your child about sex.
- *Keep talking:* Talking with your teen about sex is not a one-and-done discussion. These conversations, communications, and honesty must continue as long as you parent, and for most of us, that is a lifetime.
- *Know the village:* Know your children's friends and their parents, if possible. It takes a community to lead your child through the challenges of the teenage years and beyond. Seek and cherish fellow parents who share your Christian values, and be courageous, for your child's sake and for your faith, to be both an educator and an advocate to your child's community in what God desires for a healthy teen and healthy families.
- *Overall general health:* As we have discussed repeatedly, encourage healthy exercise, healthy eating, rest, stress management, and diligence in homework and school, and stay involved as a family in church and community service.
- *Love and forgiveness*: The bedrock of your relationship with your child must be love and forgiveness, rooted in your bap-

> tismal identity as an unconditionally loved child of God. It would have been logical for Jesus to denigrate and chastise the Samaritan woman at the well (John 4:1–26). Instead, Jesus gives her "living water": He says, "I who speak to you am He [the Messiah]." She is forgiven, restored, made new in Jesus. No matter how our children fail or misstep, they can be brought back into relationship with God and with you via confession, repentance, and forgiveness, leading to a restored effort to do better before God's throne of grace and mercy and in the eyes of man.

Despite our greatest efforts and hopes and dreams, we may have a child who is considering crossing the line or has already done so (and this may happen especially if your child has been dating someone for a substantial period of time). If you are blessed with a relationship where your child comes to you for advice about taking his or her relationship further, how might you respond? With candor. Discuss exactly what it would mean for him to cross the bridge into a sexual relationship. In fact, if you have the courage and the opportunity, bring his significant other into the conversation with you. Be frank and let your views and feelings be fully known.

Discuss with your teen the health risks of being sexually active.. He should be seen by his pediatrician and screened for STIs every three months if in a nonmonogamous relationship, or every six months even if in a monogamous relationship.

If your child has already had sex—and parents are usually the last to know—try not to overreact. Communication and continued conversation remain critical. Ask some questions and be a better listener than talker. "What happened?" "Why do you think that happened?" "How has that choice affected your relationship with your girlfriend [boyfriend]?" "How do you think it will affect your relationship with us [parents]?"

As difficult as it may be, don't lecture. Assure your teen of your unconditional love and God's unconditional love through Jesus. Remind him or her of God's forgiveness and (honestly) your forgiveness, and show your forgiveness by the way you treat him or her. It may be helpful to remind your teen of Bible stories of God's forgiveness: King David after he had killed Uriah and taken Bathsheba as his wife; Paul after he had killed many Christians; Jesus forgiving those who crucified Him.

Parents should be and will be the primary models of a healthy sexual life for their family and an extraordinary conduit for God's healing in Christ. Parents do this through their words, the values they instill, and their own behaviors.

Health care providers, pastors, and youth ministers can be the parents' greatest allies. Unconditional love, forgiveness, and compassionate and ongoing conversation are essential for family life together, especially when the topic is sex.

Drug Use

Another extraordinarily stressful conversation for parents and their teens concerns the devastating effects of drugs and the accompanying destruction of wellness, including death. Marijuana, opiates, fentanyl, heroin, methamphetamine, and cocaine are in prevalent use in our society.

Communication is the most powerful tool for parents, and just as when the topic is sex, the conversation needs to be compassionate and focused on the well-being of both the child and the family. Drug education must begin early in elementary school but really ramp up in the high school years. Fortunately, our public and private educational systems aggressively address the dangers of drug use and addiction. But school doesn't replace parents; they must mutually support each other's efforts.

In all situations where your teen might be challenged by peer pressure to compromise his principles, it is helpful to have a code word or phrase known only to you and your teen that he can use to communicate to you verbally or by text to signal that he feels uncomfortable and needs you to intervene. Make it a word that won't be subject to ridicule by friends, like *stomachache*, *dizziness*, or *nauseated*. If your child says or texts the code word, you know you need to show up and remove him from the situation. Rescue your child!

If you have concerns that your child might be using drugs, here are a few warning signs that should lead you to thoughtful but strenuous attention:

- *Behavioral change:* reduced academic, athletic, or extracurricular performance, or attendance; change in friends; hostility and defiance; secretive behavior; concern expressed by teachers
- *Personality change:* mood swings, memory loss, trouble concentrating or extreme drowsiness, loud and offensive language; many drugs have psychotropic effects
- *Physical change:* sudden weight loss or gain, insomnia, thirst, nausea and vomiting, excessive sweating, headaches, tremors, seizures without a history of epilepsy, nosebleeds, or body odor
- *Hygienic change:* teeth clenching, bloodshot eyes, runny nose, scratching (might signal opiates), incoordination, track marks on legs or arms (a sign of IV use), the smell of marijuana or alcohol
- *Telltale findings:* paraphernalia; drug residue, seeds or powder; missing cash; missing prescription medications

These alarms must trigger a calm and compassionate conversation with your teen, immediately followed by counseling with professional drug or mental health therapists, physician, pastor, and perhaps teachers and principal. Drug abuse is a disorder of the body, mind, emotion, and spirit, and the addicted teen needs experts in all of these disciplines. You as the parent, however, will be your teen's and your family's best advocate and leader.

Smoking: 9 out of 10 cigarette smokers try their first cigarette by age 18, and every day, nearly 200 people under age 18 will become daily smokers. About 5.6 million teens will die early from smoking-related illness.[21] It's a problem. The Mayo Clinic, long a leader in preventative care, suggests the following to help curb this habitual and addictive habit:[22]

- Set a good example by not smoking yourself.
- Understand the attraction and discuss the marketing methods advertisers use to encourage smoking in teens.
- Disapprove. Say no; it may have more impact than you think.
- Discuss the longer-term health risks: lung damage, heart damage, and cancer.

- Talk about the disturbing social qualities such as bad breath and yellowed teeth and nails.
- Talk about the financial cost of smoking.
- Talk about the peer pressure that may result when your teen says, "No, I don't smoke."
- Talk seriously about the issue of addiction: once you've started, it is so difficult to stop.
- Personally get involved in public efforts to stem this major health issue; be vocal.

Vaping, dabbing: Nearly half of US teens have tried electronic nicotine delivery systems (ENDS). They come as electronic devices: e-cigarettes, e-pens, e-hookahs, vape pipes and pens, and "juice." ENDS are marketed as being safer than cigarettes, but recent reports of illness and deaths make these claims unreliable. They come in bright colors, with appealing packaging, attractive flavors, and highly concentrated nicotine. They also contain clouds of chemicals and carcinogens. Dabbing involves a heated and vaporized concentrate of cannabis oil via a pipe device.

Deaths and substantial lung damage due to vaping are being reported, especially when THC is included in the product. The Centers for Disease Control and Prevention recommends that all vaping be suspended until further studies can clarify the details of the dangerous consequences.[23]

The Influence of Media and Electronic Communication

The spectrum of modern media includes print materials, TV, movies, video games, music, and the internet, and it connects us by cell phones, tablets, and computers. Average teens use devices for sending and receiving information more than six hours each day. This time could be and is used for good, but teens are greatly challenged by profound negative effects because they are still developing their full behavioral, intellectual, emotional, and social attitudes and responses.

One profound issue of media is that it can cause teens to have difficulty differentiating reality from fantasy. This is especially true among younger teens who are not mature enough to think with discernment, especially regarding violence and sex. The use of media also robs teens of spending time with sports, community service, reading, and face-to-face communication with family and friends. Children who use media heavily are at risk of becoming socially isolated. Furthermore, the propensity to use alcohol[24] is fueled by media glorification of alcohol consumption. We have evidence that marijuana use is increased by the lyrics and tunes our teens are exposed to daily.[25] Finally, it is known that exposure to sexual activity in media can predict the initiation of sexual activity in teens.[26]

Pornography

Pornography is pervasive in our culture. Pornography quickly can become as addictive as any drug, and excessive use may require professional intervention. Focus on the Family offers a few suggestions for helping your teen deal with pornography:[27]

- Explain that using pornography instead of healthier outlets for stress—like sports, hobbies, and exercise—is harmful to body, mind, and spirit.
- Limit the use of technology and explain the importance of those boundaries.
- Emphasize an "open device" policy so you can monitor what is being viewed.
- Have the tough talk about sex and provide healthy and positive direction for sexual behavior, reminding your child how pornography distorts sexual arousal and function. Sex is a positive gift of God to a loving and giving relationship; pornography promotes self-focus. Healthy sexual function requires truthful thinking, not fantasy.
- Model and encourage a healthy relationship with God and others.

There is clear documentation that media can have direct influence on risky sexual behavior.[28]

But can media also be used as a positive influence? Actually, it can—but how can we make that happen? A first step might be considering the way we spend our parental dollar. Media needs to get the clear message that we parents care about the content being streamed to our children, and that this content has grave consequences for the health of our children and society. We must insist that media show the real consequences of teen pregnancy, drug use and abuse, suicide spurred by bullying, and the lifelong tragic consequences of gun violence; and that they de-legitimize behavioral practices that harm our kids.

Second, we can sit down and watch TV and videos with our teens. Make these opportunities "teachable moments."

Third, as tough as it will be, firmly limit the amount of time your teen is allowed to play video games, view TV, use social media, or sit in his or her room and absorb music. This is increasingly a challenge, as media has moved from 10 feet away—the distance from the couch to the TV in the 1960s—to 10 inches away—the distance from the mobile phone to the face at present. You can strive to limit your home to one TV in the common family room and limit access to internet and video games, and you can take time to discuss programming.

Fourth, be a good role model yourself. This is particularly relevant with regard to viewing programs with heavy sexual or violent content.

There will be continual struggles for Christian parents as media and technology evolve. As parents striving to raise children in the way of Christ, we can keep a few simple messages imprinted on our hearts:

> Our bodies are temples of the Holy Spirit.
>
> (1 Corinthians 6:19)

> As we put on Christ, we don't have to submit to temptations.
>
> (Mark 1:12–13)

> By the power of the Holy Spirit, we can put on the mind and eyes and ears of Christ.
>
> (Philippians 2:5–8)

Bullying

There is enormous public awareness of bullying. Bullying occurs daily in the lives of many children, whether they are the victims or the aggressors in this abusive, intimidating, and dominating behavior. The bullied child or teen typically has trouble defending herself and usually has done nothing to cause the bullying. It may occur because of his appearance, race, religion, behavior, social status, popularity, sexual identity, or simply because he is in the line of vision of the bully. Bullies and their colleagues make the determination that, for whatever reason, the victim is a target.

Bullies can be boys or girls. They may be very aggressive and forthright in threatening another person face-to-face; more often, though, they are quiet and sneaky—for example, by starting rumors to damage the victim's reputation. They may appear friendly, but falsely so; they may pretend to be a friend so the child confides in them, then do hurtful things behind the child's back. Generally, bullies like to appear in charge, are self-focused, can't get along with others, lack empathy, or are themselves the victims of bullying. They truly don't understand normal social emotions. They require intervention from a responsible adult, such as a teacher, school administrator, mental health or social worker, or pastor.

Bullying takes many forms:

- Verbal taunting or teasing
- Physical harm through tripping, shoving, punching, or any unwanted contact
- Psychological intimidation through staring, gossiping, or degrading comments
- Cyberbullying by texting or using social media platforms can come in the form of posting photos, memes, or derogatory comments, or it may be videos or personal information meant to hurt or embarrass another child

All of these physical, emotional, and spiritual attacks leave victims frightened, shamed, depressed, anxious, struggling with schoolwork and relationships, and perhaps even suicidal. Parents certainly want to and must intervene on behalf of their children and should not hesitate to reach out to school authorities.

To help prepare children to protect themselves in a potential bullying situation, parents can instill these strategies and attitudes in children:

- If your child is experiencing or witnessing bullying, encourage him or her to be unafraid and unashamed to seek the help of an authority: parent, coach, teacher, pastor, or youth director.
- Urge your child to have the courage to walk away from the bully. Often bullies are seeking attention from others. Help your child learn to let the bully know it won't work (Matthew 5:39).
- Encourage your child to avoid trying to "outfight" the bully if things get physical; your child is more likely to be physically hurt than the bully. Be cautious about telling your child to defend himself or herself by fighting back. In many instances, school discipline includes suspension or expulsion for *anyone* who engages in fighting, whether or not they "started it."
- Revenge and malice come from anger, and Jesus has clear comments regarding our response: "Love your enemies, do good to those who hate you, bless those who curse you, pray for those who abuse you" (Luke 6:27–28). Encourage an attitude of compassion in your home. Do not let your child hear you express anger or vengeful thoughts.
- It is important for your child to stand up for others who are being bullied; this may expose her to similar derision, but usually defenders help the one being bullied (1 Thessalonians 5:14).
- Emphasize reaching out and talking about a bullying situation. Children should feel comfortable telling a teacher or principal, coach, other classmates, or parents and siblings. The worst scenario is a child who becomes increasingly isolated; he or she is at great risk for depression and suicide. See if your child's school has a violence or bullying prevention program or team, and if they don't, perhaps your child can be involved in starting one.

If you discover that your child is being bullied or is being a bully, it is imperative that you contact school authorities to intervene. This might mean getting involved with police or other legal officials. The media is filled with accounts of families who appeared unaware of their child's fate until permanent harm or death was the end result. That is truly sad.

If Your Child Is a Bully

We often think that bullies are big, wear dark clothes, have low self-esteem, or have a hair-trigger temper. Be aware that a bully can just as easily be a petite cheerleader or an honor student. Behavior, not appearance, defines bullying. A bully can come from any gender, race, socioeconomic class, family circumstance, or religion.

These signs might alert you to the fact that your child might be bullying others:

- He has undeveloped social skills.
- She has been bullied herself.
- He is quick to blame others or is unwilling to accept responsibility for his own actions.
- She lacks understanding of or compassion for others' feelings.
- He hangs out with other kids who encourage bullying.

If you are informed by school officials or other parents that your child is doing the bullying, there are several things you must do:

- Begin by having a forthright conversation with your child.
- Consult your pastor.
- Speak with school authorities.
- Consult a professional counselor or therapist for your child.
- Talk with a professional counselor or therapist yourself. You and your spouse will be affected by the news that your child is hurting someone. The ripple effect in your life cannot be underestimated.
- Pray for and with your child.
- Set parameters for behavior and stick to them.
- Forgive, but do not forget.
- Do not harangue, threaten, or bully your child.

It is imperative that as a Christian parent, you strongly lead your child to understand how bullying affects others and how it injures your child's very nature. It may require that you enjoin significant consequences for your child if he or she persists in this dangerous and harmful behavior.[29]

Look for the reason behind the behavior and seek to resolve what caused your child to act out. There is always a root cause. Although it may be uncomfortable or even difficult for you to work through this issue with your child, it is critical to his or her overall wellness.

Teen Mental Health and Suicide

The rate of anxiety and depression continues to rise in our country and certainly among teens. We addressed this earlier (see page 30), but I want to make an additional note about suicide in this chapter dedicated to teens.

Many teens who attempt suicide are dealing with underlying mental health disorders (e.g., depression, bipolar mood disorders) or shame. They have trouble coping with stress, failure, rejection, or conflict, and they may not realize that there are resources to help them turn their life around. Some teens are dealing with physical or sexual abuse, pregnancy, sexually transmitted infections, bullying, gender identification issues, or family histories of mood disorders.[30]

Further, it is important to be aware that many depressed or anxious teens may be taking antidepressants. Be cautioned that while such medications can help significantly in the long term, they come with a caveat: teens and young adults under age 25 may experience increased thoughts of suicide while on an antidepressant, especially during the first few weeks. They *need* to be *carefully monitored* by both parents and physicians.

We know that cognitive and spiritual counseling are key therapies and must be started as soon as parents recognize possible mental or mood disorders or suspects their child is having suicidal thoughts.

Here are a few warning signs:

- Talking or writing about suicide (don't be afraid to talk to your teen or to use the word *suicide*; you won't implant this idea in her brain)

- Dramatic mood swings
- Withdrawal
- Increased alcohol or drug abuse
- Change in eating or sleeping patterns
- Risky behavior
- Giving away possessions

Not all teens will show these symptoms, however. Some will appear to be confident and comfortable, adopting a façade of happiness that covers the turmoil underneath. Therefore, it is important to be sensitive to your teen's nuances of personality and behaviors. Strive to create an atmosphere of open, honest communication so your teen feels safe talking with you (or another adult) about fears, anxieties, failures, and flaws.

If you suspect your teen is suicidal, immediately call 911 or a local hotline, or call the National Suicide Prevention Hotline: 800-273-TALK or 800-273-8255.

Do not dismiss your child's feelings or behaviors. Be proactive. Offer your help and the help of professional medical, behavioral, and spiritual counselors. Remove or store firearms, personal medications, and alcohol. Be vigilant so you know where your teen is and whether he or she is alone or with others. Pay attention! Seek and stay with the treatment plan. Pray for and with your teen.

PURPOSEFUL AND MISSIONAL LIVING IN HIGH SCHOOLERS

I have emphasized the importance of social studies curricula in preparing elementary children to serve purposefully in a democratic society. Those same learning modules and personal interactions are intensified in high school, but I will not repeat a topic we've already covered. I will emphasize, though, that it's essential for a high school student to be equipped to live and serve in the world, beginning with the vocational, familial calling God has prepared in advance for him or her in Christ. Teens become increasingly autonomous, but they remain members of the family; their vocations as child, sibling, and student continue. Parental guidance, academic instruction, and congregational life serve to prepare teens to enter the adult world with a clear understanding of the truth about life, creation and its inhabitants, and their particular place in it. They are to have a deep conviction of their role as stewards of all the gifts of God to this world. To do that requires that your teenager understands the truth of the Bible and has faith that the Word of God is the standard for truth. Jesus is Lord of all, including every aspect of education and living. Jesus calls each of us to be transforming agents and influencers of society in His name. The Lord provides us with the tools to care well for our own body, mind, emotions, and heart so that we can glorify and serve Him with vitality and joy.

These aspects of Christian life are in the hands of Spirit-led parents and grandparents. But Christian education for teens, whether at a Christian high school or in the context of the home, supports parents to gird their children with a worldview from a Christ-purposed perspective. This perspective also realizes that we will encounter daily (as Christ did) those with different and sometimes strongly divergent views of life and the world. Compassion and respect are critical elements of Christian life; compromising Christian faith is not.

We want our children to see God everywhere, in each subject they study, as part of each relationship they have, and in every phase of preparation for vocations and service. We want our children to understand that their faith submits them to Jesus and is founded and energized by the Holy Spirit. That Spirit is molding and sculpting them to care in real and material ways as the hands and feet of the Savior to bless the world.

To accomplish this, our teens must develop a "love rhetoric" to communicate and converse with an often unloving world. And to be able to speak the truth in love, they need to embrace what they believe as true. They need to be able to articulate Christ's unconditional love for them and their capacity to fear, love, and trust Christ themselves.

> We love because He first loved us.
>
> (1 John 4:19)

This assurance is the anchor that allows our children to live and move and serve in myriad settings. It gives them the power to flourish in whatever vocation they are called to and whatever profession or service they pursue, in the home and family and in any corner of the universe. Christ's love serves as the model of the servant posture for living.

How do we encourage a servant heart in teenagers? We begin by letting them see us in prayer, turning over all our tensions and challenges to God, and looking to Him with trust and thanksgiving. Pray for your child in his presence. Pray with her for opportunities for service.

As you watch your child grow, you will perceive the gifts God has given him or her and will begin to think about how He wants your teen to use those gifts. Be a lens to help your teen focus those gifts in service, and be an encourager.

Share with your teen how God works in the world when His people are interdependent, when they work and serve together. There is great strength in encouraging one another, particularly as family members. Working together requires relational skills that are learned; it takes energy, and it doesn't just happen.

Help your child understand your strengths and weaknesses as a parent, that you are not perfect. Ask for forgiveness when you have erred, and ask for help when you need it.

Finally, use every opportunity to serve together with your teen around your home, in your local congregation, at school, and in the community. Help him or her understand that what drives your service is not duty; rather it flows out of a relationship based in your love for your Creator, for your child, and for all God's people and creation. "WE love because He first loved us."

You have parented your child through most of the tender years of development. And as you have learned, your vocation as parent changes to accommodate your child's development. Your teen may be leaving your home soon to pursue further education or to enter the workforce. But your role as parent doesn't end when he or she moves out of the home. Your guidance, wisdom, and love will continue to be important.

However, just like with Timothy's grandmother, Lois (2 Timothy 1:5), Laban and his grandchildren (Genesis 31:55), or even Naomi's care of a nongenetic grandson (Ruth 4:16), God may have one more task for you—grandparenting. It is a challenging but rewarding calling from a gracious God. Let us look at grandparenting in its lush complexities and blessings.

NOTES

1. See p. 127, "Faith and Family in the Toddler's Life."
2. "Athletic Scholarship Statistics," (accessed Feb. 19, 2020) scholarshipowl.com/blog/find-scholarships/athletic-scholarship-statistics.
3. "Teenagers and Sleep: How Much Sleep Is Enough?" Johns Hopkins Medicine, https://www.hopkinsmedicine.org/health/wellness-and-prevention/teenagers-and-sleep-how-much-sleep-is-enough.
4. "School Start Time for Adolescents," American Academy of Pediatrics Adolescent Sleep Working Group and Committee on Adolescence and Council on School Health policy statement, https://teensneedsleep.files.wordpress/2011/08/aap-school-start-times.
5. "Teens Say Parents Most Influence Their Decisions about Sex: New Survey Data of Teens and Adults Released," press release from The National Campaign (Washington, DC), 2012, https://thenationalcampaign.org/press-release/teen-say-parents-most-influence-their-decision-about-sex.
6. Stan Jones and Brenna Jones, "What Parents Need to Know—And Do—About Teenage Sexuality," https://fullerstudio.fuller.edu/what-parents-need-to-know-and-do-about-teenage-sexuality/.
7. "Teen Pregnancy," Guttmacher Institute, https://live.guttmacher.org/united-states/teens/teen-pregnancy.
8. "Over Half of U.S. Teens Have Had Sexual Intercourse by Age 18, New Report Shows," National Center for Health Statistics (June 22, 2017), cdc.gov/nchs/pressroom/nchs_press_releases/2017/201706_NSFG.htm.
9. K. Kost, I. Maddow-Zimet, and A. Arpaia, "Pregnancies, Births and Abortion among Adolescents and Young Women in the United States, 2013: National and State Trends by Age, Race and Ethnicity" (August 2017), Guttmacher Institute, guttmacher.org.
10. Stan Jones and Brenna Jones, "What Parents Need to Know—And Do. . . ."
11. Vincent Guilamo-Ramos et al., "Paternal Influences on Adolescent Sexual Risk Behaviors: A Structured Literature Review," *Pediatrics* 130, no. 5 (November 2012), e1313–e1325, https://www.cdc.gov/healthyyouth/protective/pdf/fathers_influence.pdf.
12. D. A. deVries, J. Peter, H. deGraff, et al., *Journal of Youth and Adolescence* 45 (2016), 211.
13. Preston Ni, "7 Predictors of Long-Term Relationship Success," *Psychology Today* (February 2013), https://www.psychologytoday.com/us/blog/communication-success/201302/7-predictors-long-term-relationship-success.
14. "Sexual Identity, Sex of Sexual Contacts, and Health-Risk Behaviors among Students in Grades 9–12: Youth Risk Behavior Surveillance," Centers for Disease Control and Prevention (2016), https://www.cdc.gov/mmwr/volumes/65/ss/pdfs/ss6509.pdf.
15. "Adolescent Sexual Orientation," *Pediatrics & Child Health* 13, no. 7 (September 2008), 619–23, NCBI, NIH, https://www.ncbi.nim.nih.gov/pmc/articles/PMC2603519/.
16. Jeff Johnson, "Is My Teen Struggling with Homosexuality?" Focus on the Family, www.focusonthefamily.com.
17. "Sexual Orientation (for Parents)," KidsHealth, www.kidshealth.org.

18. Daniel Puls, *A Christian Perspective on Homosexuality* (St. Louis: Concordia Publishing House, 1996).

19. P. S. Karofsky, L. Zeng, and M. R. Kosorok, "Relationships between Adolescent-Parental Communication and Initiation of First Intercourse by Adolescents," *Journal of Adolescent Health* 28, no. 1 (January 2001), 41–45.

20. https://www.lcms.org/about/beliefs/faqs/lcms-views#masturbation.

21. See www.cdc.gov/tobacco/data_statistical/fact_sheets/youth_data/tobacco_use/index.htm.

22. "Teen Smoking: 10 Ways to Keep Teens Smoke-Free," Mayo Clinic, www.mayoclinic.org/healthy-lifestyle/tween-and-teen-health/in-depth/teen-smoking/art-20047069.

23. https://www.woodtv.com/news/grand-rapids/cdc-collecting-more-data-on-vaping-illnesses, Sept. 5, 2019.

24. J. W. Grube and E. Waiters, "Alcohol in the Media: Content and Effects on Drinking Beliefs and Behaviors among Youth," *Adolescent Medicine Clinics* 16 (June 2005), 327–343.

25. B. A. Primack, K. L. Kraeer, M. J. Fine, and M. A. Dalton, "Association between Media Exposure and Marijuana and Alcohol Use in Adolescents," *Journal of Adolescent Health* 2008: 42:S3.

26. R. I. Collins et al., "Watching Sex on Television Predicts Adolescent Initiation of Sexual Behavior," *Pediatrics* 114, no. 3 (September 2004), e280–c289. www.pediatrics.aappublications.or/content/114/3/e280.

27. Danny Huerta, "Seven Strategies to Combat Teen Porn Use," Focus on the Family, (August 14, 2018) www.focusonthefamily.com/parenting/seen-strategies-to-combat-teen-porn-use/.

28. M. Ray and K. R. Jat, "Effect of Electronic Media on Children," *Indian Pediatrics* 47, no. 7 (July 2010), 561–568.

29. Mary L. Gavin, "Dealing with Bullying," *TeensHealth* from Nemours, www.kidshealth.org/en/teens/bullies.html.

30. "Teen Suicide: What Parents Need to Know," mayoclinic.org/healthy-lifestyle/tween-and-teen-health/in-depth/teen-suicide/art-20044308.

ADDITIONAL READING

- Kenneth Ginsburg and Susan FitzGerald, *Letting Go with Love and Confidence: Raising Responsible, Resilient, Self-Sufficient Teens in the 21st Century* (Avery Press, Penguin Books, 2011).
- Lauren Krasny Brown, *What's the Big Secret? Talking about Sex with Girls and Boys* (Little, Brown Books for Young Readers, 1997).
- Lenore Buth, *How to Talk Confidently with Your Child About Sex* (St. Louis: Concordia Publishing House, 2008).
- Shahid Ali, Charles P. Mouton, et al., "Early Detection of Illicit Drug Use in Teenagers," *Innovations in Clinical Neuroscience* 8 (December 2011), 24–28, heep://www.ncbi.nlm.nih.gov/pmc/articles/PMC3257983/.

CHAPTER 16

Grandparenting Wellness

Grandparenting is a marvelous calling from God. A solemn privilege, it can be an enormous responsibility. It can be frustrating but extraordinarily joyous and deeply gratifying.

Probably the best starting point for talking about grandparenting is to assure you, as a grandparent, that your role matters! Grandparents are indispensable parts of families; they always have been and always will be.[1]

Parents have the primary responsibility for raising their children. God planned for grandparents to be helpers. Consider just a few of the perspectives for your role from our Creator:

> But the steadfast love of the Lord is from everlasting to everlasting on those who fear Him, and His righteousness to children's children.
>
> (Psalm 103:17)

> Grandchildren are the crown of the aged, and the glory of children is their fathers.
>
> (Proverbs 17:6)

> Only take care, and keep your soul diligently, lest you forget the things that your eyes have seen, and lest they depart from your heart all the days of your life. Make them known to your children and your children's children.
>
> (Deuteronomy 4:9)

As a grandparent empowered by Holy Spirit, you are a guardian and transmitter of a legacy of faith based on the Word of God. Grandparents model for their grown children and grandchildren an active faith based on fear, love, and trust in God—Creator, Redeemer, and Sanctifier.

> I am reminded of your sincere faith, a faith that dwelt first in your grandmother Lois and your mother Eunice and now, I am sure, dwells in you as well.
>
> (2 Timothy 1:5)

You bring wisdom, patience, and experience to the role of parent helper, yet we never truly finish parenting our own children. Instead, we transition to a new role in the family circle. We may be sad or happy about getting older, retiring, and releasing some of our obligations. But these are self-imposed perspectives. Grandparenting today is often a next chapter and not an end to the story. You are old only when you see yourself as being antiquated; useless only if you perceive yourself as obsolete—all regardless of societal designations.

Grandparents need to honestly express to themselves and their children how they feel in this new role. Take some time to think about it during those precious prenatal months, and talk it over with your spouse. What are the boundaries you wish to set for yourself regarding your children and grandchildren? Are you comfortable and desirous of being a babysitter? Do you have the energy to have your grandchildren stay overnight with you? Do you wish to help support your grandchildren with money for preschool, grade school, high school, or college? Are you financially able to take them out to eat or to buy them clothes, sports equipment, or music lessons? Have these discussions early and often with your children.

Here are some of the pragmatic topics grandparents need to address; other understandings will evolve over time:

- *What is your moniker?* What do you want to be called? There is the traditional Grandma and Grandpa, Oma and Opa, or variations thereof. Usually your grandchild will call you what he or she can pronounce, but make your preference known.

- *Involvement:* How involved do you want to be? Some of this may be determined by whether you live in the same community as your grandchild. If you live nearby and have retired, do you want to offer child care so both parents can work? If you have more than one child and more than one grandchild, will you offer the same kind of care for all of them? If you are in a distant community, how will you stay connected on a regular basis? Are you a family that vacations together? Would you enjoy taking your grandchildren on vacation or for weekends without their parents? How is your health? Do you have the energy or stamina to deal with babies and young children?
- *Who's primary?* You are *not* the parent; you can give grandchildren back! In all seriousness, though, it's important to recognize that parenting expectations and practices have changed in the last two or three decades. Some of these practices may be smarter and scientifically safer than when your children were young. Your children are likely to be aware of the latest knowledge, follow the latest guidelines, and be just as capable as you were when you were parenting. Your new vocation as grandparent means that you defer to their desires and understandings, which may require that you bite your tongue.
- *Nonconfrontation policy:* Don't confront your children with differences of opinion on a particular child-rearing subject, especially in front of your grandchildren. This undercuts closeness and respect in the family. Show your grandchildren that you honor and respect their parents; this is edifying for everyone's relationship. In fact, it is not wise to tell your children that they are doing it wrong. Unless there is domestic violence or other dangerous situations—in which you are obligated to intervene—the best approach is to be respectful and supportive of your children's parenting style. Remember your God-given role is to be a helper. No one benefits from family friction.
- *Who makes the rules?* This particularly pertains to your children's expressed rules regarding meals, snacks, bedtimes, use of video games, and so forth. If your children have dos and don'ts, do not deviate or be permissive.
- *Spoiling:* As tough as it is, don't over-spoil your grandchildren. Note I did not say *not* to spoil them, but don't over-spoil them. Don't

become an easy mark, a pushover. And please ask your children's permission to take your grandchildren somewhere special or if you can give a particularly generous gift. Follow your children's wishes and respect the boundaries.

- *Favoritism:* This is a tough dictum but one that will save everyone heartache. If you are blessed with more than one grandchild, you will undoubtedly love each the same. Yet some grandparents discover that one grandchild just seems special. Some grandchildren seem easier to relate to and get along with. Children and grandchildren notice favoritism. They feel hurt and even angry. At its worst, favoritism leads to estrangement and feuding. Strive to treat all children and grandchildren the same at all times.
- *Keeping an even keel:* Raising children in today's world is considerably more challenging than it was a generation ago. Because you have a few more years of wisdom and experience, you can help your children and grandchildren keep highlights and low points in their lives in perspective. You can be a nonanxious, nonjudgmental voice in the midst of the controversies and growing pains of family life.
- *Have their back:* Always be there for your children and grandchildren. Be in their corner, and let them both know you've got their back. Be a superb listener. Show them how to go about making choices in life and how to live with the consequences. When things don't go perfectly as a result of their decisions, teach them not to blame others for negative consequences.
- *Keeper of the flame:* Be a keeper of the family stories and be a teller of those tales. Your grandchildren will hear and see lots of stories, but nothing is more important than to hear it from Grandpa's and Grandma's lips to their ears. Children delight in hearing about their parents' lives and their own baby years. Your influence is powerful.
- *Documenter extraordinaire:* Create a written, photographic, or video history of your relationship with your grandchildren. Our ability to share these images is remarkable, thanks to today's technology, and your family will be thankful that you thought so much of them to document your lives together.
- *Spiritual one:* As you are able, take your grandchildren outside into God's beautiful nature to play, hike, and observe. Teach them to see

God's presence in all things. Show them how God preserves and restores His creation. Tell them how God is active in all things. Read to them from the Bible and Bible story books. Share with them how God has worked and still works in your life.

- *Solomon:* Use your wisdom and experience to introduce them to life lessons. There may be times when children listen more to grandparents than their own parents. Some of the greatest life lessons are the importance of being altruistic, that is, being of service to others. Supporting your children in their vocation as parents is a beautiful example of altruism. Another is the significance of acting from principle rather than convenience. A third is being empathetic, seeing the world through the eyes of others. You teach these lessons by living this way and by focusing conversation on these important life learnings. Teach them to be relational, calm, and optimistic. Teach them to be resilient—to try, and if they fail, to try again.
- *Gifting:* When giving grandkids gifts, it is helpful to them and to their parents if you consider whether the gift is educational, fun, healthy, or otherwise helpful. Another consideration is whether the gift is wanted. (We can all think of times when a gift giver was well-meaning but misguided.) If the answer is yes, and if it's okay with their parents, then go for it.
- *Be LOVE:* Make your home a comfortable place by providing toys, books, and games they like. As they are older, prepare a place where they can also be alone if needed. Make it truly a safe zone, a door that is always open, a refuge where there is love and care, and a place where they know Jesus is trusted. Let your grandchildren know that you love them unconditionally, no matter how low they might feel, no matter how far they have strayed, no matter what trials and troubles they are facing in their relationships with their parents, friends, or school. Tell them often that "Grandma and Grandpa love you."

A GRANDPARENT'S PRAYER

Lord of Life, I thank You for the gift of my grandchild. Thank You for the gift of Your own Son that I may have the hope and assurance to live into eternity with You, my children, and my grandchildren.

Grant my grandchild safety through every walk in life. Let [him/her] be loving and faithful, resilient, of high integrity, Christ-purposed, forgiving, and giving.

Grant [him/her] health in body, mind, and spirit; hope in Your Son; and happiness in living the life of a faithful servant.

Grant [him/her] wholeness when [his/her] heart is broken, shelter when [he/she] seeks safety, and light when [he/she] stumbles in darkness. Let [him/her] know that You are [his/her] "refuge and strength, a very present help in trouble," a mighty fortress (Psalm 46).

Make me a reflection of Jesus for [him/her], an example of unconditional love.

And for the day when I am no longer able to walk by [his/her] side, fill [him/her] with the assurance that I am resting and waiting in the arms of our Savior and Redeemer; and in the blink of an eye, we will be together again.

I ask this in Jesus' holy name. Amen.

NOTES

1. Christine Crosby, "Characteristics of Effective Grandparents," *Grand*, August 2012, https:www .grandmagazine.com/2012/08/effective-grandparenting.

SECTION 5

Helpful Additions to Your Conversations as Parents

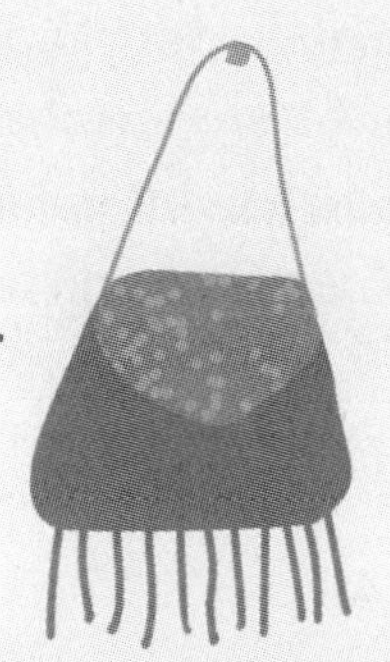

Epilogue

Parenting has been and always will be one of the most profound undertakings for any of us. We want to do our best, apply our full spectrum of child-raising resources, and express our love for our children through deliberate, compassionate, and impactful leadership and care. As parents living in our baptismal covenant, we are not alone in our striving. We have the faith-building energy of the Spirit, the restoration and advocacy of the Son, and the unconditional, active love and presence of the Father. We are surrounded by a cloud of witnesses who pledge their faith and action to lift up our parenting arms. I will continue to pray for your faithful service, and I ask your prayers for mine.

Appendix: Discussion Guides and Bible Studies

Chapter 1: Does your family value democratic ideals?

Be subject for the Lord's sake to every human institution, whether it be to the emperor as supreme, or to governors as sent by him to punish those who do evil and to praise those who do good. For this is the will of God, that by doing good you should put to silence the ignorance of foolish people. Live as people who are free, not using your freedom as a cover-up for evil, but living as servants of God. Honor everyone. Love the brotherhood. Fear God. Honor the emperor. (1 Peter 2:13–17)

What then, brothers? When you come together, each one has a hymn, a lesson, a revelation, a tongue, or an interpretation. Let all things be done for building up. (1 Corinthians 14:26)

1. Do the Scriptures speak of democratic principles? If you are unsure, re-examine the Bible references above.
2. What organizational guidelines have you found useful within your family for instilling a sense of honor and respect for all people?
3. How have you explained the differences in your power and role as a parent as opposed to the role and power of your children? How do you instill a sense of equality and specific roles as being for the good of the family?
4. How do you, as leader of your family, address problems of inequality and injustice concerning gender, race, disabilities, and other inequities that are at the forefront in society's awareness and conversation?

Chapter 2: How do we build a faith-filled family?

Let love be genuine. . . . Love one another with brotherly affection. Outdo one another in showing honor. . . . Contribute to the needs of the saints and seek to show hospitality. . . . Live in harmony with one another. Do not be haughty, but associate with the lowly. . . . If possible, so far as it depends on you, live peaceably with all. (Romans 12:9–18)

1. For families facing the challenges of both parents working outside the home and the hectic schedules that can bring, what strategies for having everyone gather for mealtimes work best?

2. Have you established a regular devotional life within your family? If so, what resources work best? If not, what is preventing regular devotions?

3. How often—outside of confirmation preparation—do you review the parts of the worship service and Luther's Small Catechism with your children?

4. How do you remind children of God's presence in their daily life, in the family's life, in school, and in nature?

5. How does your family live your faith? What attitudes or projects does your family embrace, or how do you serve in the congregation or community? How do you live out your beliefs in a society filled with political division and conflict?

Chapter 3: What strategies and behaviors encourage or discourage?

Be strong and courageous. Do not fear or be in dread of them, for it is the Lord your God who goes with you. He will not leave you or forsake you. (Deuteronomy 31:6)

1. Has your family ever had to make a courageous decision? What was the process that you as a parent used to arrive at that decision? Were there pitfalls or negative consequences of that decision?
2. How have you tried to instill courage in your child?
3. Can you recall a time when you might have discouraged your child? What were your child's short-term and long-term responses? Did it change the dynamic between you? Did you make adjustments after the fact?
4. In what ways do you see an encouraged or discouraged child's behavior play out as it relates to you or others?
5. What strategies are you using to help a discouraged child regain courage, resilience, and confidence?

Chapter 4: How do we deal with positive and negative consequences of our decisions?

> Do not be conformed to this world, but be transformed by the renewal of your mind, that by testing you may discern what is the will of God, what is good and acceptable and perfect. (Romans 12:2)

1. Can you share a time when you saw positive consequences from a health decision? How about a time when you realized negative consequences of a decision?
2. Have you ever let your child fail as a result of a decision? If so, how did you approach him or her after that failure? Did you reprimand? encourage your child to try again? use it as a teachable moment?

3. How do you help your children realize that their choices affect the family as well as themselves? If they are disrespectful, how does that affect your whole family?

4. Can you share an example of the positive or negative ramifications of your acting honorably (or dishonorably) and what you learned from that experience?

Chapter 5: How can we instill a deep sense of safety, mission, and purpose?

You are a hiding place for me; You preserve me from trouble; You surround me with shouts of deliverance. (Psalm 32:7)

So then you are no longer strangers and aliens, but you are fellow citizens with the saints and members of the household of God, built on the foundation of the apostles and prophets, Christ Jesus Himself being the cornerstone, in which the whole structure, being joined together, grows into a holy temple in the Lord. In Him you also are being built together into a dwelling place for God by the Spirit. (Ephesians 2:19–22)

1. What steps do you emphasize in your home to keep everyone safe and secure?

2. What biblical lessons or prayers do you use regularly to teach your children about God's faithful presence in all circumstances?

3. Does your family talk about a family purpose or something that makes your family unique, with specific gifts to contribute to your church, school, or society?

4. Do you talk with each child about his or her current vocations (as son or daughter, student, sibling) and what God may have called your child to do with his or her life? If so, at what age did you begin this discussion?

5. Do you talk about the gifts God has given each member of the family that differentiate each person and allow each to contribute to the family in different ways?

Chapter 6: How do we guide children toward living as WE rather than self-focused ME?

If anyone says, "I love God," and hates his brother, he is a liar; for he who does not love his brother whom he has seen cannot love God whom he has not seen. (1 John 4:20)

But the steadfast love of the Lord is from everlasting to everlasting on those who fear Him, and His righteousness to children's children, to those who keep His covenant and remember to do His commandments. (Psalm 103:17–18)

Train up a child in the way he should go; even when he is old he will not depart from it. (Proverbs 22:6)

But if anyone does not provide for his relatives, and especially for members of his household, he has denied the faith and is worse than an unbeliever. (1 Timothy 5:8)

1. How can a child contribute in a meaningful way to family life?
2. Do you define the talents, abilities, and gifts of each member of the family and discuss how that can contribute to family good?
3. Do you hold regular family meetings? Share specifically how that works in your family.
4. How do you reinforce or reward positive contributions or compassionate caring of family members? Conversely, how do you deal with negative contributions to family life by any of its members?

5. How can you teach civic responsibility to your children? What if your Christian faith is at odds with societal practice or laws?

6. Do you have fun in your family? Share resources and strategies that seem to work best for your family that all seem to enjoy and from which all gain benefit.

Chapter 7: How do wellness values relate to wellness behaviors?

I appeal to you therefore, brothers, by the mercies of God, to present your bodies as a living sacrifice, holy and acceptable to God, which is your spiritual worship. (Romans 12:1)

1. What does it mean to "present your bodies as a living sacrifice"? What was the purpose of a sacrifice in the Old Testament, and how does that relate to Christ on the cross in the New Testament?

2. What does stewardship of self have to do with spiritual worship?

3. What is the difference between a wellness prescription and a wellness outcome, particularly from the viewpoint of understanding the working of the Holy Spirit?

4. Can you think of any other wellness behaviors that you want to explore based on your reading or media search?

Chapter 8: What can we learn about wellness from the Blue Zones?

I appeal to you therefore, brothers, by the mercies of God, to present your bodies as a living sacrifice, holy and acceptable to God, which is your spiritual worship. Do not be conformed to this world, but be transformed by the renewal of your mind, that by testing you may discern what is the will of God, what is good and acceptable and perfect. (Romans 12:1–2)

> Jesus revealed Himself again to the disciples by the Sea of Tiberias. . . . Just as day was breaking, Jesus stood on the shore. . . . He said to them, "Cast the net on the right side of the boat, and you will find some [fish]." . . . When [the disciples] got out on land, they saw a charcoal fire in place, with fish laid out on it, and bread. . . . Jesus said to them, "Come and have breakfast." (John 21:1–12)

1. What healthy behaviors are you trying to instill in your children? What are a few ideas from the Blue Zones that interest you?

2. If you promote the following five healthy behaviors for you and your children flowing out of the Blue Zone data, what difficulties do you anticipate in instituting these behaviors in your family?

- Daily exercise and opportunities for more movement
- A predominantly plant-based diet
- Adequate sleep for every member of the family and daily periods for rest throughout the day
- An intentional effort to focus on family, and frequent opportunities to focus on faith formation in the home
- Developing a family "mission statement" and setting aside times to discuss and teach missional/purposeful living to your children

3. What healthy behaviors could be instilled in your church or school? Who would be the individuals of influence you would have to convince, and how would you participate in producing healthier choices for your faith community?

Chapter 9: Are we dealing with a child with developmental challenges?

1. Are you struggling with developmental issues regarding where you child might fall on a bell-shaped curve for any growth issue? If so, how are you and your physician strategizing to address your concerns?

Chapters 10–15: How can we promote wellness in our child(ren) at each growth stage?

1. The following questions are appropriate for each developmental age. Apply these questions to the particular age you are addressing in your thoughts and discussions.
2. How have you designed your home and family life to encourage movement in your child? Is it working?
3. Discuss what your family is doing to encourage plant-based nutrition. What are the greatest challenges to good nutrition?
4. How have you designed your home and your child's routine to assure adequate rest? What helpful suggestions can you share for providing pause points within your daily schedule?
5. What do you do to encourage closeness and faith bonds within your family? If you are a single parent, what particular challenges (today, this week) rob joy from your parenting, and what help is available from your community?
6. Do you ever discuss purpose and mission as a family? What special ways do you try to intentionally build purposeful living in your child?

7. What particular issue(s) are you struggling with at your child's age? What resources from media, school, church, or community do you recommend that help you parent?

Chapter 16: What are the challenges to being a good—no, *great*—grandparent?

1. What issues related to your relationship with your grandchildren are you struggling with?
2. Are you finding any challenges or struggles, like jealousy or competition for your time or resources, with grandparenting multiple grandchildren ?
3. How do you manage different parenting strategies you have with your children?
4. What are the best ways to share your resources with your grandchildren in the short term and in the future?
5. How do you share your faith with your grandchildren? with your grown children?

Biography

John D. Eckrich, MD, is a board-certified internist and gastroenterologist who has served the St. Louis, Missouri, community at large and especially professional Christian church workers and their families for over forty years. In 1999, he founded Grace Place Wellness Ministries, a retreat-based program to encourage stewardship of body, mind, and spirit among Lutheran pastors and teachers and their families, equipping them to lead healthy and joyful lives of service. He is an author and speaker on wellness topics from a Christian perspective and has three wellness books to his credit: *Vocation and Wellness; Fear, Anxiety and Wellness;* and *Resilient Aging and Wellness.* He resides in St. Louis with his wife, three children and their spouses, and two grandchildren. He is a longtime member of Concordia Lutheran Church (LCMS), Kirkwood, Missouri.